40 Years of Democracy in Botswana

1965-2005

EDITED BY

ZIBANI MAUNDENI

Mmegi Publishing House

40 Years of Democracy in Botswana: 1965 - 2005

First Published in 2005 by Mmegi Publishing House,
P/Bag Br 298, Gaborone, Botswana

ISBN: 99912-526-3-0

Cover design by: Resolution
Layout and design by: Resolution
Printed and bound by: Mills Litho, Cape Town, South Africa

40 Years
of Democracy
in Botswana

1965-2005

EDITED BY

ZIBANI MAUNDENI

CONTENTS

SECTION THREE

ACKNOWLEDGEMENTS

I want to take this opportunity to thank my colleagues in the Democracy Research Project (DRP). I thank you for accepting my invitation to contribute chapters and for cooperating with me until the final product was realised. This is a significant achievement comparable to the 1989 book that was coordinated by the DRP with chapters from members of the public. The current book is slightly different in that it was authored by DRP members themselves. I thank you for your cooperation, your willingness to revise the chapters in the light of comments by external reviewers and myself and for your patience throughout the delays of the editing and publishing process. Let us celebrate this significant achievement together with new DRP members who found this project well advanced and missed the opportunity of contributing chapters. With so many academic doctors and professors in the DRP, there is no doubt that other books will follow and new members will have the opportunity to contribute. We should all look forward to better days ahead.

All the chapters in this book were reviewed by a number of professors and other scholars from the University of Botswana who made valuable comments that helped in the revision exercise. Some professors were heavily burdened as they had to review more than one chapter. I want to thank Professors Frank Youngman, Kenneth Good, Roger Tangri, for their insightful reviews which significantly helped in the sharpening and re-focusing of some of the chapters. I also thank Dr. Bertha Osei-Hwedie and Elsie Alexander, who reviewed the chapters on gender and youth and I thank all the other reviewers whose names I might have omitted here. I thank all of you on behalf of the authors and myself for your huge contribution towards the success of this book.

Lastly, I want to thank Friedrich Ebert Foundation for supporting the production of the book. I also thank the publisher for agreeing to its publication.

Zibani Maundeni
April 2005

CONTRIBUTORS

Mogopodi Lekorwe, PhD. is a Senior Lecturer and Director of the Centre of Specialisation in Public Administration and Management (CESPAM). He has published a number of papers and lectures at the University of Botswana. Dr Lekorwe has been involved in several professional fora, research projects and educational programmes. In his present role as Director of CESPAM, he has been instrumental in launching and being the catalyst for a number of professional development programmes, primarily for public administration within SADC. He holds degrees in Politics and Administration and a doctorate in Development Administration.

Zibani Maundeni, PhD. is a senior lecturer in political science at the University of Botswana. He is the Coordinator of the Democracy Research Project. Dr Maundeni is the author of the book, *Civil Society, Politics and the State in Botswana* (2004). He has also published a number of articles in reputable journals. His research interests are: democracy and democratisation, state and development, civil society, elections, and local democracy.

Adam Mfundisi is a lecturer in Public Administration at the University of Botswana. He has ten years of teaching and researching at University of Botswana. Since 1993 he has been lecturing in Public Administration in the Department of Political and Administrative Studies at the University. Mr Mfundisi's major research interests focus on decentralisation and local governance, public enterprise management and public administration in Botswana.

Wilford Molefe A statistician by profession, Mr Molefe is currently a lecturer in the Department of Statistics at the University of Botswana. Mr Molefe is a member of the Democracy Research Project and the Afrobarometer Botswana Chapter specialising on methodology issues.

Mpho Molomo, PhD is an Associate Professor in the Department of Political and Administrative Studies and Director of the Centre for Strategic Studies. His research interests are: democracy, political parties, electoral systems, land, ethnicity and security sector reform.

Patrick Molutsi, PhD. was appointed Executive Secretary of the Tertiary Education Council in October 2003. Before joining the Tertiary Education Council, he was working for the International Institute for Democracy and Electoral Assistance (IDEA) in Stockholm, Sweden from 1999 to 2003. Starting as Head of Applied Research, in 2001 he was promoted to the position of Director of Field Programmes. In 2002, after the restructuring of IDEA, Dr Molutsi was appointed Director of two major programmes related to democracy assessment and assistance. Between 1980 and 1999, Dr Molutsi worked at the University of Botswana, Department of Sociology of the Faculty of Social Sciences, rising to the rank of Senior Lecturer and to the positions of Head of Department of Sociology, and Dean of Faculty of Social Sciences. Dr Molutsi received his first degree at the University of Botswana in Sociology and History and a concurrent Diploma in Education, a Post-Graduate Diploma in Population Studies (Ghana), M.Phil (Oxford), D.Phil (Oxford) both in Sociology of Development and a Diploma in Public International Law (Woverhampton/Holborn College). Dr Molutsi has researched and written on a wide range of issues including democracy, education, election, rural development, human development, poverty and governance.

Tidimane Ntsabane is a Senior Lecturer in the Department of Sociology at the University of Botswana. His research areas are social and economic development, the family, social problems and democracy and electoral issues in Botswana.

Dolly Ntseane, PhD. is a lecturer in the Department of Social Work. She received her PhD in Social Policy from Brandeis University, School of Social Welfare in 1997. Prior to joining the University of Botswana in 1987, she worked as a Senior Social Welfare Officer in the Ministry of Local Government and Lands. Dr Ntseane has done extensive research in the areas of: work and family issues, HIV/AIDS, social security, women and politics, and gender and development. She has published articles in journals and has written chapters in books in these areas. Dr Ntseane participates actively in both professional and community activities. She has been instrumental in the formation of the Task Force on Social Security which is now driving social security reforms in the country. Her area of specialisation includes; social research, social policy analysis, children and youth issues, women and politics and gender and HIV/AIDS.

David Sebudubudu, PhD. is a political Science lecturer in the Department of Political and Administrative Studies at the University of Botswana. He teaches at undergraduate and graduate levels. He is also a member of the Democracy Research Project (DRP) of the University of Botswana.

Joel Sentsho, PhD. is a lecturer in the Department of Economics. He holds a PhD from the University of Strathclyde, Scotland. He has researched extensively in the areas of exports and economic growth, the state and economic development, industrial development and poverty reduction, problems of income disparity and gender inequality as well as quantitative economic analysis and econometric modeling. Most of his research is based on the Botswana economy, and how it compares with other high growth performing economies like those of east Asia. He has also written extensively on the role of the state in the use of economic incentives for development. Dr Sentsho is currently the President of the Botswana Economic Association (BEA) and Editor of the *Botswana Journal of Economics* (BOJE).

Onkemetse Tshosa, LL.B (UB), LL.M (Lund), PhD (Edinburgh), Senior Lecturer-in-Law, Department of Law, University of Botswana

INTRODUCTION

B otswana and the Friedrich Ebert Foundation celebrate 40 years (1965-2005) and 80 years (1925 - 2005) respectively of practising and promoting democratic electoral politics. The Democracy Research Project (DRP) as the leading democracy research agency takes this opportunity to document the democratic achievements, failures, reversals and challenges of Botswana. Although Botswana was not the first African country to achieve independence, it has been one of the few that has sustained democratic politics during the last 40 years. It has demonstrated the fallacy of much international thinking that held that electoral democracy was only achievable in rich, western Europe and north America.

Botswana held its first election in 1965, at a time when it was classified as one of the three poorest countries in the world, without a promising economic future and without an electoral democratic culture to lean on. Its first election was followed by a devastating drought during which one-third of the livestock (then the mainstay of the economy) perished, massive crop production failure resulted and severe water shortages occurred. In the initial chapters, the authors analyse issues ranging from how far Botswana is still a leading democratic nation in the region, through electoral systems and the evolution of election management, to transparency in the electoral system.

The second election was due to take place in 1970, but was called earlier in 1969. This was partly because President Seretse Khama sought to restore the legitimacy of his government in the face of accusations of being responsible for all the ills that faced the nation at that time. Towards the end of the 1960s, chiefs (whose powers over the allocation of land and rural administration had been shared between other institutions) and opposition parties (accusing the BDP government of neo-colonialism) heavily criticised the government for the policies it was pursuing, prompting President Khama to call for an early election. Khama's party won the 1969 election, but his vice president and minister of development, Quett Masire, lost his seat to a former chief who had resigned and joined the newly formed opposition Botswana National Front (BNF). The electoral loss of the vice president and minister of development was the kind of setback which might have prompted governments in other African states to declare a one party state and to outlaw the opposition. But the ruling Botswana Democratic Party (BDP) saw the electoral loss of the vice president as an electoral reform issue rather than a national security one, prompting it to introduce electoral reforms that

6

prevented retiring chiefs from immediately entering into politics and absolving presidents from standing for parliamentary elections. Other chiefs who were critical of the government were either retired or appointed into ambassadorial positions in far away countries. Thus, Botswana's electoral democracy (unlike Lesotho and Swaziland) survived its biggest challenge from the traditional leaders and fine tuned its electoral system.

The third election was held in the fifth year after the second election (1974) as required by the constitution and there were signs of the emergence of civil society. By the time of the 1989 election, civil society organisations were emerging but their role in the political system was restricted and un-analysed.

In **Chapter One**, Patrick Molutsi compares Botswana's electoral democracy with that of the region. His central question is whether Botswana is still the leader in democratic politics and whether there are lessons that other countries could learn from Botswana's experience of democratic politics. In **Chapter Two**, Mpho Molomo compares electoral systems and demonstrates how alternative systems could have shaped Botswana politics. Molomo draws the conclusion that the first-past-the-post system is no longer adequate for Botswana's needs. In **Chapter Three**, Mogopodi Lekorwe and Onkemetse Tshosa analyse the evolution of the electoral management body that culminated in the Independent Electoral Commission. In **Chapter Four**, David Sebudubudu evaluates improvements to transparency in electoral management and the manner in which electoral disputes have been handled over the years.

Section Two of the book focuses on the political parties and the politics of succession. In **Chapter Five** Zibani Maundeni discusses the rules and principles guiding succession to high office in Botswana, showing the continuity with Tswana political culture. In **Chapter Six**, Mpho Molomo and Wilford Molefe analyse voting trends and the electoral performances of the parties. They conclude that opposition unity would either see a change of government or result in the opposition winning the popular vote and losing the election with a likelihood of plunging the country into a Lesotho kind of crisis. In **Chapter Seven**, Mogopodi Lekorwe discusses the organisation of the main political parties, the BDP and the BNF, showing how they run their congresses and how this has contributed to or subtracted from internal party democracy. Section Two ends with **Chapter Eight** in which Mpho Molomo and David Sebudubudu discuss the need for the state to fund political parties.

Section Three begins with **Chapter Nine** which looks at the importance of stakeholders fully participating in the electoral process. In **Chapter Ten**, Zibani Maundeni shows that civil society played a crucial role in the democratisation process and dismisses the literature that gave it a negative portrayal. In **Chapter Eleven**, Dolly Ntseane and Joel Sentsho make a comparative analysis of gender representation in parliament, analyse the role played by women-based NGOs and show that Botswana made significant gains in this area and then partly lost them. In **Chapter Twelve**, Tidimane Ntsabane analyses the youth, particularly their apathy in electoral politics, and calls for stakeholders to encourage them to participate more fully. In **Chapter Thirteen**, Dolly Ntseane discusses the marginal presence of women in political party structures, highlighting the impediments to their full participation.

In the concluding **Chapter Fourteen**, Zibani Maundeni draws from the latest elections in the region and from the various chapters in the book to show how some new democracies are seriously challenging Botswana's leadership in democratic politics, and how others are having serious problems of their own that may ultimately even lead to democratic reversals. Maundeni re-visits the issue of alternative electoral systems and shows that countries practising proportional representation (PR) such as South Africa and multi-member proportional system (MMP) such as Lesotho, still suffer the setbacks that Botswana's first-past-the-post system (FPTP) generates. The book contains a significant amount of previously unpublished material and so makes an important contribution to understanding and knowledge of Botswana's politics and political science in general. Students and researchers will therefore find it very useful.

This section focuses on electoral trends in the region, comparative electoral systems, the organisation of elections in Botswana and the settling of electoral disputes. It compares the electoral experiences of Botswana with those of other countries in the region, highlighting instances in which Botswana and the region performed well or poorly. It also compares electoral systems and highlights the importance of a periodic review of the electoral system in Botswana. The section further analyses the history of reforming the management of elections and discusses the manner in which electoral disputes are handled.

CHAPTER 1

BOTSWANA'S DEMOCRACY IN A SOUTHERN AFRICAN REGIONAL PERSPECTIVE: PROGRESS OR DECLINE?

Patrick Molutsi

INTRODUCTION

The general elections of 2004 in Botswana were the ninth since the country attained independence from Britain in 1965 and completed forty years of democratic governance. On all counts it is evident that electoral democracy has become a part of the country's political culture. On the whole, the electoral process has been successfully implemented and has helped to reinforce and maintain the separation of powers between the legislature, the executive and the judiciary. Every election has meant a new parliament, a new executive and often some changes in the judiciary as well. The system of political parties in Botswana has also taken shape. Over recent years the country has developed a three party system with political parties of varying strengths and different ideological persuasions.

The fourth pillar of democracy, the media, has evolved from state-dominated newspaper and radio to one private daily and a number of weekly private newspapers and local radio stations all of which are prepared to take a critical stance against the government on a number of different issues. The civil society groups have increased in number, diversity and complexity. At another level however, we can observe that the voices of traditional leaders and local councils which used to be critical on certain issues, now appear to have disappeared or to have been silenced. In the early years following independence the chiefs in particular and the opposition-led councils constituted an important voice of conscience on issues of land, culture, social justice and equity.

In the past one and a half decades Botswana has introduced a new layer of institutions, known as watchdog institutions, whose main function is to safeguard democracy, promote transparency and guard against corruption. Among these are the Independent Electoral Commission, the Ombudsman and the Directorate on Corruption and Economic Crime. This chapter examines the state of democracy in Botswana in the context of the southern African region and the broader post-1989 democratisation process in less developed countries. The question is whether, given the years of democratic development, Botswana is more democratic than her newly-democratising neighbours. If so, what lessons can the countries in the region, and the newly-democratising countries around the world learn from Botswana? Compared to the rest of the Southern African Development Community (SADC) member states, Botswana should have many experiences and practical lessons on democracy to share with the region. Many of the countries in the region re-introduced multi-party democratic elections only in the early 1990s. For instance, Namibia, Zambia, Malawi, Mozambique, South Africa and Tanzania held their first such elections in 1989, 1991, 1994, 1994, 1994 and 1995 respectively. These countries are by any measure newcomers to electoral democracy when compared to Botswana.

This chapter focuses on five areas of democracy development in Botswana and the SADC region. At the political level, it focuses on three core processes and institutions, the socio-economic agenda or what is called the instrumental dimension of democracy. Here, it addresses economic development policies and programmes and their effects on economic growth; poverty and the unemployment situation. Finally, the role of SADC and NEPAD as possible vehicles for political and economic integration of the region is addressed. In this context the extent to which Botswana has provided a democratic leadership role in the region is examined. The analysis focuses on two broad aspects of the state of democracy.

The chapter is divided into two parts. The first part focuses on political democracy and its quality. That is, it evaluates the institutional processes and infrastructure of democracy in Botswana using what Armatya Sen (1999) has called the *intrinsic* dimension of democracy. The second part discusses the socio-economic aspects of democracy or, what is termed the *instrumental* dimension of democracy or its ability to deliver not just the political but the social and economic goods – social welfare programme for the majority of the otherwise impoverished population. It is argued that it is on the basis of both its intrinsic and instrumental values that the quality and sustainability of democracy in Botswana - and in any country for that matter - will be determined.

THE TOOLS OF ANALYSIS

The analysis to be used as a point of departure is a simple approach to democracy derived from Armatya Sen (1999). He described democracy as having two dimensions or functions. These he said were the intrinsic and instrumental dimensions. The intrinsic value of a political system refers to its ability to provide security to the people individually and collectively, to protect and promote their human and political rights, to enshrine their rights to participate freely in the political processes of their country and ensure they are treated equally and fairly before the law. Any political system which fails to meet basic security, political freedoms and human rights of its citizens is not intrinsically of value to its citizens. Democracy is considered generally superior to other political systems in that it claims to give priority to people's security, freedoms and human rights. Beetham *et al*, (2002) correctly noted that democracy is basically about two core principles of citizen equality and their ability/authority to remove leaders and institute a government of majority choice through elections. The instrumental dimension refers to the ability of a democratic system to deliver the economic welfare to the often poor and needy population. Using this approach it will become evident that the success of any political system, but particularly that of a less developed country, has to be measured in terms of both its intrinsic and instrumental values.

In the comparative analysis of Botswana and its neighbours, this simple distinction between intrinsic and instrumental dimensions of democracy will be used to assess not only achievement in the politico-legal arena but achievement in the economic development and social welfare fields. It is acknowledged that this is only one of several approaches that can be used to carry out an evaluation of democracy in any country and that this approach departs significantly from the 'original' meaning and intentions of democracy. Some will strongly argue that this approach unnecessarily burdens the political system, and democracy in particular, with functions and goals which do not belong to it. They will probably argue that democracy is about governance and political stability and much less about economic development and social welfare. The counter position to such arguments is that definitions of human rights and human security, the primary requirement of a stable and functioning political system, have also changed. They now include the socio-economic opportunities available to the population. In other words, security is not just physical protection against invasion, violation and violence, etc., it is also about the absence of and/or denial of opportunities to shelter, a piece of land, a source of income, etc. Similarly, human rights are not merely civil and political. They increasingly include what are commonly termed the 'third generation' of rights which refers to rights to development, a clean environment, education and other necessities of life.

Understood from this perspective, a democracy that ignores the socio-economic needs of society will be both fragile and unsustainable. It should further be recalled that one party states and other undemocratic regimes in southern Africa collapsed in the 1990s largely because they failed to deliver basic welfare programmes against unemployment and poverty, and structural adjustment programmes actually reduced state spending on health, education, water and housing for the poor. Even what were originally perceived as militarily invincible regimes, such the Apartheid regime in pre-1994 South Africa crumbled even faster partly because of the effects of externally induced economic crises. In short, democracy assessment must necessarily include economic performance as an indicator.

PART 1: INTRINSIC DEMOCRACY DIMENSION

This section evaluates the extent to which governments and peoples of southern Africa have embraced democracy as a political system. It assesses the extent of the entrenchment of democratic principles, the operations of democratic processes, the strength and performance of institutions and the extent to which individual countries of the region, and the region as a whole, promote democracy at regional, continental and global levels. In this context the intention is to establish whether or not Botswana, as one of the oldest democracies in the region, has been able to lead both by example and proactively.

REGIONAL COMMITMENT TO DEMOCRACY

Roughly one and half decades since the fall of the Berlin Wall and the spread of democracy around the world, many countries which were previously ruled by different types of undemocratic regimes have held three successive multi-party elections. In this regard, it would appear that time is opportune for the pro-democracy movement in less developed countries, and their partners in developed democracies, to take a careful look at what is happening to democracy on the ground. They must ask themselves a series of weighty but necessary questions relating to whether or not progress has been made. If so, what type of progress and will it be sustainable in the light of daunting challenges of poverty, unequal terms of trade, slow economic growth and continuing conflicts and disease in regions of Africa, Asia, Latin America and the former Soviet Union. Perhaps even more important for assessing the state of democracy in these countries is the need to establish whether or not the practice on the ground lives up to the rhetorical statements of leaders that they are committed to democracy. It has been observed that academic researchers and civil society groups, central enough to the process of democratisation to be termed 'drivers of democracy', have become increasingly sceptical of the quality of democracy in their countries. Their reports suggest that in many cases elections are fraudulent, media is restricted and the opposition is starved of necessary resources to enable it to campaign.

However, when it comes to the countries of southern Africa it can justifiably be argued that although many of the countries in this region were themselves not multi-party democracies in the 1970s and 1980s, they nevertheless committed themselves to, and defended the principles of majority rule way back to the 1950s and 1960s. The struggles against colonialism, apartheid and white minority regimes in South Africa, Angola, Mozambique, Namibia and Zimbabwe were all struggles for democracy. While, after independence, many countries in the region including Tanzania, Zambia, Malawi and Mozambique opted for one party rule, this decision was based more on political expediency and political inexperience than on principle. Many of the leaders knew that in the process they were violating the democratic principles for which they had fought. In fact, some countries such as Tanzania and Zambia continued to hold regular elections in an attempt to show that theirs was still a participatory system where leaders could be recalled. Within the region only Botswana and Mauritius maintained multi-party democratic system without interruptions. These two countries are today among the oldest and most stable democracies with an impressive record of economic growth and good overall development (UNDP, 2002). Are these countries economically successful because they were democratic or were they democratic because they had strategic economic resources that drove their economic development and thereby induced political stability? This is an old and controversial question which neither economists nor political scientists have been able to answer satisfactorily. The conclusions of this chapter will come back to this question and show that the relationship between the political system and economic performance is a complex one.

In the past fifteen years or so, SADC countries have joined the global trend and committed themselves to democracy and the promotion of democracy. In fact, the region boasts of some of the most creative constitutions in the world. The constitutions of South Africa and Namibia in particular, are often cited as among the most comprehensive and dynamic constitutions in the world. Through the Commonwealth's Harare Declaration of 1991, the Africa Union Constitution, the UN resolutions in the 1990s, SADC member states have committed themselves to democratic governance. For example, the SADC Protocol on Gender Equality is a significant tool in the hands of citizens to pressure their governments to bring about democratic equality between men and women in the region. Some governments and political parties in countries such as South Africa, Namibia and Mozambique have gone further and set a target of 30 per cent for gender equality in the areas of political representation and high level decision-making.

However, it has been observed that as a mature democracy, Botswana trails behind a number of newly-democratising countries in the region on the measure of gender equality. Both the government and the ruling BDP have declined to set the target for achieving at least 30 per cent women representation in the party's leadership positions, parliamentary and council representation.

DEMOCRATIC PRACTICE AND POLITICAL PARTICIPATION

Three areas are discussed below, as evidence of the practice of democracy by the governments and the peoples of the SADC region. First the regularity of the elections, secondly the level of citizen participation in the elections and thirdly whether or not the people see the value of democracy. This section concludes by identifying areas of inequality in the participation of women and opposition parties and highlights differences between the countries.

TABLE 1.1: Schedule of elections in SADC countries

Country	Year 1	Year 2	Year 3	Type of Electoral System	Voting Age
Angola	1992	-	-	PR	18
Botswana	1994	1999	2004	FPTP	18
Lesotho	1998	2003	-	MMP	18
Malawi	1994	1999	2004	FPTP	18
Mozambique	1994	1999	2004	List PR	18
Namibia	1994	1999	2004	List PR	18
South Africa	1994	1999	2004	List PR	18
Tanzania	1995	2000	2005	FPTP	18
Zambia	1991	1996	2001	FPTP	18
Zimbabwe	1995	2000	2005	FPTP	18

Source: *International IDEA, Global Voter Turnout Report*, 2002

Elections have become a common feature of the political calendars of most SADC countries. In the past fifteen years most countries held elections in the years shown in **Table 1.1.** Two types of electoral systems are commonly used in the region: the first-past-the-post system (FPTP) and list proportional representation system (List PR). Only Lesotho changed its electoral system for a multi-member proportional system (MMP). This followed the disastrous experience with the FPTP system in 1998 when one party won 99 per cent of the parliamentary seats with less than 70 per cent of the votes. The voting age in all the countries is 18 years, although interestingly, Botswana was the last of the countries to lower its voting age from 21 to 18 years in 1998. In terms of electoral outcomes, the type of electoral system seems to have made only marginal differences on the results. The significant difference was in women's political participation. In all the countries the opposition remains weak and marginally represented in parliament. However, in the List PR countries the relationship between votes received and seats allocated was more directly related to seats gained in parliament. This had the effect that many smaller parties were represented in parliament in countries practising List PR than in FPTP countries. In all FPTP countries the largest number of parties in parliament averaged three for example in Botswana, Malawi, Tanzania, Zambia and Zimbabwe. By contrast, the List PR countries have had an average of five political parties represented in parliament over the last three successive elections. Thus it could be argued that the List PR electoral system is more effective in ensuring both enhanced gender participation and more diversity in political representation in parliament.

Botswana has scored poorly on both counts. Since independence there have been, on average, only three political parties represented in parliament. The first time Botswana had three parties directly elected into parliament was in 1969 and the third party has almost always been represented by not more that one person. The exception was in 1998 when the BNF's first split in parliament created representation of two persons for the third party in parliament.

Female representation in Botswana's parliament took much longer than in other SADC countries as shown in **Table 1.2.** It took three successive elections from 1965 to 1979 before the first woman was elected to the Botswana parliament. Since then, female representation has remained low, ranging between 10 per cent and 17 per cent and much lower than the newly democratising countries of Mozambique, South Africa, Namibia and Tanzania. In the most recent elections held in 2004, only four women out of a total of 57 constituencies (three per cent) were directly elected to parliament. However, as in the previous election in 1999, parliament attempted to remedy this anomalous situation by electing women into three of the four positions of specially elected members of parliament. Interestingly, all the three women and two of the directly elected ones were given either full or assistant ministerial positions.

Country	Year women received vote	First woman stood for election	First woman elected/ appointed to parliament	Women in govt. at ministerial level: per cent	Percentage of women in lower house	Percentage of women in upper house
Mauritius (67)	1956	1956	1976 (E)	9.1	5.7	-
South Africa (107)	(1930) 1994	(1930) 1994	1933 (E)	38.1	29.8	31.5
Namibia (122)	1989	1989	1989 (E)	16.3	25.0	7.7
Swaziland (125)	1968	1968	1972 (E+A)	12.5	3.1	13.3
Botswana (126)	1965	1965	1979 (E)	26.7	17.0	-
Zimbabwe (128)	1957	1978	1980 (E+A)	36.0	10.0	-
Lesotho (132)	1965	1965	1965 (A)	-	3.8	27.3
Tanzania (151)	1959	1959	-	-	22.3	-
Zambia (153)	1962	1962	1964 (E+A)	6.2	1.0	-
Angola (161)	1975	1975	1980 (E)	14.7	15.5	-
Malawi (163)	1961	1961	1964 (E)	11.8	9.3	-
Mozambique (170)	1975	1975	1979 (E)	-	30.0	-

TABLE 1.2: Women's political parties in SADC countries

Notes: The table derives from UNDP Human Development Report (2002) on *Deepening Democracy in a Fragmented World* pp.239-242
*Nos in brackets refer to Human Development Index Rank. E is elected and A is appointed.

In assessing political participation and determining the extent of popular support for democracy it is necessary to examine more closely the level of voter turnout in SADC countries. Voter turnout is one of the measures of citizen participation in politics. As a general principle, voter turnout might indicate the extent to which ordinary voters perceive and value the electoral process. However, I want to agree with Dieter Nohlen (2002) that:

- Where there are high levels of social inequality as in many SADC countries high levels of voter turnout do not necessarily indicate a perception of elections as a tool for political empowerment of the poor but rather indicate perception of an opportunity to trade votes for material profit or favour.

- Established democracies with strong democratic culture do not necessarily display high levels of voter turnout, for example the USA.

- Voter turnout should be interpreted against the background of what other non-democratic means exist in society for the leaders to achieve their goals without depending on popular support.

• Voter turnout may indicate public confidence and trust on political institutions. High turnouts may show both legitimacy and high quality of a democracy.

Table 1.3 below shows comparative statistics on voter turnout in SADC member states based on one election per country, though this is not necessarily the latest election. The statistical differences between elections within the same country over time is minimal. Thus, although ideally one might wish to work out the averages over the years, the data below is still fairly representative of trends in individual countries. Three conclusions can be drawn from the analysis of this table. Firstly, the level of voter turnout across the region is quite high ranging between 60 per cent and 80 per cent of those registered to vote. The highest level of voter turnout was recorded in Malawi at 92 per cent in 1999 and the lowest in Zimbabwe at the 48 per cent in the controversial 2000 election. These two results represented two potentially different interpretations of the value of elections. In Zimbabwe the population was clearly recording a protest mixed with fear: protest against the economic collapse of the country and fear of violence being unleashed against the opposition.

TABLE 1.3: Level of participation in the most recent election						
Country	Election Year	Total Vote	Total Registered	Percentage that Voted	Voting Age Pop (VAP)	Percentage of Voted to VAP
Angola	1992	4 402 575	4 828 486	91.2	4 986 230	88.3
Botswana	1999	354 463	459 662	77.1	844 338	42.0
DRC	1992	874 296	1 232 384	70.9	1 161 790	75.3
Lesotho	1998	617 738	860 000	71.8	1 001 034	61.7
Malawi	1999	4 680 262	5 071 822	92.3	4 419 210	105.9
Mauritius	2000	630 292	779 033	80.9	792 125	79.6
Mozambique	1999	4 833 761	7 099 105	68.1	8 303 686	58.2
Namibia	1999	541 114	861 848	62.8	878 828	61.7
South Africa	1999	16 228 462	18 177 000	89.3	25 411 573	63.9
Tanzania	2000	7 341 067	10 088 484	72.8	16 055 200	45.7
Zambia	1996	1 779 607	2 267 382	78.5	4 467 520	39.8
Zimbabwe	2000	2 556 261	5 288 804	48.3	6 392 195	40.0

Source: International IDEA, *Global Voter Turnout Report*, 2002

The second conclusion drawn from **Table 1.3** is that a significant proportion of eligible voters (voting age population) do not vote. The largest measure of voter apathy was recorded in Zambia at 60 per cent not voting and the smallest in Angola at 12 per cent. The third conclusion is that Botswana does not emerge as being any different from these newly democratising countries. In fact, Botswana has one of the highest voter apathy rates in the region.

Several studies have been conducted across the world on public perceptions of democracy. Among these has been the research conducted in Eastern Europe, Asia and Africa following the 'third wave' of democracy. These inter-regional studies on perceptions of, and commitment to, democracy show impressive support by ordinary people for democracy. In southern Africa, the African Barometer studies have been conducted in Botswana, Namibia, South Africa and Zambia. In these four SADC countries the peoples' perceptions of, and commitment to, democracy as a political system are very high, ranging between 60 per cent and 80 per cent. The people of Botswana with their long experience of democratic governance still appear to be moderately committed to democracy compared to Namibians and South Africans.

Evidently, with democratic systems and processes in place, levels of public and political party participation in elections relatively high and people's perceptions of and commitment to democracy also high, we can conclude that the prospects for democracy in this region are good. However, these prospects will further depend on the successes in improving the quality of democracy on the one hand and the ability of democratic governments to sustain and deliver economic welfare for the masses of the voters on the other hand.

THE STATE OF DEMOCRATIC INSTITUTIONS – THE QUALITY OF POLITICAL PLURALISM

There is no intention of undervaluing the democratic changes that have taken place in formerly non-democratic societies. However, it must be noted that it will be self deception on the part of the initiators of democratisation to assume that they have so far achieved much democracy. It has often been said that the project for democracy development is a long term one. Democracy development becomes even more complex in a situation in which it is not only the political but also the economic system which is vulnerable and unpredictable. So far, the achievements of democratisation in southern Africa can be summarised as follows:

- Existence of political pluralism in public debates and in parliaments
- Regular, though imperfect elections

- Functioning, though weak multi-party parliaments
- Smooth and democratic change of governments and leaders at party and national levels
- Existence of relatively autonomous, custodian institutions of democracy such as election management bodies, ombudsperson institutions and the courts of law
- Existence of a striving and critical civil society
- Increased attention to democracy development by universities and research institutions
- Sustained donor interest in democracy support and poverty alleviation
- An evolving culture of democracy

Southern Africa has not only held regular elections and undertaken constitutional reforms but also has had the largest number of democratically replaced leaders. The ruling parties in Botswana, South Africa, Malawi, Mozambique, Zambia and Namibia have, with the exception of Malawi and Zambia where some conflict between the former and the new leaders occurred, successfully transferred power to the new leader.

TABLE 1.4: Major issues affecting political competitiveness in SADC countries					
Country	Election year	Ruling party per cent of popular vote	Ruling party per cent of seats in Parliament	Type of electoral system	Is there public funding of parties?
Angola	1992	-	58	List PR	No
Botswana	1999	54	83	FPTP	No
Lesotho	1998	61	99	MMP	No
Malawi	1999	47	48	FPTP	Yes
Mozambique	1999	49	53	List PR	Yes
Namibia	1999	76	78	List PR	Yes
South Africa	1999	66	67	List PR	Yes
Tanzania	1995	59	78	FPTP	Yes
Zambia	1996	60	87	FPTP	No
Zimbabwe	1995	81	98	FPTP	Yes

Source: Various National Elections Reports

It can also be noted that the transfer of power from the ruling to the opposition party as in the experiences of Ghana and Kenya has not happened in any of the SADC countries since the re-introduction of multi-party elections. It is here that major questions about the quality of democracy in SADC countries can be raised. **Table 1.4** highlights some of the major constraints facing the opposition parties in their struggle to attain political power.

The first observation here is that, based on the evidence provided in **Table 1.4,** SADC parliaments are predominantly one-party parliaments. The second observation is that the first-past-the-post (FPTP) electoral system is contributing to the weak opposition in parliaments. It is observed that in all the FPTP countries there is a percentage points gap of between 16 and 38 between the percentage of popular vote gained and the percentage of seats obtained by the majority party. The same huge difference has not been observed in the List PR countries where the variance is between one and four. Incidentally, Botswana is one country where the FPTP has advantaged the ruling party most over the years. It has also been observed that political funding of parties on the other hand does not seem to be an important differentiating factor in opposition party performance. This is probably because party funding is almost always based on electoral performance in the previous elections and thereby most of the funding tends to go to the dominant parties.

Several other factors have also been noted, including limited access to the media, poor organisation and fragmentation of opposition political parties and their limited experience which contribute to the failure of such parties to evolve into viable contenders of power. It is suggested that the quality of intrinsic democracy in SADC depends more on the roles of media, civil society and watchdog institutions than the formal political opposition. The success of democracy in the region is also seen as continuing to depend on international pressure and the benevolence of individual political leaders. If leaders choose to limit democracy and induce violence in society as has been the case in Zimbabwe since 2000, then the danger is that even the regional body has little, if any, power to force them to change. The view is that the Lesotho experience of post-1998 where SADC countries sent a joint military force to dislodge the army mutiny is unlikely to be repeated in Zimbabwe.

PART 2: INSTRUMENTAL DEMOCRACY IN SADC – IS DEMOCRACY MAKING A DIFFERENCE TO THE QUALITY OF LIFE?

Democratisation in less developed countries has been a product of two key processes. The first comprises the long term struggles for democracy fought against colonialism and other unpopular regimes. The second process which gave impetus to democratic reforms in many countries especially in the late 1980s and early 1990s is made up of the economic crises associated with poor world economic trends and the fall of commodity prices. Understood in this context, it is clear that the success of democracy in any country goes beyond its best practice at a politico-legal and institutional level. The point is that democracy is expected to deliver economic development and equitably distribute opportunities for employment, income generation and basic social services. Furthermore, it is argued that this welfare programme has been imposed on many countries by the Millennium Development Goals (MDGs) adopted by the UN and signed by all member states in 2000. The key question is whether or not many of these countries are in a position to deliver the material imperatives of democracy and thereby sustain it? This section discusses the economic situation of SADC countries in order to determine whether or not they are in a position to meet the requirements of the MDGs in 2015 and thereby materially sustain democracy. However, the first general observation is that there have been little if any positive improvements in economic growth, job creation and integration of the SADC economies into the global market economy.

The majority of the countries of Africa, Asia, Latin America and some parts of the former Soviet Union region remain with varying degrees, peripheral to the drivers of the world economy. The latest World Bank's Report for instance, shows that Africa's per capita income is likely to grow by 1.6 per cent in 2005. While describing this level of growth as encouraging, the Bank immediately cautioned that these levels of growth are unlikely to enable the affected countries to attain their Millennium Development Goals. Consequently, it can be concluded that in Africa and Asia the quality of life crudely measured by the Human Development Index has either stagnated or fallen thus making the attainment of the Millennium Development Goals in 2015 a pipe dream. Democracy cannot be sustainable in the midst of under-development and poverty.

TABLE 1.5: Key economic indicators in SADC				
Country	% GDP per capita growth- 1990-2000	Avge annual change in consumer price index % in 2000	Debt service as % of export of goods and services – 2000	Net inflow of FDI as % of GDP -2000
Angola	-1.8	325.0	15.1	19.2
Botswana	2.3	8.6	1.8	0.6
Lesotho	2.1	6.1	12.1	-0.7
Malawi	1.8	29.5	11.7	2.7
Mauritius	4.0	4.2	20.8	6.1
Mozambique	3.9	-	11.4	3.7
Namibia	1.8	-	-	-
South Africa	-	5.3	10.0	0.8
Swaziland	0.2	12.2	2.3	-3.0
Tanzania	0.1	5.9	16.2	2.1
Zambia	-2.1	-	18.7	6.9
Zimbabwe	0.4	-	22.1	1.1

Table 1.5 on SADC economies shows that none of the countries in the region, apart from Mauritius and Mozambique, are growing enough to create more job opportunities and generate income for financing social development. Between 1990 and 2000, per capita income growth was marginal, stagnant or falling in the cases of Angola and Zambia. Meanwhile annual consumer index prices increased rapidly reaching as high as 325 per cent in Angola and almost 30 per cent in Malawi. The fact that many of the countries spend on average 15 per cent of their earned income on debt servicing suggests that economic difficulties will continue across the region. On the other hand, direct foreign investment remained very low. The SADC economies have clearly not yet reaped the democratic dividends widely expected from stable democratic economies. Expected foreign investment, perceived by many countries in the region as a critical factor to the success of their economic development strategy, has not been forthcoming. Efforts to generate local revenue sources to finance development have also been hampered by slow economic growth and low levels of domestic savings.

Given the above state of the region's economic performance, the question becomes, can these economies deliver the minimum social welfare expected of the MDGs? Clearly unemployment, poverty and limited self-supporting opportunities in less developed countries mean that more and more individuals and families will depend on the state for their basic survival needs. Dependency on the state and associated limits on personal rights and freedom does not augur well for democracy in less developed countries. From peasant farmers and students to business people, everyone increasingly looks to the state to provide assistance, jobs, and business services or to be given preferential treatment. The concern is that this type of population is captive to the state and some of the states use their economic power to stifle democracy and economic growth as a result of this dependency. For instance, government critics are few and can easily be ostracised for expressing views which contradict those of the government. Indeed some countries, including the fairly stable and maturing democracies of Botswana and Namibia, have refused to place government advertising in private newspapers because they were too critical of certain individuals within government (E.g. Botswana Guardian versus Government of Botswana – High Court of Botswana, 2003).

TABLE 1.6: State expenditure on basic services

Country	Education exp as % of GNP - 1997	Health exp as % of GNP- 97	ODA most recent year 2000	Human poverty index 2000 -%	Gini
Angola	-	-	23.3	-	-
Botswana	8.6	2.5	19.9	-	56.0*
Lesotho	-	-	20.4	25.7	56.0
Malawi	5.4	2.8	39.4	42.5	-
Mauritius	4.6	1.8	17.6	11.3	-
Mozambique	-	2.8	47.9	47.9	39.6
Namibia	9.1	3.3	11.3	34.5	-
South Africa	7.6	3.3	86.3	-	59.3
Swaziland	5.7	2.5	14.3	-	60.9
Tanzania	-	1.6	29.7	32.7	38.2
Zambia	2.2	3.6	76.3	40.0	52.6
Zimbabwe	-	-	14.1	36.1	50.1

* Estimate based on past local survey.

Table 1.6 shows two important aspects of the economic situation of SADC countries. On the one hand it is clear that these are needy populations where between 30 per cent and 40 per cent of the people live in income poverty. On the other hand, inequality of income is very high ranging between 40 per cent and 60 per cent. Clearly we are dealing with poor and unequal societies which, as noted above, tend to sell their democratic vote for short term material needs. Indeed, in many of the countries large numbers of poor people are still living as farm labourers where farm owners dictate their voting patterns or deny them access to alternative political views. These are some of the practical constraints still limiting the freedom and fairness of elections in many countries.

It is observed that Botswana, the oldest democracy in the region with relatively good economic indicators on growth, per capita income and lower debt servicing burden, has however not done much better than other countries in the areas of employment creation, foreign direct investment or poverty alleviation. While Botswana has done very well in providing free education, highly subsidised health care and provision of clean water to the majority of rural and urban poor in the past, recent economic trends show that government is unable to sustain this provision. The continuing poverty and its impact on the lives of many people in Botswana might actually be the reason why the ruling party's (BDP) popular vote has declined in the past three elections from 57 per cent (1994) to 52 per cent (2004), rather than the effectiveness of the opposition message. It was interesting that in the 2004 election the opposition BNF won four of its thirteen seats from traditional BDP strongholds of Kgalagadi North, Letlhakeng East, Letlhakeng North and Ngwaketse West. These are the regions where the impact of both poverty and inequality are strongly felt. In addition, in other north-west rural areas, Kgalagadi South, Gantsi North and South, Boteti North and South, Okavango and Chobe, the ruling party won by much smaller margins than ever before. However, it is important to add that inequality in the country is not seen merely in economic terms. It is also political-ethnic inequality which is felt by ethnic minorities in the north-western regions of the country.

BOTSWANA AND DEMOCRACY PROMOTION ABROAD

Given its long record of democratic practice over the past three and half decades, Botswana was well placed to be a regional and international promoter of democracy around the world. A combination of a stable democracy and successful economy placed Botswana in a strategic position given the general state of both economy and politics in the region and Africa as a whole during the decades of the 1970s and 1980s. Indeed in the earlier years, Botswana worked hard to lead the anti-apartheid and anti-minority rule movement that culminated in the establishment of the Southern African Development Community. However, it must also be noted that on the whole, Botswana has remained a reluctant player but certainly not a leader in democracy promotion. When Botswana was approached to lead, as in the case of the Commonwealth –

Zimbabwe issue it was found wanting and reluctant. This slowness to engage in international affairs has also been evident in the length of time Botswana took to sign many of the International Conventions. True, Botswana is a member of a number of international bodies such as SADC, the African Union, the Commonwealth, International IDEA and others, but for most of the time Botswana has not displayed the leadership currently being displayed by South Africa. From this perspective it could be argued that Botswana has failed to use its political capital to promote itself internationally.

CONCLUSIONS

In this chapter, the characteristics, performance and quality of Botswana's democracy have been analysed in comparison to her neighbouring southern African countries. Botswana has been practising democracy since independence in 1965 and as the oldest democracy in the region is an unparalleled success. Overall, the electoral process in Botswana has been free and fair, attracting the sustained participation of both the political parties and the electorate. The management of elections has been improving both organisationally and in terms of autonomy from government control as will be shown in another chapter by Lekorwe and Tshosa. In general, Botswana's democracy has shown increased confidence in the electoral process and the parliamentary system over the past three decades. It can also be concluded that a democratic culture characterised by a multi-party system and regular elections has evolved and is firmly established. In the past fifteen years the political system has also demonstrated capacity to reform when, for example, the independence of the electoral body was established, the voting age was lowered to eighteen years and the presidential term of office was limited to two terms of five years. These reforms brought the country, comparatively, closer to the new democracies in the region.

However, compared to the recent progress made by other countries in the region, Botswana's democracy does not stand out as more progressive or comprehensively developed. This is because several of the weaknesses evident in the rest of the countries of the region and beyond are apparent in Botswana's more mature democracy as well. Indeed in a number of areas Botswana performs worse than countries like Namibia, South Africa and Mauritius. The areas of democratic weakness in most of the countries discussed in this chapter include a dominant ruling party with numerous, but relatively weak, opposition groups, unequal access to the media and unequal access to financial resources and information by the opposition during election campaigns. Although political participation is still relatively high across the region, there are signs of decreasing levels of citizen participation in both elections and other democratic processes such as referenda. In some of the countries, including Botswana, weak parliaments are a result of the combination of weak opposition and the unfairness of the first-past-the post electoral system.

Botswana thus has much work to do in order to sustain confidence in its democratic system which has not yet experienced a change from one political party to another. The current system continues to breed frustration as the party which won 52 per cent of the popular vote is still able to receive over 70 per cent of the parliamentary seats as happened in the 2004 Botswana election. The funding of political parties is yet another important issue for reform and Molomo and Sebudubudu will discuss this in detail in their chapter. But it should be noted that around the world funding for political parties is provided by the state. The study of the funding of parties conducted by International IDEA (in 2003) showed that close to 60 per cent of the 144 countries surveyed had one form or another of party funding. In southern Africa around 60 per cent of the countries have political party funding. These include Angola, Lesotho, Malawi, Mozambique, Namibia, South Africa, Tanzania and Zimbabwe.

However, in the area which, in the context of this chapter has been described as the intrinsic dimension of democracy, Botswana has generally done well. But continuous reform at this level will be important to sustain public confidence in the system in the years to come. Perhaps the area where Botswana has excelled the most is the one referred to as the instrumental dimension of democracy. In this area Botswana trails only Mauritius and sometimes Namibia in its successful economic stability, overall economic performance and delivery of services such as education, health care, clean water supply and efforts toward poverty alleviation. Nevertheless, the question of sustaining the achievements of the past decades in this area is high on the agenda of Botswana's democracy as it is in other poorer countries in the region. Poverty remains persistent as unemployment, the impact of HIV/AIDS, slow economic growth and inequality become worse. The challenge of sustainability has led, in the case of Botswana, to some reversal of the mini-welfare system evident in the re-introduction of partial schools and other cost recovery measures in the social sector. These measures are bound to generate a lot of political debate and possibly create a backlash against the ruling BDP.

Finally, this chapter shows that Botswana has been a reluctant and slow political player in SADC and in the world. In this regard Botswana has failed to take the opportunity to be a democratic leader promoting democracy worldwide. This lost opportunity has now been taken aggressively by the newly democratic South Africa which is now reaping the rewards of her democratic leadership. Democracy is a process that is best demonstrated at home and promoted abroad. Perhaps Botswana can still take a more proactive role in promoting democracy in southern Africa and in the world: many countries look to Botswana for leadership but often do so in vain.

REFERENCES

Carothers, T. (1999) *Aiding Democracy Abroad: The Learning Curve.* Washington DC, Carnegie Endowment for International Peace

IDEA (2003) *Funding of Political Parties and Elections Campaigns*, Handbook Series, Stockholm, Sweden, IDEA,

IDEA (2002) *Voter Turnout in Western Europe Since 1945: A Global Report*, Stockholm, Sweden IDEA

IDEA (2000) *Towards Sustainable Democratic Institutions in Southern Africa*, Conference Report, Gaborone, Botswana

Mark Payne, J. et al (2002), *Democracies in Development: Politics and Reform in Latin America*, Washington DC, John Hopkins University Press

Ngware, S. et al (2002) *Multipartism and People's Participation: Case Studies from Kenya, Malawi, Tanzania*, Dar es Salaam, Tanzania, Tema Publishing Company Ltd

Nohlen, Dieter; (1996) *Elections and Electoral Systems*, 2nd Edition, Bonn, Germany, Friedrick Ebert Foundation,

Nohlen, Dieter; (2002) *IDEA Voter Turnout Since 1945, a Global Report*

NUPI, *Forum for Development Studies*, Olso, Norway, Norwegian Institute of International Affairs

Molutsi, P. (2004) 'Botswana: The Path to Democracy and Development' in E. Gyimah-Boadi, *Democratic Reform in Africa*, Boulder, Colorado, USA, Lynne Rienner Publishers

Sen, Armatya; (1999) 'Democracy and Development', *Journal of Democracy*

UNDP (2002) *Human Development Report: Deepening Democracy in a Fragmented World*, New York, UNDP

CHAPTER 2

ELECTORAL SYSTEMS AND DEMOCRACY IN BOTSWANA

Mpho Molomo

INTRODUCTION

Following Huntington's (1991) notion of the 'third wave' of democratisation, it is observed that there has been a resurgence of liberal democratic ideals. This has meant the opening up of the political sphere to ensure regular free and fair elections; the enjoyment of civil liberties in the form of freedom of association, assembly, and expression; the upholding of the rule of law and the absence of human rights abuses; and the existence of independent bodies within civil society to hold government accountable. Moreover, since the 1990s, elections have become the primary method of regime change in most of Africa and there has been a movement away from one party to multi-party governments and towards the consolidation and deepening of democracy. The latter entails, among other things, popular participation, political openness, free choice, equal competition, transparency and accountability in government.

Without question, Botswana is widely acclaimed as a front-runner in democratic politics in southern Africa, with every passing election exemplifying the embodiment of democratic ideals and good governance. Since the independence elections of 1965, Botswana has held nine successive elections, in an open, free and fair atmosphere but a close inspection does, however, reveal serious limitations. For instance, through no fault of theirs the ruling BDP has been in power since the independence election 40 years ago. It should be appreciated that democracy is an ever-evolving process that is under continual construction and reconstruction and must always be improved, partly through reforming the electoral system.

The central argument in this chapter is that democracy is fundamentally about freedom of choice, effective political participation, unfettered political competition, effective representation, transparency, accountability and the existence of the rule of law. It is argued that democracy in Botswana presents itself in a dialectical way, raising political expectations for greater political space, and resistance to demands calling for more democratic freedoms. It is also argued that it is perhaps the resolution of this dialectic that will determine the depth of democracy and its consolidation. It is asserted that a citizen's vote is as much a function of personal choice and social influence, as it is of the electoral system. In discussing the dialectic that promotes and encumbers democracy in Botswana, three broad areas are addressed.

First Botswana's electoral system is situated within a broader framework of alternative electoral systems. The pros and cons of the various systems are comprehensively debated with a view to suggesting an alternative model for Botswana. Secondly, areas that are perceived to be weak points in the country's democracy are isolated including the first-past-the-post system (FPTP), the absence of direct presidential elections and the lack of inner party democracy. Thirdly, it is noted that most of these limitations could be addressed through electoral reform. In addressing these issues, the chapter begins by laying out the contextual framework for understanding Botswana's electoral system.

CONTEXTUAL FRAMEWORK

In 1965, Botswana adopted a republican constitution, which operates a unicameral Westminster-style parliamentary system based on a single member district or the first-past-the-post (FPTP) electoral system. Following the 2001 National Population and Housing Census, which recorded a population increase to about 1.7 million, it transpired that the threshold of constituencies had shifted, necessitating a realignment and redrawing of constituency and ward boundaries. Parliament[1], acting on this information, increased the parliamentary seats from 40 to 57 and council seats from 406 to 490. Following the provisions of 64 (2) (b) of the Botswana Constitution, a Delimitation Commission was appointed by the Judicial Services Commission in July 2002, redrawing the constituency boundaries.

Here, the argument is that the liberal democracy that Botswana espouses can effectively take place when there is effective political competition. For it to take place there must be political parties and free and fair elections. Although elections are a

---

1 It comprises of 57 elected members and four members specially elected by parliament, the speaker, the attorney general and the president.

prima facie condition for democracy, the argument is that democracy is not only about having free and fair elections, but also having a fair electoral system in place as well.

Following the categories developed by Sartori (1976), party systems can be classified into four main types: a predominant one party system where one party wins the majority of seats in the legislature; two-party systems where two parties are dominant, of course with the possibility of the existence of several smaller parties; moderate multi-party systems are characterised by the existence of several parties, with possibilities of winning an election; and a polarised multi-party system that is characterised by the existence of several political parties with sharp ideological or regional polarity.

As shown in **Table 2.1** below, the FPTP system has ensured that Botswana operates a predominant one party system, in which the BDP has won all elections by decisive majorities. In 1965 it won 28 of the 32 seats, and in 1969 it won 24 out of 31 seats. In 1974, the BDP increased its margin by winning 27 of the 32 seats. The BDP's electoral fortunes continued to grow in 1979, when it won 29 of the 32 seats. These gains were despite the fact that its popular vote was falling. In contrast, the opposition started to make some gains in 1984 by winning 6 of the 34 constituencies, but still leaving the BDP very much in control of the political landscape. In 1989, the BDP recorded yet another decisive win of parliamentary seats, this time sweeping 31 of the 34 constituencies, but with a low popular vote. Perhaps the 1994 election could be seen as a turning point in Botswana's electoral history as, for the first time, the opposition won close to half the seats polled by the BDP – 13 out of 40 seats. During the 1999 election, the BNF poll, which constitutes the main opposition, dropped as a result of the split it experienced in 1997. In that election the opposition parties won 7 seats altogether in comparison to BDP's 33 seats. Eight political parties[2], and a few independent candidates contested the 2004 election. Of these eight, only three are represented in parliament. In 2004 election, the opposition increased its poll by winning 13 seats and the BDP 44 seats.

Following from the above discussion, it is clear that Botswana is a predominant one party system. Only one political party, the BDP, has won all elections. Huntington's formulation suggests that democracy is entrenched only when there has been a double turn over of government. But I want to make a broader analysis of Botswana's political

---

2 These are Botswana Democratic Party, Botswana National Front, Botswana Congress Party, Botswana Alliance Movement, Botswana Peoples Party, New Democratic Front, MELS Movement of Botswana, and Social Democratic Party

situation by comparing electoral systems and showing how the country's politics could have changed.

In spite of the manifestation of political pluralism marked by the existence of several political parties, in terms of parliamentary seats Botswana's democratic system is characterised by a weak opposition. The point is that a strong opposition characterised by more representation in parliament is an indispensable part of a democracy as it keeps government in check and accountable to the people. However, splits and factionalism, appear to be a weakening factor of opposition parties (although the BDP has also had its fair share of factionalism). With the exception of the Botswana Alliance Movement, breakaway factions from the BNF have significantly reduced its growth in parliament.

The second point is that even though the opposition is weak in parliament, the BNF has increased its electoral fortunes in terms of the popular vote since the 1994 election. In that election, the opposition won 42 per cent of the popular vote and this is a sign of a strong opposition. During the 1999 election, due to a split in the opposition, its poll of the popular vote only dropped slightly to 41 per cent.

TABLE 2.1: Party support (1965 – 2004) in the parliamentary elections									
Number of seats FPTP									
Party	1965	1969	1974	1979	1984	1989	1994	1999	2004
BDP	28	24	27	29	28	31	27	33	44
BNF	-	3	2	2	5	3	13	6	12
BIP/IFP	0	1	1	0	0	0	0	-	-
BPU	0	0	0	0	0	0	-	-	-
BPP	3	3	2	1	1	0	0	-	-
BCP	-	-	-	-	-	-	-	1	1
BAM	-	-	-	-	-	-	0	0	0
NDF	-	-	-	-	-	-	-	-	0
MELS	-	-	-	-	-	-	0	0	0
Total Seats	31	31	32	32	34	34	40	40	57
Number of seats PR									
BDP	25	21	25	24	23	22	22	23	30
BNF	-	4	4	4	7	9	15	10	15
BIP/IFP	2	2	1	2	1	1	1	-	-
BPU	0	0	0	0	0	0	-	-	-

TABLE 2.1: Party support (1965 – 2004) in the parliamentary elections

Number of seats PR

Party	1965	1969	1974	1979	1984	1989	1994	1999	2004
BPP	4	4	2	2	2	2	2	-	-
BCP	-	-	-	-	-	-	-	5	10
BAM	-	-	-	-	-	-	0	2	2
NDF	-	-	-	-	-	-	-	-	0
MELS	-	-	-	-	-	-	0	0	0
Total Seats	31	31	32	32	34	34	40	40	57

% of FPTP seats

BDP	90	77	84	91	82	91	67	83	77
BNF	-	10	7	6	15	9	33	15	21
BIP/IFP	0	3	2	0	0	0	-	-	-
BPU	0	0	0	0	0	0	-	-	-
BPP	10	10	7	3	3	0	0	-	-
BCP	-	-	-	-	-	-	-	2	2
BAM	-	-	-	-	-	-	0	0	0
NDF	-	-	-	-	-	-	-	-	0
MELS	-	-	-	-	-	-	0	0	0
Independent	0	0	0	0	0	0	0	0	-
TOTAL	100	100	100	100	100	100	100	100	100

% of Popular Vote

BDP	80	68	77	75	68	65	54	54	51
BNF	-	14	11	13	20	27	37	25	26
BIP/IFP	5	6	5	4	3	2	-	-	-
BPU	-	-	-	-	1	1	1	-	-
BPP	14*	12	7	7	7	4	4	-	-
BCP	-	-	-	-	-	-	-	11	16
BAM	-	-	-	-	-	-	-	5	3
NDF	-	-	-	-	-	-	-	-	0.8
MELS	-	-	-	-	-	-	0	0	0
Rejected	-	-	-	-	-	-	-	5	2
TOTAL per cent vote	99	100	100	99	99	99	96	100	100

In the 2004 election, the opposition consolidated its growth, increasing its share of the popular vote to 46 per cent. However, while the popular vote of the opposition increased, the BNF's vote grew by only 1 per cent from the 1999 election, accounting for 26 per cent of the popular vote. In relative terms, the BCP experienced the highest growth of 5 per cent. But considering the fact that the BCP is a splinter group from the BNF, it must be emphasised that its growth is at the expense of BNF. Despite this small nuance caused by the BCP, and contrary to Molutsi's argument in Chapter One, a pattern that has emerged since 1994 is that of a two party system. It is further noted that in about 12 constituencies that the BDP won, it was a result of a split in the opposition vote between the BNF and the BCP.

The predominant party system that has been evident in Botswana's political practice is a result of the FPTP electoral system and of vote splitting between the opposition parties. In the first instance, the system precipitates an uneven political playing field, generously rewarding the ruling party with parliamentary seats even though its popular vote is decreasing. In the second instance, the BDP aided in part by the failure of opposition parties to present themselves as credible alternative governments, due to their propensity to fracture and split the opposition vote, have made political participation uncompetitive and uninteresting. Essentially, voters are motivated by uncertainty; where they feel that their vote might make a difference, they turnout in large numbers and vote. But where the outcomes can be predicted a priori, they tend to be disinterested in voting.

Fair political competition is the hallmark of liberal democratic practice. Robert Dahl (1961) and Maurice Duverger (1954) see the greatest setback to democracy as manifestations of political oligarchies. In the case of Botswana, where the system operates a predominant party system, political competition between political parties is limited. The circulation of the elite, as suggested by Mosca (1939) and Pareto (1935), is more pronounced in the BDP and limited in the opposition parties, partly due to limited inner party democracy. However, Dalton (1996:44) argues that political competition has a high motivational influence in voter turnout. Campaigning is an activity that generates a lot of momentum, having a snowball effect that motivates even the uninterested, to participate. However in Botswana, political competition is one-sided, with only the BDP winning most seats most of the time.

Here the point must be made that the 'third wave' of democratisation has brought in a new momentum of institutional and capacity building with a view to deepen democracy to ensure democratic governance. Following a referendum in 1997, electoral reforms were instituted and they provided for the absentee ballot, the establishment of the Independent Electoral Commission (IEC), and the lowering of the voting age from 21 to 18 years. However, it must be noted that the political playing field in Botswana cannot be said to be level on a number of accounts. The central point is that perhaps the FPTP electoral system is weighted heavily in favour of the ruling party.

ELECTORAL SYSTEMS

Electoral systems are the basic instruments that govern the conduct of elections. As discussed in Reynolds and Reilly (1997:7), electoral systems are said to be manipulative instruments because they determine how elections are won and lost. They constitute the basic infrastructure upon which democratic discourse takes place.

The choice of an electoral system is always a political decision, and therefore underscores the nature of the political system. In the case of Botswana, the country emulated the example of the UK by adopting a constitution and electoral laws similar to theirs at the time of independence. These served the country well during the first few decades of independence as they have contributed to the political stability and tranquillity that the country has enjoyed over the years. However, a close analysis of the current electoral model demonstrates that the system is wanting in some respects. The FPTP electoral system does not provide for effective political representation; council and parliamentary electoral outcomes do not reflect the broad interests represented in society, and its winner-takes-all phenomenon provides the basis for exclusion of some interests in society. Moreover, the system tends to promote a sense of voter apathy, as one party dominates the electoral process, and supporters of opposing parties tend to get somewhat disillusioned, and withdraw from participation in politics.

The electoral system informs the basic structure of the electoral law. It specifies, among other things, the constituency size, how voters express their political choice, the minimum number of votes a candidate needs to win a ward or seat or for a party to secure representation, how ballots are counted to allocate seats and who wins the race. In what Norris (2004:4) refers to as 'electoral engineering', it is evident that attempts to deepen, consolidate and strengthen democratic governance have focused on the 'basic design of the electoral systems...on issues of electoral administration, on voter education, on election observation, and on party capacity building' (Norris, 2004:4). More broadly, electoral engineering has focused on an attempt to attain a 'balance between greater governmental accountability through majoritarian systems and wider parliamentary diversity through proportional representation.' Basically debates on electoral systems have focused on ideal types, and these are classified in three broad categories: majoritarian, proportional representation, and the combined or hybrid type, and of course each one of these has sub-categories.

Electoral procedures are also important because they regulate the manner in which elections are conducted. Through continental and regional bodies such as the Electoral Institute of Southern Africa (EISA), the SADC Parliamentary Forum and the SADC Electoral Commissioners Forum, among others, attempts have been made to set up regional norms and standards that regulate the conduct of elections. Under the framework of the New Partnership for Africa (NEPAD), a peer review mechanism, which Botswana refuses to ratify, has put in place measures to ensure that democratic governance is entrenched. These electoral standards cover a wide terrain; they serve as official guidelines for those mandated to execute the electoral law, as a code of conduct for running elections and as a code of conduct for political players. Electoral procedures set guidelines for the demarcation and distribution of polling stations, nomination of candidates, eligibility to vote, voter registration[3], voter education[4], procedures of casting a ballot, design and preparation of the ballot paper, and regulations governing the disclosure of campaign finance and media access.

PRESIDENTIAL AND PARLIAMENTARY SYSTEMS

It may be thought that electoral-engineering is perhaps more fundamentally influenced by the constitutional structure which spells out the nature of the political regime. Governments come in two basic forms; they can be presidential or parliamentary. Manifesting the extent of power sharing, the legislature may be either unicameral or bicameral, and regarding the concentration or dispersal of political power, a

---

3 Perhaps we could take a leaf from western democracies which tend to have a high voter turnout. Due to well developed national data bases, the voters roll is prepared automatically by government or electoral commissions when the electorate reaches a voting age. As a result, voters are not encumbered by the lengthy voter registration exercise, and voters stand a greater chance of casting their ballot.

4 Following the Voter Apathy Report of 2002, which recommended a vigorous voter education campaign, the IEC went all out to 'brand' itself as the sole agent empowered by the Electoral Act to administer, and also educate people about the electoral process. In its publicity campaign, the IEC used 'Mmutlanyana-wa-ditlhopho', which suggests that it is wise and noble to vote. Through the Botswana Television (Btv) programme, Matlho-a-phage, which generated a lot of dialogue and debate around elections and political issues, the IEC provided a forum and an opportunity for the electorate to learn more about political parties and the political process. The IEC, in addition to numerous other campaign messages and slogans, composed an election song, which enjoyed wide appeal.

government may be either unitary or federal.

Theorists on presidential and parliamentary systems (Lijpart, 1991; 1992; Linz, 1990; Larderyret, 1991; Quarde, 1991) have debated the pros and cons of the two systems and argue that, while presidential systems have strong and independent executives where the legislature is not controlled by the same party, they are characterised by executive-legislature stalemate. On the other hand, where the same party controls both houses, there is greater propensity to unilateralism and insensitivity to public opinion. In the parliamentary systems where all parties have a fair share of the seats, there is a sense of inclusion in the policy making process. However, Botswana presents a parliamentary system which manifests a predominant party system in which one party dominates both the executive and legislature. In theory a prime minister should head a parliamentary system but a president heads Botswana's parliamentary system, and this creates a lack of balance. Actually, the independence constitution defined the head of state as prime minister but this was amended after independence to be president but without an accompanying presidential system where the president is directly elected. In Botswana the president is indirectly elected by virtue of being the presidential candidate of the majority party in parliament. Although the president is not directly elected, he wields extensive executive powers which come directly from the constitution and not from parliament.

MAJORITARIAN PARLIAMENTARY SYSTEM

Theories of majoritarian electoral systems, which in the case of Botswana are manifested by the first-past-the-post (FPTP) electoral system, emphasise government accountability and effectiveness. This system produces single party cabinets, which take the credit for all the good work and blame for government failure. However, critics of this system argue that it makes the losers feel disempowered and alienated from the political system. The argument here is that a win by a simple majority affords the winner an opportunity to impose their will on the rest of the population. According to Norris (1999:220), 'in majoritarian democracies, winners who supported the governing party consistently expressed far higher satisfaction with democracy than losers'. This is to say that the majoritarian system inspires confidence and trust in the supporters of the dominant party and despair in the supporters of loosing parties.

The other point is that electoral systems influence the manner in which voters express their choices. The ballot links the voter to the party and the candidate. In the single-member district propounded by the FPTP electoral system, each voter is given a single ballot, and casts the vote for both the party and candidate[5]. This system brings the representative into direct contact with the electorate, and has the propensity to encourage candidates to deliver when they are in office as the electorate know whom to hold accountable, and the representatives are motivated to provide ward and constituency service. This sort of engagement encourages representatives to provide personalised support, and always ensure they maintain visibility during weddings, funerals[6] and other public gatherings. But often, this personalised service takes precedence over the core business of debating and approving government policy. Moreover, candidates develop personal attachments with wards and constituencies, and jealously guard their interests in the area such that when they lose primary elections, they often do not accept the verdict, appealing the results and if the outcomes are still not in their favour, defecting to opposing parties or standing as independent candidates.

This personalised attachment to wards, constituencies and political parties tends to produce political demagogues and personality cults. Campaign songs mostly sing praise poems about the leaders and to a lesser extent about the political parties themselves. The fragmentation of political parties in Botswana is in large measure a function of personalities and personal differences rather than substantive procedural and ideological differences. The most recent manifestation of this development is the break away of Dr Kenneth Koma[7] from the BNF[8] - although he was its founder member, its theoretician and mentor and respected leader for many years - to form the New Democratic Front (NDF).

---

5 It is said that an old man at a political gathering once asked Sir Seretse Khama a simple and yet philosophical question of how they could vote for him but not vote for their Member of Parliament. Khama had difficulties answering the question but urged the old man to continue voting for the MP because it was the only way he could vote for him.

6 The electorate tends to reward candidates who show compassion more than those who are aloof but are effective in council and parliament.

7 In 1997 when there were major disturbances in the BNF leading to the break away of the parliamentary caucus group to form the BCP, Johnson Motshwarakgole, a trade unionist and a stalwart member of the BNF personified the party with Koma. He said Koma was the BNF and the BNF was Koma. This reminds me of the time in Ghana when Kwame Nkhrumah said the Conventions Peoples Party was Ghana and Ghana was the Conventions Peoples Party. In a similar manner Kenneth Kaunda of Zambia in asserting the omnipresence of the United Independence Party said One Zambia one nation, one party one leader.

8 This development was a culmination of a split that resulted from differences between two factions within the BNF - the Concerned Group and the Party Line. The Concerned Group was a faction of young party enthusiasts who wanted to challenge Koma's hegemonic control of the party and also questioned the building of a personality cult of its leader. The Party Line consisted of those who continued to hero worship Koma, and counted on his support to assume the leadership of the party. These differences, which were not as such ideological, came to the head at the Kanye Congress of November 2001, in which the concerned group swept all the Central Committee positions by wide margins. On allegations of rigging, the Party Line refused to accept the results and after a number of exchanges, which involved their suspension and subsequent expulsion from the party, formed a new party - NDF.

Figure 2.1 below presents election outcomes using the FPTP electoral system from 1965 to 2004. This figure presents a graphic picture that the FPTP electoral system produces a predominant party system. In all these elections, except for 1994, the combined poll of the opposition in terms of parliamentary seats won was minuscule. In 1994 the opposition polled close to half the seats of the ruling party, and in 2004 the combined poll of the opposition was just under a third of the BDP.

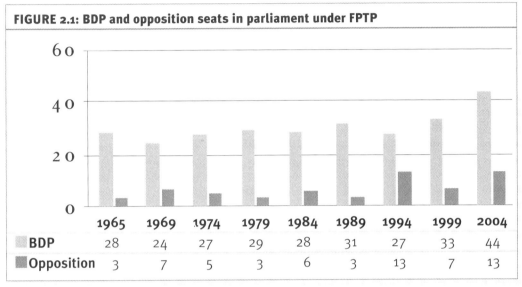

FIGURE 2.1: BDP and opposition seats in parliament under FPTP

	1965	1969	1974	1979	1984	1989	1994	1999	2004
BDP	28	24	27	29	28	31	27	33	44
Opposition	3	7	5	3	6	3	13	7	13

Source: Election Reports

It is strongly contended that the FPTP electoral system creates a feeling of exclusion for those who vote for opposition parties. **Figures 2.1, 2.2, 2.3** and **2.4,** compute election results using different electoral systems and produce different results. Starting with 1994, the BDP polled 27 of the 40 seats; the combined opposition won 13 seats. But when the popular vote is computed using PR, assuming a threshold of five per cent, it can be seen that the BDP would have won 22 seats and the opposition, would have won 18 seats in total. This scenario reflects proportional representation or rather reality because during those elections, the BDP polled 54 per cent of the popular vote and the opposition polled 42 per cent altogether. The same trend continues well into the 1999 election. In those elections, the BDP won 33 of the 40 parliamentary seats, while the opposition polled only 7 seats. However, PR reflects that the BDP share of the popular vote remained constant at 54 per cent and that of the opposition dropped to 41 per cent: a PR system would have given the BDP 23 seats and the BNF 17 seats. The 2004 election reflected the continued preponderance of the BDP at the polls; it won 44 of the 57 parliamentary constituencies under the FPTP system and the opposition won only 13 seats. In percentage terms the BDP won 77 per cent of the seats and the opposition 23 per cent. But the picture changes dramatically when the results are examined under PR. Under a PR system the BDP would have got 30 seats while the opposition would have got 27 seats. Thus, despite the show of strength by the BDP in terms of seats won, its poll of the popular vote declined to 51 per cent and that of the opposition increased to 46 per cent.

The conclusion to be drawn from the FPTP electoral system is that it encourages a predominant party system, and exaggerates the weaknesses of opposition parties. The winner-take-all phenomenon of the FPTP system has the effect of forming legislative bodies that are not reflective of the popular vote and of the will of the people. Invariably, the results show that the incumbent party tends to benefit from a windfall of seats compared to their proportion of the popular vote and this gain tends to run against the principles of representative and popular democracy.

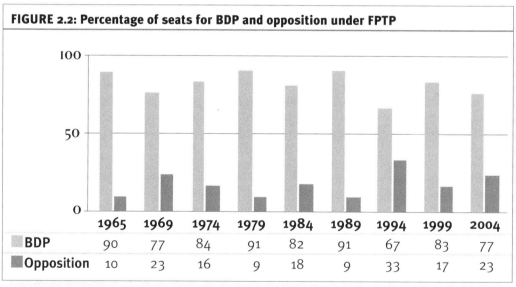

FIGURE 2.2: Percentage of seats for BDP and opposition under FPTP

	1965	1969	1974	1979	1984	1989	1994	1999	2004
BDP	90	77	84	91	82	91	67	83	77
Opposition	10	23	16	9	18	9	33	17	23

Source: Election Reports

By excluding the opposition parties from government, the FPTP system exhibits in-built tendencies of authoritarianism rather than rule by consensus. This system dilutes the most potent weapon that the electorate has – that is, their vote – and their chance to shape their political destiny. However, this system has been credited with producing stable governments that are accountable to the people and with forging effective links between representatives and the people. Nevertheless, while these benefits are enjoyed in Botswana, there are other competing interests in terms of entrenching democracy. In consideration of this we turn to PR to determine what it has to offer.

PROPORTIONAL REPRESENTATION

As already noted above, although elections are an indispensable ingredient, they are not a complete panacea for democracy. The argument here is that, reduced to simple terms, democracy is about empowering the people and giving them the power to shape their political future, and not just about electing a government. In essence, democracy is something beyond the ritual of casting a ballot and entails that institutions that are formed from the results of elections reflect the will of the people. Democracy is also about effective electoral competition, wherein political parties are not only allowed by law to contest elections, but are placed in a position that gives them as equal a chance as any other party to win the elections. The overall argument is that what obtains in Botswana is that opposition parties suffer many disabilities emanating mainly from the FPTP electoral system.

The arguments in favour of PR which, as the name suggests, is a system that allocates seats as a proportion of the popular vote, are now introduced. More than any other electoral system, it faithfully translates a party's share of the popular vote to a corresponding proportion of seats in council and parliament. Moreover, it not only advocates proportionality in the legislature but also in the executive. Of course, the degree of representation depends of the threshold[9] set by the electoral law.

Reynolds (1995) and Liphart (1999) argue that PR represents the complete opposite of the FPTP system. It is a system that believes in consensus and power sharing and widens the frontiers of democracy by ensuring that political differences that exist in society are represented in parliament in both the legislature and the executive. By virtue of its properties of narrowing the gap between winners and losers, it is highly recommended for divided societies (though it is acknowledged that Botswana is not a divided society). Since the system apportions seats according to the popular vote, even small parties make it into parliament and cabinet. Moreover, it is usually unlikely (with

---

9 A threshold can be as low as .67 per cent and as high as 10 per cent in the Netherlands and Seychelles, respectively. A low threshold accounts for extreme PR, which is more inclusive and a high threshold accounts for moderate PR. Israel and Italy are said to operate extreme PR, and Germany, Norway, Sweden, and South Africa are said to operate moderate PR. For detail see Reynolds, A. and Reilly, B. (1997) *The International IDEA Handbook of Electoral System Design* Stockholm, Sweden

the exception of South Africa) for any political party to gain an absolute majority in an election, and as a result PR systems are amenable to coalition governments.

But based on its experiences elsewhere, PR is often criticised for producing unstable governments[10]. Given the fact that the system is so open, and generously rewards even small political parties, it encourages the proliferation of political parties. Also, it is rare under this system for any one political party to win an absolute majority and form a government and as a result the PR system is amenable to coalition governments that are susceptible to collapse. Another serious weakness is the fact that coalition governments often desist from taking necessary but unpopular decisions for fear of upsetting their coalition partners. But perhaps the strongest criticism is that PR gives small parties inordinate powers because they control the 'wing seats' or are power brokers that determine the direction of the coalition.

However, one important and positive feature of this system, which surpasses the FPTP electoral system, is that by virtue of having multi-member districts it obviates the possibility of a zero-sum politics of exclusion from electoral politics. The travesty of the FPTP electoral system is that irrespective of the magnitude[11]of the poll of the losing candidates, they are excluded from the political system in which only one candidate is returned. Moreover, as discussed in another chapter in this book, all the BDP governments that have ruled the country, except for 1965 and 1984 were minority governments as they were elected by less than 50 per cent of the eligible voters. However, the electoral law in Botswana does not require a party to have an absolute majority to form government.

It should be noted that the PR system has several variations. To name two: open list PR and closed list PR. The open list system is usually preferred where the voter is entrusted with two ballots, one for the party and the other one for the preferred candidate. In this system, in addition to giving the electorate the opportunity to cast a ballot for the party, they are also given the chance to cast a ballot for their preferred candidate. This system tries to achieve a balance between the party and the candidate. Perhaps more importantly, candidates and parties that meet a certain threshold are included in government.

On the other hand, there is less preference for the closed list, multi-member district which affords the voter only one ballot for the party. In this system, the party

---

10 Italy is often cited as a most unstable government given the collapse of its coalition governments.

11 This envisages a situation whereby out of a total of 100 votes, candidates A gets 49 votes, B 48, and C 3 votes; in a winner takes all situation both B and C would be excluded from government but by any realistic measure, there is every indication that B has polled significantly to warrant representation in the political system.

ranks candidates, using whatever criteria it deems appropriate. Under the closed list PR system, the contest is essentially between political parties and not candidates who are directly recognisable to the electorate. The closed list PR system promotes authoritarianism within parties as the party often uses its control of the party list to reward loyal members and punish dissenters. On the other hand, the closed PR system may be positively used to empower women to get into positions in government. In what is often referred to as the 'zebra system', the party may deliberately rank order candidates in such a manner as to advantage women. For instance, it could require that every other candidate in the list should be a woman. In this closed PR system, the central focus is on the party, and the party manifesto and party programmes are held supreme. The strength of a campaign depends on sound programmes that a party propounds and on the charisma of the party leader.

The advantages of PR have already been discussed when the FPTP electoral system was critiqued. Suffice only to amplify a few here. Assuming a threshold of five per cent, as per **Figure 2.3** below, starting perhaps with the 1984 election, the election results would have been markedly different and the opposition poll would only have been less than half that of the BDP. In 1989 and the opposition would have polled more than half of the seats in the national assembly. In 1994, if Botswana were using PR, it would have entered a new phase in politics; only three seats would have separated the BDP from the opposition. Due to a split vote, the opposition vote dropped slightly but in 2004 it returned to the position it was at in 1994.

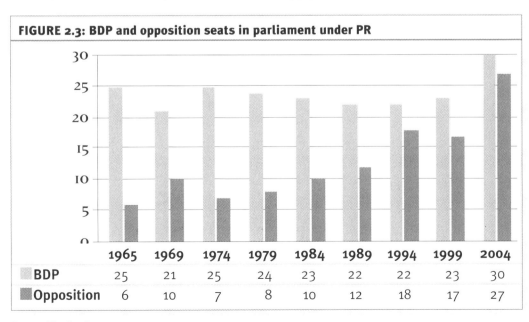

FIGURE 2.3: BDP and opposition seats in parliament under PR

	1965	1969	1974	1979	1984	1989	1994	1999	2004
BDP	25	21	25	24	23	22	22	23	30
Opposition	6	10	7	8	10	12	18	17	27

Source: Election Reports

Political debates in Botswana, especially when instigated by opposition parties argue for the introduction of political reforms in favour of greater proportionality of seats in accordance with the popular vote. **Figure 2.4** shows that since 1984, the portion of the BDP share of the popular vote has been decreasing, and that of the opposition increasing. Indications are that, assuming everything remains constant, and in line with trends of the last few, the 2009 election is likely to see the BDP's popular vote drop to 48 per cent, and that of the opposition rise to 51 per cent. But this may not help the opposition to win state power due to the FPTP system.

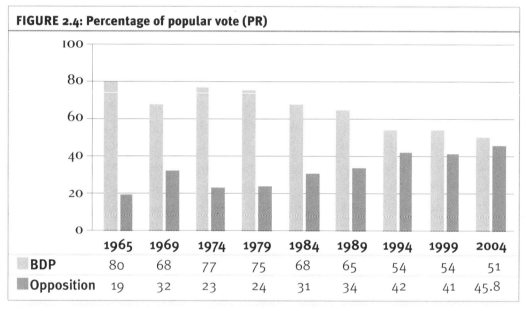

FIGURE 2.4: Percentage of popular vote (PR)

	1965	1969	1974	1979	1984	1989	1994	1999	2004
BDP	80	68	77	75	68	65	54	54	51
Opposition	19	32	23	24	31	34	42	41	45.8

Source: Election Reports

The conclusions to be drawn from PR are that if Botswana was operating PR, the notions held as characteristics of a predominant party system and a weak opposition would not hold water anymore. Perhaps given the enthusiasm and the confidence that the system would have inspired in the opposition, there would already have been a turn over of government.

MIXED MEMBER PROPORTIONALITY

With the 'third wave' of democratisation the Mixed Member Proportionality (MMP) electoral system is beginning to receive greater consideration. It is viewed it as a system that not only affords greater representation but also accountability. The system combines the best elements of the FPTP and PR. It is a system that tries to retain the effectiveness of the FPTP system in giving greater accountability by connecting the electorate to their representatives, and also introducing the greater representation and proportionality of PR. Its effect is that it would not only increase the number of seats but also provide two tiers of electoral systems. What I suggest for Botswana is an MMP system, comprising the retention of the FPTP system through which 57 seats would be filled, and to have an additional 29 seats that would be allocated according to the PR system. The MMP system would give each voter two ballots; one for the constituency to be computed according to the FPTP, and the other for the party to be computed using the PR system. Basically the constituency vote would determine who represents the constituency in the national assembly, and the PR vote would determine the overall composition of the house. The degree of proportions[12] would have to be arrived at based on the local conditions. In Lesotho during the 2002 elections, there was a total of 120 seats in which 80 were allocated according to FPTP system and 40 according to PR. The manner in which it would operate in Botswana would have to be tailored to meet the local conditions. However, the Lesotho model[13] could be explored to provide lessons for Botswana. The procedure of allocating seats in the Lesotho model is that the constituency ballots would be computed using the FPTP system. To allocate the seats proportionally, the quota has to be established first by adding up the total number of party votes cast and dividing it by the total number of seats. Then, the number of seats each party is entitled to is determined by dividing the total votes cast for that party by the quota. However, if a party has acquired more seats in the constituency election or the same number of seats they would have acquired under PR, then those seats would be considered as the final allocation. The compensatory seats work where parties get fewer seats under the constituency than they would have been entitled under PR. In such a situation, the difference between the constituency and popular vote would be added under the PR system.

Even though the situation in Botswana is not as dramatic as that of Lesotho, I still think it bears some resemblance to it (see the concluding chapter for an

---

12 In Germany 50 per cent of the seats are voted on FPTP system while the other 50 per cent are on PR. In New Zealand 58 per cent are on FPTP and 42 per cent PR.

13 Perhaps in order to appreciate the necessity of the MMP we should draw a parallel of what is likely to happen in Botswana to what happened in Lesotho. Reference to the 1993 and 1998 elections would illustrate the point. In 1993, the Basotoland Congress Party (BCP) won all 65 parliamentary seats although it had received only 74.9 per cent of the popular vote. The opposition Basotoland National Party (BNP) did not win a single seat despite the fact that it had polled 22.6 per cent of the popular vote, a factor that raised suspicion among opposition parties that government had rigged the elections. Following democratic procedures of redress, the opposition parties contested the election results in a court of law but lost, as there was no strong evidence to substantiate their claims. With time, due to internal fights, the leader of the BCP, Ntsu Mokhehle resigned from the party and formed the Lesotho Congress for Democracy (LCD). During the 1998 election there was a near repeat of the 1993 election outcome. The LCD won the election by 79 out of 80 seats while they had polled 60.7 per cent of the popular vote. The BNP, which had received 24.5 per cent of the popular vote received only 1 seat.

alternative view), and lessons can be drawn from it. The general lesson to be derived from Lesotho is that there were perceptions that both the 1993 and 1998 elections were rigged. Whatever the merits of these allegations were, it is evident from them that the FPTP system encouraged a predominant party system which excluded the opposition from government. Following the disturbances of 1998, Lesotho decided to reform its electoral system, and adopted the MMP system. And the system seems to have addressed the pertinent electoral problems (see the concluding chapter for more details). The projections made here for Botswana are that during the 2009 election, the BDP is likely to win the majority of the seats in parliament but lose the popular vote; and this is likely to fuel a political crisis in the country. Perhaps the best way for this country to avert such a crisis is to reform the electoral system.

CONCLUSION

Democracy is not an absolute. It is an evolving process that needs to be nurtured, constantly reinforced, altered and refined: reforming the electoral system is one way of enhancing democracy. The single member district FPTP electoral system operating in Botswana creates strong, accountable governments that do not adequately represent the popular will of the people. It also serves as a disincentive to small parties because they do not stand a chance of winning seats. As a result, this system produces citizens with less support for democracy. The PR system on the other hand, produces representative, inclusive and consensual governments but is often characterised by political instability.

Based on the trend of previous elections, it can be seen that the BDP poll of the popular vote is declining and that of the opposition is rising and yet the BDP still stands a good chance of winning the 2009 election if the FPTP system is used. What is problematic is the likelihood that the BDP could win more seats but lose the popular vote to the opposition. The disparity between the number of seats and the popular vote would most probably be magnified, and that would create an impression that elections are rigged, leading the country into a crisis (see the conclusion of the book for an alternative treatment of this issue).

Another possible scenario is that as it is apparent that the BDP is most likely to lose the popular vote, factionalism would compound this process by polarising the party, making its future less bright and its continued stay in power more uncertain. Perhaps the best way to guarantee the BDP's continued presence in government is to reform the electoral system, and introduce MMP as a system that would enjoy the best of the two worlds: the effectiveness of the FPTP and the representative-ness of the PR system. The overall conclusion is that an MMP system is best suited for Botswana's changing political situation and climate. A middle of the road position that mixes the two systems would produce a strong government that is based on the will of the people and deepen democracy by promoting political equality across gender, ethnic and regional divisions.

REFERENCES

Almond, G and Powell, B. (1966) *Comparative Politics: A Developmental Approach* Boston: Little Brown and Company,.

Barkan, J. (2002) 'Protracted Transitions in Africa's New Democracies', *Democratisation*, 7,3 Autumn, pp. 277-43.

Berlson, B, Lazarsfeld, P. and McPhee, W. (1954) *Voting: a Study of Opinion Formation in a Presidential Campaign*, Chicago: Chicago University Press.

Bill, J and Hardgrave, R. (1973) *Comparative Politics: the Quest for Theory*, Columbus: Charles Merill Publishing Co.

Bratton, M and Van de Wallie, N. (1997) *Democratic experiments in Africa*. Cambridge: Cambridge University Press.

Bratton, M. (1999) 'Political Participation in a New Democracy: Institutional Considerations in Zambia', *Comparative Political studies*, 32, 5, pp. 549-588.

Botswana Democratic Party (2001) Botswana Democratic Party Primary Election Rules, Gaborone.

Botswana Congress Congress Party : Manifesto 2004 – 'Botswana Can be Much Better', Gaborone, BCP 2004.

Botswana Democratic Party, BDP manifesto 2004: 'There is still no alternative, Gaborone, BDP 2004.

Chazan, N. and D. Rothchild. eds. (1988) *The Precarious Balance: State and Society in Africa*. Boulder, Colorado.

Dahl, R. (1989) *Democracy and its Critics*. New Haven: Yale University Press.

Dahl, R. (1961) *Who governs?* New Haven: Yale University Press.

Dalton, R., P. Beck and S, Flanagan (1984) *Electoral Change in Advanced Democracies,* Princeton University Press.

Diamond, L. (2000) (ed) *Democratisation in Africa*. Baltimore: John Hopkins University Press.

Diamond, L. (1996) 'Is the Third Wave Over?', *Journal of Democracy*. 7, 3 pp.20-37.

_____ (1999) *Developing Democracy: Toward Consolidation*. Baltimore: John Hopkins University Press.

_____ 1994. Rethinking Civil society: Toward Democratic Consolidation, *Journal of Democracy* 5,3 pp. 4-17.

Diamond, L. and M. Plattner (1999). *Democratisation in Africa*. Baltimore: John Hopkins University Press.

Duverger, M. (1954) *Political Parties: Their Organisation and Activities in the Modern State*. Cambridge: Cambridge University Press

Good, K. (1999) 'Enduring Elite Democracy in Botswana', *Democratisation* Vol. 6:1

Good, K. (1993) 'At the End of the Ladder: Radical Inequalities in Botswana', *Journal of Modern African Studies*, 31, 2.

_____ (1996) 'Authoritarian Liberalism: Defining Characteristic of Botswana', *Journal of Contemporary African Politics*, Vol. 14:1.

_____ (1999) 'The State of extreme Poverty in Botswana: The San and Destitutes', *Journal of Modern African Studies*, 37.

Gunther, R., N. Diamandouros and H. Puhle (1996) Democratic Consolidation: O'Donnell's "Illusions: A Rejoinder", *Journal of Democracy* 7,4 pp151-159.

Holm, J. and Molutsi, P. (1992) State-Society Relations in Botswana: Beginning Liberalization, in (eds.) G. Hyden and Bratton, M. *Governance and Politics in Africa*. Boulder, Colorado: Lynne Rienner Publishers.

Huckfeldt, R., and J, Sprangue (1985) *Citizens, Politics and Social Communication Participation and Influence in an Election Campaign* Cambridge: Cambridge University Press.

Huntington, S. (1991) 'Democracy's Third Wave', *Journal of Democracy* 2,2 pp12-34.

Juan, J. Linz and A. Stepan. (1996) *Problems of Democratic Transition and Consolidation: Southern Europe, South America, and post-Communist Europe* Baltimore.

Juan, J. Linz and A. Stepan. (1996) *Problems of Democratic Transition and Consolidation: Southern Europe, South America, and post-Communist Europe* Baltimore.

Karam, A. (1998) *Women in Parliament: Beyond Numbers* Stockholm: International IDEA Institute for Democracy and Electoral Assistance.

Leftwich, A. (1994) Governance, the State and the Politics of Development, *Development and Change*, 25:2 pp 363-386.

Lijphart, A. (1991) Double Checking the Evidence, *Journal of Democracy* 2, 3 pp.42-48.

_____ (1977) *Democracy in Plural Societies: A Comparative Exploration*. New Haven: Yale University Press.

_____ (1984) *Democracies: Patterns of Majoritarian and Concensus Government in Twenty One Countries*. New Haven: Yale University Press.

Lipset, S. (1981) *Political Man* New York: Doudleday.

Linz, J. (1990) The Perils of Presidentialism, *Journal of Democracy* 1,1

Linz, J and A. Stepan. (1996) Towards Consolidated Democracies, *Journal of Democracy* 7,2 pp 14-32.

Luckman, R. The Military, Militarisation and Democracy in Africa: A Survey of Literature and Issues in (ed) Hutchful and Bathily, *The Military and Militarism in Africa*, Codesria Books, 1998.

Mattes, R. and M. Bratton. (2003). Learning about Democracy in Africa: Awareness, Performance and Experience, Centre for Social Science Research Working Paper No. 48 University of Cape Town pp 1-42.

Michels, R. (1959) *Political Parties: A Sociological Study of Oligarchical Tendencies of Modern Democracy* New York: Dover Publications.

Molomo, M.G. (1998). 'The Role and Responsibilities of Members of Parliament in Facilitating Good Governance and Democracy', in ed. W. Edge and M. Lekorwe, *Botswana: Politics and Society. Pretoria*: J.L. van Schaik Publishers.

Mokopakgosi, B. and Molomo, M.G (2000) 'Democracy in the Face of a Weak Opposition', *Pula: Botswana Journal of African Studies* Vol. 14: 1.

Molomo, M.G (1998) 'The Political Implications of the 4 October 1997 Referendum in Botswana', *Democratisation* Vol. 5 No. 4.

Molomo, M.G. (2003) 'Political Parties and Democratic Governance in Botswana,' (ed) Mohamed Salih *African Political Parties*, London: Pluto Press.

Molomo, M. G. (2000) 'Understanding Government and Opposition Parties in Botswana,' *Commonwealth and Comparative Politics*, Vol. 38:1.

Molomo, M.G. (2000) 'Democracy Under Seige: The Presidency and Executive Powers in Botswana,' *Pula: Botswana Journal of African Studies*, Vol. 14:1.

_____ (2000) 'In Search of an Alternative Electoral System for Botswana,' *Pula: Botswana Journal of African Studies*, Vol. 14:1.

Molutsi, P. and J. Holm (1990) 'Developing Democracy When Civil Society is Weak, African Affairs, 89 pp323-340.

Mosca, G. (1939) *The Ruling Class*, Translated by Hannah D. Kahn New York, McGraw-Hill.

Norris, P (2004) 'Electoral Engineering: Voting and Rules of Political Behaviour': *Pula: Botswana Journal of African Studies*, Vol. 14:1.

_____ (2002) *Democratic Phoenix: Reinventing Political Activism* Harvard: Cambridge University Press.

Norris, P (199) *Critical Citizens: Global Support for Democratic Development,* Oxford: Oxford University Press.

O'Donnell, G. (1996) 'Illusions About Consolidation', *Journal of Democracy* 7,2: 34-51.

_____ (1996) 'Democratic Consolidation: Illusions and Conceptual Flaws' *Journal of Democracy* 7,4 pp160-168

Pareto, V. *The Mind and Society*, Translated by Andrew Bongiorus and Arthur Livingston, New York: Hartcourt, Brace and co. 1935.

Przeworski. (1991) *Democracy and the Market: Political and Economic Reform in Eastern Europe and Latin America* Cambridge: Cambridge University Press.

Przeworski, A, M. Alvearez, J. A J.A. Cheibub and F. Limongi. (1996). 'What Makes Democracies Endure?' *Journal of Democracy* 7, 1: 39-55.

Putnam, R. (1993) *Making Democracy Work: Civic Traditions in Modern Italy* Princeton: Princeton University Press.

------------ (1995) 'Bowling Alone: America's Declining Social Capital', *Journal of Democracy*, 6 pp 65-78.

Quade, Q. (1991) 'PR and Democratic Statecraft', *Journal of Democracy* 2, 3 pp. 36-41.

Reynolds, A. and Reilly, B. (1997) *The International IDEAHandbook of Electoral System Design* Stockholm: Sweden.

Rose, R. and McAllister (1986) *Voters Begin to Choose* London: Sage

Samuel Huntington (1966) *Political Order in Changing Societies* New Haven:Yale University Press.

Schlemmer, R. et al. (1997) *Realities and Strategies for the Future: Training Workshop for the Botswana* Democratic Party (Gaborone).

Shugart, M. and Taagepera, R. (1994) 'Plurality Versus Majority Election presidents: A proposal for "Double Complement Rule"', *Comparative Political Studies*, 27:3.

Samatar, A. (1999) *An African Miracle: State and Class Leadership and Colonial Legacy in Botswana's Development*. Portmouth: Herinemann.

Sartori, G. (1976) *Political Parties and Party Systems: A Framework of Analysis* New York: Cambridge University Press.

The Pact, *Manifesto 2004: Together we shall deliver*, Gaborone, The Pact 2004.

Weatherford, M. (1982) "Interpersonal Networks and Political Behaviour", *American Journal of Political Science* 26 pp117-143.

CHAPTER 3

THE ORGANISATION OF ELECTIONS
AND INSTITUTIONAL REFORMS

Mogopodi Lekorwe and Onkemetse Tshosa

INTRODUCTION

This chapter focuses on the administration of elections and departs from the previous focus on electoral systems. It is argued that in any democratic dispensation, the machinery for the administration of the elections or the electoral process is pivotal to ensuring that the elections are free and fair. It is also argued that the holding of free and fair elections is one of the main pillars of a democratic process. The discussion that follows examines the administration of elections in Botswana in the early period of independence and currently, with a view to finding out whether or not it has ensured a freer and fairer electoral process. It also examines and evaluates the role of the police in ensuring free and fair elections. It concludes that, generally, the electoral process has been free although problems continue to persist regarding the fairness of the system. Moreover, the police have played a pivotal role in ensuring that the electoral system is free.

INSTITUTIONAL FRAMEWORK: AN OVERVIEW

Upon attaining independence, Botswana established a less-autonomous machinery for the conduct and administration of elections. The role of administering elections was bestowed upon, or rather was made the responsibility of the Permanent Secretary to the President. This kind of centralisation naturally led to much dissatisfaction among opposition parties. The main complaint was that the office was essentially not independent from the office of the president since the permanent secretary was directly responsible to the president. In order to address this concern, the Supervisor of Elections was established to run the elections and provided for in the Constitution of Botswana (Otlhogile, 1991). Henceforth, the Supervisor of Elections became the institution responsible to the National Assembly for the conduct and administration of the elections and who it was argued held an independent office. This was a view with which opposition parties have never agreed.

The early electoral amendments setting up the 'Supervisor of Elections' were not adequate. The constitution was amended and Section 66(1) provided that there shall be a Supervisor of Elections whose duty it shall be to exercise jurisdiction over the registration of voters for election of Elected Members of the National Assembly and over the conduct of such elections. Thus the Supervisor of Elections had the overall charge of administration of elections in the country. But such a reform was not adequate as the opposition parties continued to register complaints.

The question of freeness of elections has never really caused much controversy because every eligible voter freely participated in the electoral process (Otlhogile, 1991; Tshosa, 1994) or stayed away from it. The thorny issue concerned the fairness of the election. The issue has arisen in relation to the appointment of the Supervisor of Elections. Section 66(2) of the Constitution unambiguously declared that 'The Supervisor of Elections shall be appointed by the President.' It was the manner of the appointment of this officer that became a pertinent issue of concern. First, the presidential appointment of the Supervisor of Elections was not subject to approval by anybody or authority. It was the prerogative of the president to appoint any individual whom he deemed fit (the only qualifications were that the appointee had to be a citizen of Botswana and should have held a senior office in or outside the public service in any country; should not have been declared insolvent or otherwise adjudged bankruptcy by a court of law and should not have been convicted of any offence involving dishonesty in any country) (Botswana Constitution, Section 66 (30 (a) to (c)). Obviously, this raised several questions regarding the criterion that the president used in appointing the Supervisor of Elections. It made the appointment very subjective and subject to abuse. As a matter of fact, this issue was discussed in political circles including various all-party conferences where the opposition parties, in particular, questioned the appointment procedure and hence the independence of the Supervisor of Elections. It should be emphasized that opposition parties never agreed with the ruling party's position that the Supervisor of Elections was independent. This was because not only was he appointed by the president but also because prior to the formation of the IEC, which will be discussed later, the office-holder was a former BDP activist who had once contested a parliamentary seat under the BDP ticket. Moreover, the elections office never had sufficient facilities and personnel to run the elections independently of the government.

Secondly, the unsupervised presidential appointment of the Supervisor of Elections undermined the notion of fair elections because as the leader of a political party, it raised the potential, or even the likelihood that the president would appoint a political favourite. As one author has aptly put it in another context:

> The vesting of an apparently unfettered discretion in the State President in the appointment of the Chief Justice and the President of the Court of Appeal has also been criticised although Botswana does not stand out alone in this regard. It is not known what factors are taken into account in exercising this discretion and the possibility of political consideration cannot be ruled out (Quansah, 1997: 202).

For this reason, we hold the view that the whole issue of the appointment of the Supervisor of Elections meant that the independence of that office was left much in doubt and tainted the fairness of the electoral process. This issue can be closely connected to the fact that the Supervisor of Elections was a department in the Office of the President. As such, it obviously meant that it received orders and directions from the Office of the President. It is therefore concluded that it could not take independent decisions, including those decisions relating to the conduct of elections. Thus, that the complaints by the opposition parties with respect to the independence of the permanent secretary to the president in running the elections applied with equal force to the Supervisor of Elections. These concerns eventually led to the abolition of the office of the Supervisor of Elections.

INDEPENDENT ELECTORAL COMMISSION (IEC)

We are of the view that the establishment of the IEC went a long way towards addressing previous concerns about the administration of elections. Realising the political heat generated by the manner of the appointment of the Supervisor of Elections, in 1997 Parliament passed the Constitution (Amendment) Act No.18/1997, which repealed Section 66 of the Constitution and introduced a new Section 65A. The new Section 65A replaced the office of the Supervisor of Elections with the Independent Electoral Commission (hereafter the IEC) (Somolekae and Lekorwe, 2000). In terms of this clause, the IEC shall be responsible for the conduct and supervision of elections of the Elected Members of the National Assembly and members of a local authority, and conduct of a referendum; giving instructions and directions to the Secretary of the IEC, ensuring that elections are conducted efficiently, properly, freely and fairly, and performing such other functions that may be prescribed by an Act of Parliament. It is on the basis of this clause that the IEC has assumed the responsibility of its predecessor of conducting and supervising elections in the country, which mandate it has been discharging since its establishment. As its name suggests, the IEC is supposed to be an independent institution in executing its functions of administering elections. Several mechanisms are put in place to ensure the independence of the IEC.

In terms of the Constitution (Amendment Act), the IEC shall consist first of the Chairman who shall be a judge of the High Court appointed by the Judicial Service Commission (Constitution of Botswana, Section 103 [1 and 2]). Secondly, a legal practitioner appointed by the Judicial Service Commission. Thirdly, five other persons who are fit, proper and impartial and are to be appointed by the Judicial Service Commission (JSC is an independent body that recommends the appointment of judicial officers in the country) from a list of persons recommended by the All-Party Conference. It is clear that the IEC consists of people of integrity and honour such as judges. This is meant to ensure that it discharges its duties with utmost fairness and independence. In principle, members of the IEC are individuals of high professional standard and integrity. Perhaps most importantly, the requirement that the chairperson of the IEC should be a judge of the High Court further underscores the need to ensure independence in the general direction and operation of the IEC.

The appointment of all the other members of the commission from a list agreed upon by the All-party Conference was not meant to politicise the work and operation of the IEC. Rather, it is designed to strengthen its independence further by ensuring that those appointed are not members of any political party. The political parties are expected to recommend for appointment individuals of impeccable credentials and integrity.

The Constitution (Amendment) Act Section 65A (1) (a) to (c), provides that the members of the IEC shall be appointed by the JSC. The involvement of the JSC in the appointment of the IEC is an important mechanism that ensures that the appointment process is independent of any external pressure or forces. The JSC also comprises the Chief Justice, who is the chairperson, the President of the Court of Appeal (not being the Chief Justice or the most Senior Justice of the Court of Appeal), the Attorney-General, the Chairman of the Public Service Commission, a member of the Law Society and any person of integrity and experience not being a legal person appointed by the president. It is evidently clear that the membership of the JSC comprises individuals of integrity and it is reasonably expected that in making the appointment they should ensure that members of the IEC are non-partisan and that they arrive at their decisions independently and objectively.

The members of the IEC enjoy security of tenure. According to the new Section 65A (4) of the Constitution, 'The first appointments of the Chairman and the Members of the Commission shall be made not later than 31 January, 1999 and thereafter subsequent appointments shall be made at the last dissolution of every two successive lives of

Parliament.' The provision further states that 'The Chairman and other members of the Commission shall hold office for two successive lives of Parliament'. These clauses guarantee members of the IEC a security of tenure of at least ten years. This means that during this period they cannot be dismissed from the membership of the IEC. The rationale behind ensuring that members of the IEC have security of tenure is to make them feel protected in their positions and enables them to perform their duties effectively without the fear that they will be removed from office by the stroke of a pen. It also ensures that they are independent in the exercise of their responsibilities.

It is worth noting that the new legal order does not provide for circumstances under which members of the IEC may be removed from office, for instance for inability to perform their duties due to physical or mental illness or serious misconduct. This is a standard practice where security of tenure is entrenched. Its aim is to provide for legal certainty in the event that vacancy occurs during the term of office of the members under any of these circumstances.

THE SECRETARY TO THE INDEPENDENT ELECTORAL COMMISSION

Section 66 of the Constitution dealing with the Supervisor of Elections has been repealed by the above Constitution (Amendment) Act and replaced with the new clause. The new Section 66 replaces the Supervisor of Elections with the Secretary to the IEC who, in terms of paragraph (2), 'shall be appointed by the President.' In terms of paragraph (3), subject to the directions and supervision of the IEC, the functions of the Secretary to the IEC are to exercise general supervision over the registration of voters for elections; (a) the Elected Members of the National Assembly and (b) the members of any local authority and over the conduct of such elections. Thus the supervision of registration of both national and local elections is the responsibility of the Secretary to the IEC. His office ensures not only that voters are registered but also that the elections are conducted freely and fairly.

Subsection 4 of the new Section 66 provides that an individual does not qualify to be elected the Secretary to the IEC if (a) he is not a citizen of Botswana, (b) he has been declared insolvent or bankrupt under any law and (c) he has been convicted of any offence involving dishonesty in any country. These criteria ensure that only individuals of high repute are appointed to the office of the Secretary to the IEC

In order to ensure the independence of the Secretary to the IEC, the position is subject to tenure protection. Subsection 7 of the new Section provides that the Secretary shall vacate the office on attaining the age of 65 years or such other age as may be prescribed by an Act of Parliament. This means that before attaining 65 years the

Secretary to the IEC may not be retired. However, in Subsection 8, where he is unable to discharge his functions due to infirmity of body and mind or from other cause or misbehaviour he may be removed from office. The Act does not define what 'any other cause' means for purposes of the removal of the Secretary from his office. But where he cannot fully perform his duties he may be removed from office. In such situations Subsection 9 of the new Section 66 requires the president to appoint a tribunal to investigate the matter. If the tribunal recommends removal, then the president would cause the Secretary to be removed from office. It should be noted that this mechanism is not unusual for individuals holding positions such as the one held by the Secretary to the IEC which require some degree of independence from the office. For instance, judges of the High Court and the Court of Appeal are generally subjected to the same procedure should they be unable to discharge their duties due to misbehaviour or misconduct.

Although the constitutional amendment is meant to ensure that the Secretary discharges his functions or exercises general supervision over the registration of voters, the position is tainted by the fact that his appointment is only done by the president who is not assisted by anybody in the appointment procedure which may affect the independence of the Secretary to the IEC. One way of ensuring the independence of the Secretary may be that he should be appointed by the IEC and be made accountable to it instead of to the president.

CALL FOR MORE ELECTORAL REFORMS

A number of electoral reforms were made prior to the 1999 elections: the setting up of the IEC and its mandate to run the 1999 elections; the reduction of the voting age from 21 to 18 years old; the abandonment of the voting disc and the adoption of the ballot paper. The 1999 elections were run under these changed circumstances and were conducted by the IEC.

Although the franchise was opened to citizens of age 18 and above, foreigners, irrespective of the length of time they have resided in the country and despite the fact that they pay tax, were not allowed to vote. (Note that civil servants are not allowed to stand for political office, and to that extent the principles of free and fair elections are compromised (Molomo, 2000; Holm, 1986)). In addition, the constitution gives the president the power to determine the timing and the date of elections. This prompted opposition parties to complain that the government was too involved in the running of the elections. This made the opposition parties uncomfortable as they felt that the BDP could use state machinery to rig the elections.

A closely related issue was the independence of the IEC especially from the government. First, it is argued that the IEC should not fall under the Minister for Presidential Affairs and Public Administration. The placement of the IEC under this ministry taints its independence. The IEC and Secretary thereof should not only be independent but should also be seen to be independent. Secondly, the method that was used for the selection of the Secretary of the IEC is questioned (Somolekae and Lekorwe, 2000). It is noted that under the present system the State President alone appoints the Secretary. The main argument is that the whole system is subject to manipulation by the government of the day.

Another concern is with regard to the demarcation of constituencies. The constitution provides that the country should be divided into as many constituencies as there are members of the National Assembly. The delimitation of constituencies is to take place at intervals of five to ten years. Following the population census, the delimitation of constituencies is conducted by a commission which is appointed by the Judicial Service Commission. The chairperson of the Delimitation Commission is normally a high-ranking judicial office. Other members of the commission are people who have not been active in partisan politics for the preceding five years, nor have been members of the National Assembly or public service. In theory therefore, the composition of the commission gives some measure of independence and confidence within the public at large. However, the point is that the chairmanship of the commission was monopolised by foreigners, creating some discomfort as they would never understand the dynamics of Tswana Society (Otlhogile: 1991). The practice should be understood in its proper historical context in which there were no local judges. This has been changing as the latest Delimitation Commission (2002) was chaired by a local judge.

THE ROLE OF THE POLICE IN THE ELECTORAL SYSTEM

It is noted that the general function of the police is to ensure that there is law and order in society. In other words, the main responsibility of the police is to maintain peace in the country. The Botswana police operate under, and derive their powers from, the Police Act, Cap. 21:01. The Act constitutes the main legislative instrument that deals with the general functions, duties and powers of the police force in the country. It is the legal source of authority for the police in carrying out their functions. Section 6 of the Act provides that the force shall be employed in and throughout Botswana to protect life and property, prevent and detect crimes, repress internal disturbances, maintain security and *public tranquillity*, apprehend offenders, bring offenders to justice and duly enforce all written laws with which it is directly charged and generally *maintain the peace*. (*Emphasis supplied*). In addition, Section 16 (2) proclaims that it shall be the duty of every police officer at all times to protect life and property, prevent and detect crimes, repress internal disturbance, maintain security and *public tranquillity*, apprehend offenders, bring offenders to justice and duly enforce all written laws with which the force is directly charged and generally *maintain the peace. (Emphasis supplied)*. The generality of these clauses provides the necessary scope for the police even to ensure that the elections are conducted in a peaceful manner.

The Police Act is reinforced and complemented by the Public Order Act, Cap 22:02. The Act is also a legal tool for the police to use during elections to suppress activities that are likely to disrupt the conduct of elections. The preamble states that the aim of the Act is to regulate and control public meetings. Section 2 thereof defines a public meeting to mean any meeting in a public place and any meeting which the public or any section thereof are permitted to attend, whether on payment or otherwise. This definition covers meetings called by political parties, including those held for campaign purposes. Section 3 of the Act gives the police powers to preserve public order on the occasion of public meetings and public processions. Moreover, Section 4 of the Act indirectly gives the police power to regulate public meetings and public procession so as to preserve public peace and order. In terms of Section 8(3) any person who violates the Act shall be guilty of an offence and liable to a fine or imprisonment.

The Public Order Act however exempts certain meetings from the application of Sections 4, 5 and 6 of the Act. Section 7(2) of the Act states that the Act shall not apply to public meetings convened (a) by or on behalf of a candidate for election in any parliamentary or city, town or district council election after the issue of the writ of election. The effect of this exemption seems to be that, in principle, the powers of the police to maintain public peace and order do not extend to meetings under this provision. But the exemption is only limited to public meetings held after the issue of the writ of election presumably so as to allow the candidates to engage in political activities unimpeded. This does not mean that where the public meetings get out of control and in the process threaten public order and peace the police are powerless. They have the general powers to maintain peace, order and tranquillity.

The Penal Code Cap. 08:01 also gives the police power under certain circumstances to regulate and prosecute crimes related to, or which may have a bearing on, elections. They may prosecute individuals who engage in unlawful activities for purposes of disturbing or inciting to the disturbance of peace and order in any part of Botswana, unlawful assembly, and threat to the breach of peace. Thus these legislative instruments give the police in the country power to preserve and maintain peace generally including during elections. The police do have a specific code of practice or conduct that deals directly with elections. In fact, since independence they have mainly relied on the Police Act and the Public Order Act to control political meetings and gatherings before and during elections. The authors are not aware of any complaints that the police disrupted political meetings.

CONCLUSION

It is concluded that the administration of elections has a direct bearing on the fairness and freeness of the elections. By and large, and in comparison with other countries in the southern African region, it is satisfying to note that the mechanism for the administration of elections in Botswana has realised these objectives and has generally ensured that the electoral process, particularly the voting system, is free. Furthermore, we also conclude that the police have played a crucial role in ensuring that the electoral system is free. They have ensured that places of political activity such as political rallies are generally peaceful and orderly. However, the concern is with respect to the continued domination of the government in the administration of the election such as the presidential appointment of the Secretary of the IEC. The removal of the government involvement, directly or indirectly, in the administration of the electoral process will go a long way to ensuring that the system is not only free but that it is also fair.

REFERENCES

Brownlie, I. (1994) *Basic Documents on Human Rights*, Oxford: Clarendon Press.

Clarke, H.W. (1971) *Constitutional and Administrative Law*, London: Sweet & Maxwell.

Otlhogile, B. (1991) *A History of Higher Courts in Botswana: 1912-1990*, Gaborone: Mmegi Publishing Company.

Otlhogile, B. The Administration of Elections in Botswana (unpublished).

Somolekae, G and M. Lekorwe. *An Evaluation of the 1999 Elections: Proceedings of a Workshop held 26-27 June, 2000*, Gaborone: Grand Palm Hotel.

Tshosa, OB, (1994) 'Freedom of Political Activity: Law and Practice in Botswana', *CLISA* 27, 371.

Quansah, (1997) 'The Independence of the Judiciary in Botswana: The Law and the Reality' ASICL 9, 196.

CHAPTER 4

TRANSPARENCY AND SETTLING OF DISPUTES IN THE BOTSWANA ELECTORAL SYSTEM

David Sebudubudu

INTRODUCTION

This chapter looks at the level of transparency in the elections and the manner in which electoral disputes are handled. As an attempt to address the concerns of opposition parties and to promote transparency, it is noted that the administration of elections was reformed as shown in the previous chapters. The concern in this chapter is with the introduction of election observers and monitors. However, it also analyses the court system that is the primary mechanism for addressing complaints related to electoral outcomes or maladministration.

This chapter first examines the role of election observers and monitors as a way of promoting transparency in the Botswana electoral system. It is argued that election observers and monitors have significantly improved transparency and accountability in the Botswana electoral process especially in recent past years. Secondly, the laws for settling electoral disputes through the modern court system are discussed. Although the role of the courts in settling electoral disputes is appreciated, the court system involves considerable expense and may inhibit the delivery of justice involving electoral cases.

ELECTION OBSERVERS AND MONITORS

Election observation and monitoring have become highly contentious issues in recent years especially with the linking of political reforms to economic aid. Most donor organisations and governments have since become interested in the reports of election observers and monitors because election observation and monitoring have become the most important ways to judge if elections were free and fair.

A free electoral process 'is one where fundamental human rights and freedoms are respected' and a fair one is 'where the playing field is reasonably level and accessible to all electors and parties' (Common Borders, 21/04/2004: bhttp://www.commonborders.org/free_and _fair.htm). Free and fair elections are seen internationally as the basis of good governance and also give legitimacy to the victor. They are also of central importance to the sustenance of democracy. It is in this sense that election observation and monitoring have gained popularity and acceptance internationally. Despite the above definition and the existence of widely accepted credible standards of judging an electoral process, what constitutes a free and fair election remains an issue of controversy. This is especially the case whereby observer groups issue conflicting reports as in Zimbabwe in 2002. My personal view of Zimbabwe's 2002 presidential election was that it was unfair and fraudulent, and the fact that President Robert Mugabe and his party claim differently does not change the judgment. In Russia, Bruce George the President of the Parliamentary Assembly of the Organisation for Security and Co-operation in Europe (OSCE) which had 400 observers in that country's election in 2003 noted that 'our main impression of the overall process was ... one of regression in the democratisation of that country' as it was 'overwhelmingly distorted' (BBC News, 8/12/2003:http://news.bbc.co.uk/2/hi/Europe/3300483). Thus, the freeness and fairness of elections can now depend on what international observers say.

Although it is not precisely clear what election observation and monitoring means, Otlhogile defines it as 'an attempt by the international community at closely overseeing (a decision-making process such as an election), in order to ensure that every eligible member of that particular nation is afforded an opportunity... to participate in the decision-making in their country, and that the wishes of the majority determine the outcome' (1994: 294). Otlhogile (1994) also observed that the purpose of such an exercise is to authenticate elections and re-establish confidence among political contenders. According to Harris, an election observer 'is not involved directly in the operation of the election process, has no right to demand changes but does have a role in drawing attention to irregularities and publicising their requests for appropriate action to be taken'. An election monitor on the other hand 'is not directly involved in the election process and therefore only has the right to demand changes and to publicise the fact that these demands have been made' (1997: 27). As the United Nations (UN) Code of Practice puts it, observation entails;

> the purposeful gathering of information regarding an electoral process, and the making of informed judgments on the conduct of such a process on the basis of the information collected, by persons who are not

inherently authorised to intervene in the process, whose involvement in mediation or technical assistance activities (is unofficial and) should not be such as to jeopardise their main observation responsibilities (UN Code of Practice quoted in Harris, 1997: 27).

Thus, election observers and monitors are not only central but have also become part and parcel of the electoral process worldwide especially in emerging or young democracies as a way of promoting transparency in the electoral process and encouraging free and fair elections. As Dugard (1998) noted, openness is an essential element of ensuring confidence in the election process. Election observation and monitoring are important activities that help to strengthen the democratic process and institutions, the value of elections and instil confidence in an election. This is because they are believed to monitor and observe elections on a non-partisan basis and therefore all interested parties generally accept their judgment of the elections. For an election observation to thrive, it has to be credible in the eyes of contesting parties, and that trustworthiness comes from the refusal to take sides and the impartial and fair-minded nature of the observation endeavour. Transparency in the electoral process is of critical importance in ensuring public confidence in the election system and recognition of the election outcome (Dundas, 1994). For Totemeyer and Kadima, 'election observation, builds citizen confidence in the integrity of the election process, which encourages them to exercise their voting rights (2000: 4).

Similarly, Ramadhani (1999) pointed out that election observers might persuade nervous citizens as well as suspicious opposition politicians to take part in the electoral process rather than to resort to violence, as was the case in Angola and Mozambique. In Zambia in 1991, the involvement of observers is thought to have calmed intense disagreements over electoral rules and regulations by asking for concessions from government and electoral officials on areas of disagreement (National Democratic Institute for International Affairs, 1992). Thus, election observers and monitors can perform a constructive function in generating an environment favourable for everyone to take part in general elections (Totemeyer and Kadima, 2000). They can add more value to the whole electoral process and thereby give it greater legitimacy. Moreover, their involvement may also encourage the government to recognise the outcome and therefore step down. Nicaragua in 1990 under President Daniel Ortega and Zambia in 1991 under President Kenneth Kaunda are cases in point. In this way, election observers and monitors help to promote stability.

As the National Democratic Institute for International Affairs (1992) noted, international observers may be asked to arbitrate in disagreements among contesting political organisations in an attempt to lessen hostilities prior to elections, throughout and subsequent to the elections. For an election outcome to be acceptable to all interested parties it should not only be seen as free and fair but it should also not be marred by allegations of fraud. Thus, although free and fair elections are not a sufficient condition towards democratic consolidation, they are central because of 'their ability to jump-start the process of democratisation and boost the morale of pro-democracy forces' (Nevitte & Canton, 1997: 51). Election observers and monitors are one way of trying to attain this.

Previously, journalists, academics as well as embassy staff observed elections in foreign countries. However, following the Second World War, political participation in government came to be accepted as a fundamental right and since then election observation has been institutionalised internationally. The United Nations initially took part in election observation in South Korea in 1948 because it was considered essential to monitor the elections in countries coming out of dictatorial/military regimes or authoritarian communist rule. Since then, election observation has become common and is equally put into use in the developed countries (Ramadhani, 1999). Subsequently, a number of organisations became involved in election observation and monitoring because there has been an increasing acceptance of the probable support international observers make to an election process internationally.

Otlhogile (1994) correctly traces the origins of the Commonwealth observation of elections to the 1971 Singapore Declaration. The essence of this declaration was to advance individual freedom in countries that are members of the Commonwealth. In 1989, the Commonwealth adopted yet another declaration - The Kuala Lumpur Declaration - in which it pledged to promote democratic values in member countries. The Commonwealth proposed in the Kuala Lumpur Declaration 'that one of [its] contributions to strengthening democracy might be the provision of Commonwealth assistance in helping member countries to reinforce their election and other constitutional processes through a facility for mounting observer missions at the request of member governments, and in responding to such requests in other relevant ways' (Otlhogile, 1994: 295). The promise to promote democratic values within the Commonwealth was repeated two years afterwards in Harare (Otlhogile, 1994). This demonstrates the concern to support and encourage free and fair elections within the Commonwealth. However, the implementation of this proposition has always been a thorny issue. The problem with this proposition is that it relied heavily on the government of the country conducting an election. This renders the Commonwealth a weak organisation in the process of election monitoring.

Likewise, in June 1990, the Conference on Security and Cooperation in Europe, which comprises all European countries, Canada and the United States, embraced a declaration which calls for member states to recognise the need to involve international observers in national elections. This was followed by the endorsement of the practice by the United Nations General Assembly and the Secretary General of the U.N. in an attempt to boost the efficiency of the rule of regular and indisputable elections (National Democratic Institute for International Affairs, 1992). As Ramadhani has observed, the aim of election observation in emerging democracies

> is to enhance internal and international credibility of the electoral process. A basic function of international election observation is detecting and, if possible deterring electoral fraud. Election observation has helped to expose fraud in the Philippines in 1986 and in Panama in 1989 as well as in Zimbabwe in 2002. At times, apart from publishing electoral fraud, election observation has also contributed to prevent it. Political authorities may abandon election rigging out of fear of being caught by observers. Moreover, election observation may help to hold together shaky electoral processes in new democracies (1999: 104).

Similarly, Kupe (2000) correctly notes that the participation of observers could help to decrease propensities toward improper practices by over-zealous political parties or government administrators in charge of elections. Dundas (1994) observed that the involvement of observers during voting and at the count can help to calm down the election environment, and is thought to encourage the openness of both the polling and counting of the ballot papers. The National Democratic Institute for International Affairs (1992) stated that the presence of international observers is intended to give confidence in the process, to discourage electoral irregularities and to give an account of the impartiality of the elections to the international community. In the view of the Executive Secretary of the Botswana Democratic Party (BDP), 'observers [international] are so important because they are a stamp of approval in a democratic process, that is whether the electoral outcome is acceptable or not' (Interview, 19 June 2003). Thus, election observation and monitoring are of special importance because, 'the presence of observers has a primary focus on promoting an atmosphere of openness and transparency, thus enhancing public confidence in the election processes and their outcomes. [In this way], observer access to voting processes acts as a deterrent to improper practices and attempts at fraud' (Aceproject, 24 June, 2003:

http://www.aceproject.org/main/english/po/poa03/default.htm). This explains why election observation and monitoring have become so important in recent years especially in countries undergoing political change. Moreover, election observation ensures that the electoral outcome is credible internationally in the light of donor conditionality: economic aid has come to be linked to democracy and good governance. Furthermore, taxpayers in donor countries would like to know if their money has been used properly because they provide for some of the expenses of conducting elections. And in established democracies, election observation seeks to act as an example to emerging democracies (Ramadhani, 1999). Election observation is not merely about verifying the fairness of an election but instead, and more crucially, broadens the access to democratic norms and procedures for thousands of people, and thus help in building and strengthening a culture of democracy (Green-Thompson, 2001). It is in this context that election observation and monitoring have come to be accepted as a key part of the democratic process because they seek to promote transparency and accountability – the central tenets of democracy.

Election observer and monitor missions take different shapes. Their diversity depends on the type and size of the organisation involved, its period of stay in the country holding elections as well as the kind of report they produce after the elections (Ramadhani, 1999). Nevertheless there are certain experienced and credible election observers – e.g. the Commonwealth, the European Union, the Jimmy Carter Group – that have a greater capacity as observers than others such as the SADC Parliamentary Forum that relies on ruling and opposition parliamentarians within the SADC, and the Electoral Institute of Southern Africa that depends on scholars and human rights activists around the African continent. Generally, election observers observe the administrative arrangements, the preparedness of the electoral authority, the behaviour of election officials, the police, party agents, the voters, the sealing of ballot boxes before and after voting, escorting boxes to counting centre, and counting as well as balancing (The Catholic Justice and Peace Commission, 1994). The observers are expected to produce individual reports, which highlight the positive aspects of the election, noting problems as well as recommending measures for improvement. They are also expected to pronounce on whether the elections were free and fair. Kupe has rightly observed that election observers are 'watchdogs working for the electorate and the political parties involved in the elections. It is their business to make sure that elections are conducted properly during the prescribed times and at the designated venues' (2000: 102).

One can identify two main types of observer and monitoring groups: local and international groups / organisations. Local observers, who are normally citizens of the country whose elections are being monitored can have the edge over international observers, because they are familiar with the country concerned. However, although local observers promote transparency in the electoral process, they can often be treated with suspicion as having their own agenda and thus not seen as impartial by governments. On the other hand, international observers 'have added a new dimension to election transparency' (Dundas, 1994: 45). Nevitte & Canton observed that 'public confidence in internationally driven [observation] efforts characteristically hinges on the reputation and legitimacy of the international or regional organisation involved, and derives in large part from the multinational membership of the observation team in place' (1997: 50). For Camay and Gordon 'international observers bring an added credibility to the monitoring and assessment of elections, in that they are able to refer to their experience elsewhere and apply international standards of good practice wherever they go' (1999: 259). International observers can thus be seen as giving a stamp of approval.

Observer groups can use different approaches to observe elections. These can take the form of regular short visits, permanent groups, mobile teams or stationery teams (Ramadhani, 1999). Nevertheless, election observers face a number of limitations. Firstly, as Dundas noted, 'there are limitations to the extent to which observers generally can impact on the transparency of the system, since they are not in charge of the machinery which runs the election. Secondly, 'they have a limited time to see only the final days of the campaign leading up to the polls, and sometimes many leave before the final results are known (1994: 45). This in a way compromises the role of election observers in promoting transparency and accountability in the electoral process.

Botswana, despite being the longest and most stable democracy in Africa, did not catch the attention of most international observer organisations and the international media until 2004. Part of the reason why international observers had ignored Botswana was because of the 'peace and tranquillity' that the country has enjoyed over the years and the perception that 'elections have always been successful' (Molomo & Somolekae, n.d: 111). As Elago noted, 'where the political environment in a given country proves stable and peaceful enough for the local institutions to organise elections, the presence of international observers and monitors has not been a conditional requirement' (1999: 115). Indeed, international observers did not even observe the Botswana 2004 election. Harris observed that election observers were initially meant to provide legitimacy where 'a state was emerging from a long period of autocratic rule' (1997: 28). As one senior official of the Independent Electoral Commission (IEC) of Botswana puts it, 'international observers are not yet interested in Botswana elections because there were no incidents of serious concern' (Telephonic Interview, 19 June 2003). In the view of the Executive Secretary of the Botswana Democratic Party (BDP), Botswana's elections have not yet caught the attention of international observers because 'international observers are attracted to elections where there is potential for conflict or where conflict preceded elections' (Interview, 19 June 2003). One member of the BNF Central Committee believes that there is a combination of factors why Botswana has not yet interested international observers. He observed that 'Botswana is unique because it has not yet experienced violence since independence and has not had serious [electoral] disputes and the opposition has always accepted defeat even where they felt cheated. Moreover, Botswana is regarded as a strong adherent of the rule of law' (Interview, 25 June 2003). These factors are rarely present in most African countries that urgently need international election observers. The most recent example of a country that has been sliding into political violence is Zimbabwe following the 2002 presidential elections whose outcome was rejected by the main opposition party. As a result there was pressure on the government of Zimbabwe to hold a fresh election because its government was internationally perceived as illegitimate. However, President Mugabe has resisted and went on to hold the 2005 parliamentary elections and excluded most of the credible international observers.

The foregoing features make Botswana a unique country envied by many in a continent characterised by political turmoil and where international observers are denied entry, as in Zimbabwe in 2005. Otlhogile (1994) notes that: 'not all elections are observed. The international community is committed to circumstances where for instance, there has been an absence of power sharing, or where there have been autocratic or despotic rulers, or the country has gone through turbulent periods in its history, perhaps accompanied by human rights violations', which is not the case for Botswana. Thus, election monitoring and observation are common in countries undergoing political transformation - from autocratic regimes to multi-party systems - because in such countries, elections 'often take place in an atmosphere of uncertainty, confusion and concern about the ability of election administrators to deliver an accurate and impartial electoral result'.

As the National Democratic Institute for International Affairs stated, 'previously, international observation of elections in Africa had taken place in the context of a transition from colonial rule, as in Zimbabwe in 1980 and in Namibia in 1989, or in the absence of a centrally controlled authority, as in Uganda in 1980'. Zambia was the first independent African country to ask for the involvement of international observers during the 1991 elections (1992: 62). In such conditions, both local and external election observers 'play an increasingly important role in promoting free and fair elections that can lead to the establishment of accountable, effective governance' (National Democratic Institute for International Affairs, 1992: 61). For Nevitte & Canton, transitional democracies interest international observers because 'they not only constitute a litmus test of a regime's devotion to a variety of democratic values and procedural norms, but also provide critical opportunities for voters to weaken or break the grip of authoritarian governments' (1997: 47).

In that sense, it is true that 'monitors and observers are mostly interested in overseeing an election in suspect areas' (Elago, 1999: 116). Thus, countries undergoing transformation attract international observers because there is a lot of unease surrounding an election in such a country. International observers and monitors in such countries are meant to re-establish the confidence not only amongst those contesting such an election but also amongst foreign investors. As Otlhogile puts it 'the country concerned is in the process of reconstructing itself politically and seeks the assistance of the international community. It wants to regain its position in the community of nations by allowing international observers to pass judgment that its elections were properly conducted' (1994: 294). Thus, for Otlhogile quoting Reisman, 'the purpose of the international observation is to assure the world community that the election meets the minimum requirements of an international standard' that is, the elections were 'free and fair' (Reisman, 1992, quoted in Otlhogile, 1994: 294). This largely explains why Botswana's democratic system has not yet attracted many foreign observers and monitors because it has enjoyed peace and stability since independence in 1966 and its elections have generally met internationally acceptable standards. A contributory factor to this could be that the ruling party has never faced any serious threat from the opposition which is in disarray.

Notwithstanding the importance of election monitoring and observation in promoting transparency and accountability in the electoral process, there are limits to what such monitoring can achieve. Although the role of election observers and monitors is widely appreciated, their judgements have never resulted in a re-election in any country. The April and December 2003 elections in Nigeria and Russia respectively are cases in point. Moreover, even if observers and monitors are expected to be impartial, an element of bias cannot be ruled out. However, their reports might indirectly prompt people to revolt resulting in a new election. In Georgia recently, fraudulent elections led to the storming of parliament and new elections in which the corrupt sitting president was ousted.

OBSERVING AND MONITORING OF BOTSWANA ELECTIONS

Amid controversy surrounding past elections especially the 1984 and 1989 elections, a number of organisations, including amongst others, the Catholic Justice and Peace Commission, and the Democracy Research Project (DRP) of the University of Botswana decided to observe Botswana elections. As the Catholic Justice and Peace Commission put it, its

> decision to observe [the 1994] General Elections in Botswana came in the background of a controversy that surrounded the past elections. The 1984 and 1989 elections particularly, could rightly be rated the most controversial in Botswana's political history. In each of these two elections several petitions seeking to nullify the results were brought before the High court. Although most of the petitions were rejected, often on a technicality, two crucial ones, one in 1984 and another in 1989 relating to the parliamentary elections were upheld by the court and re-elections held in Gaborone South (1984) and Mochudi (1989) (1994: 3).

Election petitions demonstrate that other interested parties are not happy about the electoral outcome suggesting that the electoral process may not be completely transparent. In an attempt to address the concerns raised by other role players, particularly opposition parties, these organisations took a deliberate decision to observe and monitor elections in Botswana with the view to make an impartial judgment on the conduct of the elections. However, due to lack of resources, the activities of these organisations (i.e. DRP and the Catholic Justice and Peace Commission) in observing elections in Botswana are limited to certain selected constituencies in the country. For instance, the Catholic Justice and Peace Commission observed elections in just sixteen constituencies in 1994 and eight constituencies in 1999.

Similarly, the DRP has been observing the Botswana elections in selected constituencies in 1989, 1994 and 1999. The DRP is a non-partisan multi-disciplinary organisation that was established in 1987 with the aim of studying and monitoring democratic processes and institutions in Botswana. For example, it observed elections in ten constituencies in 1994 and 'even within these constituencies, not all polling stations were visited' (Democracy Research Project, 1994: 3). Similarly, ten constituencies were chosen for observation in 1999 by the DRP and within the chosen constituencies, a number of polling stations were sampled (Democracy Research Project, 1999). The DRP team concluded that 'the 1999 elections were free and fair. The elections were peaceful and smoothly proceeded throughout the constituencies where observation was done (1999: 16). There were 40 constituencies in 1999. These have been increased to 57 in 2003 following a Delimitation Commission in 2002.

The Electoral Commissions Forum of the SADC countries (through its SADC missions) and the SADC Parliamentary Forum and the Electoral Institute of Southern Africa (EISA) also observed the 2004 Botswana elections at the invitation of the Independent Electoral Commission (IEC). While their first observation in the 1999 elections was limited to Gaborone, Francistown and Lobatse constituencies, their second observation was broader and covered most of the constituencies. However, unlike conventional observer groups, SADC mission's main objective 'is to act as a capacity building resource to the Electoral Authority [of the concerned country]. This means that its role will not in the first instance be to assess the correctness of the electoral process in relation to international norms and standards, but rather the development of a constructive and formative relationship which will enable the improvement of electoral processes within the region' (SADC Electoral Observation Missions, 2001: 3). Nevertheless, '...the overall goal of [SADC] missions is to contribute to the establishment and consolidations of democratic ideals and practices within the region' (Nupen, 1999: 109). Observer groups have certain criteria that they use in assessing an election. For instance, the SADC observer missions assess an election against a number of indicators which include, fairness, equality, freedom, universality, secrecy, transparency as well as accountability. These measures are used universally in assessing an election. When assessing or observing an election, SADC observer missions are governed by a code of conduct as well as a code of practice (SADC Electoral Observation Missions, 2001). The Electoral Commissions Forum (ECF) of SADC countries concluded that 'the 1999 Botswana election was very peaceful. The ECF observers did not receive any reports of violence or intimidation during the electoral campaign period' (Kadima, 1999: 16).

In 1999 the Independent Electoral Commission (IEC) of Botswana requested an external assessment of its work in conducting the 1999 parliamentary and local government elections. Following this invitation, a team of electoral experts from three Commonwealth countries led by David Zamchiya of Zimbabwe visited Botswana. The other members of this team were Dinanath Gajadhar of Trinidad & Tobago and Victor Butler of the United Kingdom. The team of experts was funded by the British Department for International Development (DFID). Similarly, the IEC asked a team comprising international and local experts Carl Dadus from the Commonwealth Secretariat, Zibani Maundeni and Tachilisa Balule, (both from the University of Botswana) to evaluate its conduct of the 2004 elections. The teams were mandated to examine the electoral laws and regulations, election operations as well as public and institutional involvement. The first team worked closely with the DRP of the University of Botswana which was conducting an exit poll in selected constituencies on polling day (Zamchiya, 2002). The second team of 2004 included the DRP coordinator. The Zamchiya Report noted that by inviting an external team, 'the IEC felt that an external view would assist the people of Botswana to improve on the electoral delivery system with the benefit of comparative experience from other countries' (2000: 2). In its report, the first Commonwealth team of experts not only made some recommendations on how the conduct of elections in Botswana can be improved, but it also observed that 'the 1999 elections [in Botswana] were not marked by high levels of conflict between the parties, and were generally conducted in a manner consistent with a peaceful and democratic society' (Zamchiya, 2000: 3). The Dandus Report of 2004 reiterated the point that was made before concerning Botswana's elections, that they were free and peaceful. However, it questioned the independence of the IEC and the manner in which boundaries were drawn. Such statements from international teams enhance Botswana's democratic process, add value to Botswana's democracy and legitimise its government. They also deepen its democracy.

A workshop that was held in 2000 to evaluate the performance of the Independent Electoral Commission (IEC) in the 1999 elections underscored the role of election observation and monitoring. The workshop noted that

> although election monitoring and observation have not historically been an important aspect in Botswana elections, it was a good practice which needed to be maintained. It was agreed [at the workshop] that election observation, particularly by external observers enhances the credibility and transparency of the electoral process, and hence it was an important aspect in delivering free and fair elections. [The workshop] also noted that observers can be helpful to the electoral process and the success of an election (Somolekae and Lekorwe, 2000: 36).

Similarly, after the 2004 election, the IEC invited Mogopodi Lekorwe and David Sebudubudu to facilitate at two workshops meant to evaluate the manner in which it handled the elections. Such reviews have proved to add value to the country's democracy.

THE COURTS AND LAWS ON SETTLING ELECTORAL DISPUTES IN BOTSWANA

This section discusses ways of settling electoral disputes in Botswana through the court system. Although a number of petitions were brought before the courts in recent years, only a few – which include two parliamentary petitions – have been successful. The two successful parliamentary petitions are discussed below because they are of political importance in Botswana's democratic process. These petitions demonstrated that the government of Botswana abides by and respects the decisions of the court.

As noted above, Botswana has held nine free and peaceful multi-party elections since independence. The country has not yet known electoral disputes which threaten the stability of the political system and which are common in most African countries. For example, in Lesotho in 1998, the opposition rejected the electoral outcome and resorted to civil disobedience. Botswana has not yet experienced electoral conflicts of this nature, which endanger the political establishment although there have been allegations of electoral cheating by the opposition. However, a number of election cases or petitions have been through the courts but only a handful have been successful with the High Court declaring election results null and void and declaring the seats vacant in the concerned constituencies. These include amongst others, two parliamentary seats; Gaborone South in 1984 and Mochudi in 1989.

The above two cases were brought to court by the opposition party, the BNF following its repeated complaints of cheating. Most of the cases or petitions that were brought before the High Court were dismissed on a technicality. The growing number of election petitions since 1984 until 1989 was an indication of the dissatisfaction that remained after elections. The section that follows examines the law under which election petitions are dealt with in Botswana.

THE ELECTORAL LAW AND PETITIONS

In democratic countries, the courts play an important role in trying to ensure free and fair elections. Under the laws of Botswana, once the Returning Officer has announced the results, the only way of contesting the results is through an election petition (Otlhogile, 1993). Election cases or petitions in Botswana are dealt with in terms of Section 69 of the Constitution of Botswana and Part X of the Electoral Act. Section 69 (1) of the Constitution of Botswana states that 'the High Court shall have jurisdiction to hear and determine any question whether – (a) any person has been validly elected as an Elected Member of the National Assembly or the seat of any such Member has become vacant'. Thus, it is only the High Court which can entertain election petitions for both parliamentary and council petitions. The procedure through which election petitions can be brought before the High Court is as spelt out in Part X of the Electoral Act. In terms of Section 114 of the Act, a voter in the constituency concerned or any person who was a contender in that election may present an election petition. An election petition may be lodged with the Registrar of the High Court 'complaining of an undue return or an undue election of a Member for any constituency by reason of want of qualification or by reason of disqualification, corrupt or illegal practice, irregularity, or by reason of any other cause whatsoever as spelt out in Section 114 of the Electoral Act. The petitioner is required to sign such a petition and it has to be presented within 30 days following the day the election results were announced by the Returning Officer in accordance with Section 115 of the Electoral Act. Section 115 (b) further provides that where a petition alleges an illegal practice, it may be presented

(i) at any time before the expiry of 21 days after the day on which the returning officer receives the return of election expenses of the person whose election is to be questioned; or

(ii) if the election petition specifically alleges a payment or money or some other act to have been made or done since that day by the Member or with the privy of the Member of his election agent in pursuance or in furtherance of the illegal practice alleged in the petition, at any time within 30 days after the date of such payment or other act.

Furthermore, Section 115 (d) requires that, when presenting such a petition or within seven days following the presentation of the petition with the High Court, the petitioner must furnish the Court with security for all the expenses the petitioner may be required to pay. But in terms of Section 117 of the Electoral Act, the successful candidate or respondent may object to the surety provided by the petitioner on the basis that it is inadequate. For Otlhogile, these requirements, 'give the impression that election petitions are private civil proceedings' (1993: 56). The issue of security and costs raises the question of affordability suggesting that the provision of election petitions as a way of promoting transparency and accountability is most likely to be pursued by those who have adequate resources because the court process in Botswana is highly expensive. This may reduce the number of contestants or voters who may want to challenge the electoral outcome. In the light of this the Zamchiya and the Dandus teams of experts (discussed above) observed that the traditional manner of resolving disputes by petition to the High Court is now regarded as too restricted, costly, and technical and not very useful where disputes are urgent. Some countries have an electoral court or an arbitration mechanism or require the commission to have a department which is qualified and empowered to resolve any disputes which may arise following an election. Thus, the reports suggested that the Electoral Act be reviewed and that Botswana should give consideration to updating the methods of resolving disputes in the electoral matters. Similarly, although Dundas sees 'the election petition procedure [as] an appropriate response to doubtful election results', he nevertheless cautioned that 'much care needs to be taken to ensure that the costs of these petitions are kept well within the reach of all candidates, including aggrieved independent candidates who have no party to help meet the cost of petitions' (1993: 35). The issue of affordability thus needs to be addressed so that the process of election petitions does not exclude those who do not have sufficient resources. This is important because electoral disputes have resulted in civil wars or civil disobedience in a number of countries in Africa.

In terms of Section 119, election petitions will take place in an open court and in the final analysis the court has to decide whether the respondent or successful candidate has been properly elected, and then award costs in accordance with the Electoral Act. Under Section 119 (h) if, at the end of the trial the High Court decides that somebody else has been properly elected rather than the successful candidate, then the successful candidate shall be considered to have vacated the seat, and the High Court will communicate its decision to the Secretary of the Independent Electoral Commission to announce in the Gazette that some other person has been accordingly elected. If the High Court decides that no one - including the successful candidate - was properly elected for a particular seat, it shall be declared vacant and the High Court shall communicate its decision to the President [if it is a parliamentary seat] in line with Section 119 (i). In the case of a council seat, the High Court shall communicate its decision to the Minister of Local Government and a new election will be held on a date to be set either by the President in the case of a parliamentary seat or the minister with respect to a council seat. Where the petitioner decides to withdraw the petition, he or she will be required to pay the costs incurred by the respondent in terms of Section 132. Moreover, if in the process of an election petition, corrupt or illegal practices are revealed or exposed, the High Court shall communicate the evidence to the Attorney General so that he or she may institute a prosecution in terms of Section 120.

ELECTION PETITIONS

Having examined the provisions under which election petitions are dealt with in Botswana, two parliamentary election petitions that have been successful – Gaborone South constituency of 1984 and the Mochudi constituency petition of 1989 – are discussed.

Gaborone South constituency petition of 1984

The Gaborone South petition of 1984, involved two powerful politicians, Peter Mmusi and Kenneth Koma representing the Botswana Democratic Party (BDP) and the Botswana National Front (BNF) respectively. Mmusi had won the elections in Gaborone South constituency and Koma was disputing the results of that election. However, 'before the [Gaborone South] petition could be heard [in court] a sealed ballot box, from the Tshiamo polling station [in Gaborone South Constituency], was discovered by the staff of the Supervisor of Elections as they were preparing to send all general elections ballot boxes to the National Archives. With this discovery both parties accepted the irregularity in the conduct of election in the constituency and agreed to a by-election' (Otlhogile, 1993: 64/5).

The Tshiamo ballot box was discovered following repeated complaints of election rigging and cheating by the opposition. Following the discovery of this ballot box, the High Court ordered a re-election, and the BNF represented by Kenneth Koma won Gaborone South constituency (Molomo, 1991). Since then, Gaborone South Constituency has been in the hands of the opposition. Molomo & Somolekae (n.d: 110) observed that 'until the discovery of the unopened ballot box of the Tshiamo Primary School polling station [in 1984] alleged irregularities in Botswana elections were always dismissed as unfounded'. Molomo & Somolekae (n.d.: 110) further noted 'the opposition claimed that the discovery of this unopened ballot box was testimony to the cheating that they have always complained about. Although not much was made of this incident internationally, it had at least registered a point that the opposition had made for years'. Thus, the Gaborone South petition was of particular importance in the sense that it did not only reinforce allegations of cheating by the opposition, but it was also the first crucial petition to be won by the opposition. From this petition, a few observations can be noted.

First, by agreeing to a by-election, the BDP wanted to demonstrate to the voters that it has nothing to hide and that it is committed to a transparent election process, thereby vindicating itself, and officials of the Supervisor of Elections, from allegations of cheating. This was particularly the case in that the sealed ballot box was not discovered by members of the opposition but by officials of the Elections Office who have always been accused of cheating by the opposition. Secondly, the BDP may also have agreed to a by-election because it believed that whatever the outcome of the election resulting from the by-election of this constituency, it would not change the position of the opposition in the National Assembly.

Mochudi constituency petition of 1989

Another petition which was made successfully to the High Court by the opposition was that of Mochudi constituency in 1989. In this case, James Pilane representing the BNF petitioned the High Court over the election results which gave the constituency to Ray Matlapeng Molomo of the BDP by a margin of 29 votes. In this case, an administrative irregularity had occurred because the Returning Officer had 'extended polling times beyond that stipulated by the relevant election laws' (Otlhogile, 1993: 63). James Pilane argued that such an extension affected the result of the election. The High Court nullified the results and ordered a re-election because the election failed the test as laid down in Section 138 of the Electoral Act (Otlhogile, 1993). Section 138 of the Electoral Act reads: 'no election shall be set aside by the High Court by reason of any mistake or non-compliance with the provisions of Part VI or Part VII, if it appears to the High Court that the election was conducted in accordance with the principles laid down in Part VI or Part VII and that such mistake or non-compliance did not affect the result of the election. In this case, the High Court felt that the administrative irregularity on the part of the Returning Officer affected the result and as such rendered the outcome invalid. However, Ray Molomo of the BDP eventually won by a margin of 104. The same argument was applied in the Lebofanye Dithebe versus Rex Mafoko in a local government election in 1989 (Republic of Botswana, 1989). In this case, the Returning Officer also committed an administrative mistake by extending voting times beyond that stated in the election laws. As a result, the result of the election in the Woodwall Ward that was won by Rex Mafoko was set aside by the High Court. Setting the election aside, Judge Barrington-Jones concluded that 'I am not satisfied that the mistake on non-compliance did not affect the result of the election, and so I find that the Respondent [successful candidate – Mafoko] was not duly elected, and I accordingly set aside his election' (Republic of Botswana, Misca No. 165 of 1989: 14).

Despite the above crucial and successful petitions, a number of other petitions were also presented before the courts following the 1994 and 1999 elections, but most if not all of them have been unsuccessful or thrown out on a point of technicality. It is worth noting that the IEC does not have the information on all the election petitions. This is in part because it is not the IEC that is petitioned but the High Court. Nevertheless, the IEC together with the successful candidate are the respondents in any election petition that is brought. The increase in the number of petitions that have been made to the courts in recent years demonstrate that the courts have a role to play in the Botswana electoral process. Where an election was not conducted in accordance with the Electoral Act, the court may order a re-election as shown in the cases of the Gaborone South Constituency in 1984 and Mochudi Constituency in 1989. Thus, the Electoral Law and the courts together with the presence of election observers in recent past years, put pressure on those responsible for the conduct of elections to be transparent and accountable because those who feel cheated may resort to the law courts. However, the provision of the courts is most likely to be utilised by those who have resources because it is an expensive procedure. As a result, although the courts may help to promote openness in the conduct of elections, the cost of going to court may also discourage those who want to challenge the election results. Moreover, the courts are not only costly and technical but they are also slow in resolving electoral disputes.

CONCLUSION

Although Botswana has held several multi-party elections since independence, election observers and monitors were not part of the electoral process until recently. The explanation for this was that Botswana's elections have been held under a peaceful atmosphere which is not regarded as suspect by international observers. However, Botswana's elections have in the recent past caught the attention of regional observers. Part of the reason why observers are developing interest in Botswana elections is the emergence of democratic regimes in southern Africa which have put Botswana's democracy under the spotlight. But part of the reason also is that SADC election observers have adopted a policy of observing all elections in the region.

Notwithstanding the importance of election monitoring and observation in promoting transparency and accountability in the electoral process, a few observations can be made about election observers and monitors. They have never resulted in a re-election in any country whatever their judgment of the election might be. In fact, they have become a standard institution that is expected to take part in the democratic process especially for the reasons discussed above. Moreover, even if they are expected to be impartial, an element of bias cannot be ruled out. At best, they only have moral significance.

Although the laws in Botswana provide for election results to be challenged in a court of law, only a few cases or petitions have been successful. Most of the petitions have been dismissed on a technicality. The court process in Botswana is not only expensive but time consuming as well and this may defeat the very purpose they were meant to serve in the first place – that is, promoting electoral transparency. The court process may also disillusion the voters. Therefore, there is a need for a quick solution to deal with electoral disputes. One such solution could be the establishment of an electoral court that will deal specifically with disputes arising from the elections. The other probable solution is the establishment of a unit within the IEC which is empowered to tackle electoral disputes. This is important because there is a need to hold a hearing while allegations are still fresh in the minds of the voters.

REFERENCES

BBC News, London, 'Monitors Condemn Russian Election', 8 December 2003 in http://news.bbc.co.uk/2/hi/Europe/3300483

Camay, P & Gordon, J, A (1999) *The People have Spoken...A Review of the 1999 South African Election*, Johannesburg: Co-operative for Research and Education.

Common Borders, Elections in Latin America, 'What Constitutes a Free and Fair Election?' 21 April 2004 in http://wwwcommonborders.org/free_and _fair.htm.

Democracy Research Project (December 1994) *A Report on the 1994 Elections*, Gaborone: Democracy Research Project,

Democracy Research Project (December 1999) *An Evaluation of the Performance of the Independent Electoral Commission* (IEC) in Botswana's 1999 Elections, Gaborone: Democracy Research Project,.

Dugard, J (1998) 'Current Issues in Election Management' in Dundas, C W (ed) *Discussion of Election Issues in Commonwealth Africa*, London: Commonwealth Secretariat.

Dundas, C, W (1993) *Organising Free and Fair Elections at Cost-Effective Levels*, London: Commonwealth Secretariat.

Dundas, C, W (1994) *Dimensions of Free and Fair Elections*, London: Commonwealth Secretariat.

Dundas, et al (2004) *Audit of the IEC. Preparedness to Conduct Legitimate and Credible Elections in October 2004*, Gaborone: IEC

Elago, A,N 'The Role of Monitors and Observers During Elections: The SADC Experience' in *SADC/EU Conference Proceedings: Strengthening and Consolidating Democracy in SADC through the Electoral Process*, Gaborone: 20th – 22nd June1999.

Election Observation: Why Observe Voting Operations Processes? in Aceproject, 24 June, 2003: http://www.aceproject.org/main/english/po/poa03/default.htm.

Green-Thompson, A (2001) 'Election Observations: Issues and Debates' in *South Africa's Local Government Elections 2000: Evaluation and Prospects*, Seminar Report, Johannesburg: No 12.

Harris, J (1997) 'Election Observation with Reference to International Observation Missions' in *NGO Roundtable – Strengthening Democracy through Civil Society*, 18 – 20 August 1997, Gaborone.

Kadima, D (1999) *Botswana Elections Observer Mission Report*, The Electoral Commissions Forum of SADC Countries, 16th October 1999.

Kupe, M (2000) 'Does Election Observation Improve the Confidence of Political Parties and the Public in Election Results?' in Dundas, C, W (ed) *Rules of Elections in Commonwealth Africa*, London: Commonwealth Secretariat.

Molomo, M, G (1991) 'Botswana's Political Process' in Molomo, M, G & Mokopakgosi, B, T (eds) *Multi-Party Democracy in Botswana*, Harare: Bardwells.

Molomo, M, G & Somolekae, G (n.d.) 'Sustainable Electoral Democracy in Botswana' a paper presented an *International IDEA-SADC Conference: 'Towards Sustainable Democratic Institutions in Southern Africa'* in http://www.idea.int/ideas_work/22_s_africa/elections_5_botswana.htm.

National Democratic Institute for International Affairs (1992) *The October 31, 1991 National Elections in Zambia*, Carter Center; Emory Univeristy.

Nevitte, N & Canton, S, A (1997) 'The Role of Domestic Observers' in *Journal of Democracy*, Vol. 8.No.3.

Nupen, D (1999) 'The Role of Monitors and Observers During Elections: The Electoral Commissions Forum of SADC countries' in *SADC/EU Conference Proceedings: Strengthening and Consolidating Democracy in SADC through the Electoral Process*, Gaborone: 20th – 22nd June1999.

Olthogile, B (1993) 'Judicial Intervention in Election Process: Botswana's Experience' in Otlhogile, B & Molutsi, P (eds) *Consolidating Democracy: The Electoral Process Under Scrutiny*, Report of the Workshop on Electoral Law and Administration of Elections in Botswana, Gaborone: 19th – 20th May 1993, Democracy Research Project.

Otlhogile, B (1994) 'Observing for Democracy: A Note on the Practices of the Commonwealth Observer Groups' in *African Journal of International and Comparative Law*, Vol. 6;2.

Ramadhani,S,L (1999) 'The Role of Monitors and Observers During Elections' in *SADC/EU Conference Proceedings: Strengthening and Consolidating Democracy in SADC through the Electoral Process*, Gaborone: 20th – 22nd June1999.

Republic of Botswana, Lebofanye Dithebe versus Rex Mafoko, MISCA No.165 of 1989.

Republic of Botswana, *Constitution of Botswana* Chapter 1, Gaborone: Government Printer.

Republic of Botswana, (1999) *Electoral Chapter* 02:07, Gaborone: Government Printer.

SADC Electoral observation missions (2001) 'Terms of Reference' in Electoral Institute of Southern Africa (ELSA) *Election Observer Missions: Terms of Reference*, Auckland Park: ELSA Library.

Somolekae, G and Lekorwe, M (2000) 'An Evaluation of the 1999 Elections', *Proceedings of A Workshop Held 26-27 June, 2000*, Gaborone: Independent Electoral Commission Botswana.

The Catholic Justice and Peace Commission, *Report of the Catholic Justice and Peace Commission on the observation of Botswana's 1994 General Elections*, Gaborone: October 1994.

The Catholic Justice and Peace Commission, *Report on Observation of Botswana 1999 General Elections*, Gaborone.

Totemeyer and Kadima (2000) *Handbook for Election Observer Missions*, Auckland Park: Electoral Institute of Southern Africa.

Zamchiya, M, D (2000) *Report of a Team of Experts on the Conduct of October 1999 Elections in Botswana*, March.

S ection Two shifts away from electoral systems, election administration and election observers. Instead, it covers various aspects concerning the participants in the election, such as political parties and their succession rules, internal party democracy and its impact on the electoral performance of the parties in electoral competition, and funding. The section starts by tracing succession rules and linking them to Tswana political culture. The section then maps internal party democracy and its effects on the electoral performance of the major political parties, showing the gains and reversals in opposition electoral performance. It further assesses the need for, and argues in favour of, state funding of political parties.

Section Two

CHAPTER 5

SUCCESSION TO HIGH OFFICE: TSWANA CULTURE AND MODERN BOTSWANA POLITICS

Zibani Maundeni

INTRODUCTION

Thabo Mbeki, the President of South Africa, holds that strong links exist between Botswana's democracy and ancient Tswana political values. In a speech to the Botswana Parliament in March 2003, Thabo Mbeki praised Botswana for its home-grown, stable and sustainable democracy. Mbeki's view is shared by some researchers (Ngcongco, 1989; Mgadla, 1998; Maundeni, 2002). Patrick Mgadla (1998:9) notes that, 'to a limited extent, characteristics of participation and consultation are traceable within the operations and duties of the chief prior to European contact'. Other researchers emphasise the point that Tswana chieftainship was a democratic institution in which the role of the chief was neither dictatorial nor autocratic but was tempered by democratic practices. 'The ruler was not above the law and his abuses could be checked, even though powerful kings tended towards despotism' (Tlou, 1998: 27). It was mandatory for the chief to consult a formal council of ward heads, many of whom were royals, or dikgosana, or to consult an informal council of advisers and to address a great council or kgotla meeting (Tlou, 1998). All these fora helped to democratise chieftan rule. Tswana state politics was characterised by consultation and participation (Holm and Molutsi, 1992). While the other observers have also praised Tswana traditions, it can be argued that it constrains the growth of the country's democracy in matters related to succession to high office.

The current chapter focuses on succession rules in Tswana states and in modern Botswana. Tlou initiated research that surveyed the Tswana rules of succession (1972) but Michael Crowder, Jack Parson and Neil Parsons (1990) initiated the comparison between Tswana succession rules with succession rules in modern Botswana. In following up their work the chapter also seeks to establish whether the system that democratised the chief's role also democratised the rules of succession. The continuities and discontinuities of Tswana political values, particularly succession rules, and their relevance in modern democratic politics are also reviewed. It is argued that Botswana's democracy is founded on Tswana succession rules.

The chapter is divided into two sections. The first section reviews the ancient Tswana political values and practices; the second looks at succession in modern Botswana in the light of traditional political values. The research is continued through the study of the continuities and discontinuities between Tswana succession rules and those that are applied in modern Botswana politics.

TSWANA SUCCESSION RULES

Michael Crowder, Jack Parson and Neil Parsons carried out studies on the succession rules in Tswana polities and related them to the rules of succession in modern democratic Botswana. They made one significant observation to the effect that, 'instances of succession in Botswana politics involve most directly the principles of traditional and legal-rational authority...' (Crowder, Parson and Parsons, 1990: 2). Traditional Tswana states had developed clear principles of succession. One key principle was, 'legitimacy-based on male primogeniture' (Crowder, Parson and Parsons, 1990: 3). In addition, 'sororate and levirate marriages ensured that there would always be an heir' (Tlou, 1998: 22). This means that the chief was necessarily male and hereditary. 'Chiefs could neither be nominated, elected nor appointed – *kgosi ke kgosi ka a tswetswe* (a chief is a chief by right of birth' (Mgadla, 1998: 3). The important point that Tswana chiefs were never elected was emphasised in the Voter Apathy Report (IEC, 2002). The obvious conclusion is that the Tswana leadership was hereditary and reserved for a male heir.

The principle of legitimacy based on male primogeniture was combined with a marriage system based on the 'great wife' *(mohumagadi)* to limit contestation for political office even among the royal brothers and cousins.

> 'A system was devised whereby heirship was determined by the seniority of the mother rather than the age of the son. The senior wife was not the one necessarily married first, but the *peelela* wife (from *beelela*, to reserve for future use). This wife was called *mohumagadi* (the great wife) or *mmadikgomo* (she for whom *bogadi* was paid). Her first son was the heir. Any woman married before the *mohumagadi* was called *mmamoleta* (she who awaits the queen) and her sons could not be heirs unless there was no *peelela* wife' (Tlou, 1972: 108).

Thus, being born of the great wife was more significant than being the eldest son of the incumbent chief or just his son. This is because the throne was constitutionally reserved for the first son of the great wife, thus limiting competition from the other sons of the chief. The effect of this was to depoliticise succession and make it a constitutional issue only.

The point on regency is that it was used to 'soften up' elder sons of other wives of the chief who could otherwise lay claim to the chieftaincy and depose the heir. The import of the regency system was an attempt to limit political struggles even among royals through cultural values and political practices (of course such limitations were not always successful, but the intent was clear). In view of the constitutional attempt to limit contestation for political office among royals, regency was used to cushion royal brothers who would otherwise never rule unless through secession or other violent means that would most likely disrupt the political system. What this meant is that leadership struggles were limited purely to constitutional-minded royal relatives in support of royal claimant who claimed that their mothers were the *mohumagadi.*

A further observation is that the other vital Tswana political principle that limited competitive politics (and therefore limited participatory democracy) was the one seeking to minimise or eliminate competition between the chief and the heir-apparent. 'The *mohumagadi* was usually married late in the king's life to prevent a possible struggle for power between him and the heir who frequently attained majority after the king's death. This is why regency was common' (Tlou, 1972: 109). Thus, the system of regency, whereby an important member of the royal family was appointed to act, filled the gap between the ageing chief and the heir apparent and ensured that the regent could rule without laying legitimate claims to the chieftainship.

The political culture of creating huge age gaps between the reigning chief and the heir apparent and the use of regents to fill the vacuum created by the system, was heavily relied upon and helped to stabilise the Tswana political system. The truth of that observation is confirmed by historical instances. For instance, Seretse Khama's father died when he was four years old and he was proclaimed as the rightful ruler of the Bangwato people. However, his young uncle, Tshekedi, became regent until Seretse had grown up and finished his education (Parsons, Henderson and Tlou, 1995: Introduction; IEC, 2002). There are two important conclusions that emerge from this short analysis. The first is that 'Beyond the Ngwato polity, pre-colonial Tswana polities generally contained within them a strong sense of constitutionalism regarding political succession, policy making, and the implementation of policy' (Crowder, Parson and Parsons, 1990:10). The second important conclusion is that the pre-colonial Tswana also had no constitutional mechanisms for allowing sustainable political competition. Thus, in the case of succession, Tswana constitutionalism was designed to limit contestation and to prevent sustained political competition.

It can therefore be emphasised that there is validity in the observation that the Tswana 'constitution was undemocratic in the liberal-democratic sense of today. Legitimate succession to high office was dependent upon birth. Large segments of the population were excluded by birth both from any part in succession as well as normal politics' (Crowder, Parson and Parsons, 1990:10). So, although the Tswana were very constitutional, theirs was a constitutionalism that promoted heredity and never accommodated sustainable peaceful competition, the hallmark of modern liberal democracy.

The point is that even where systematic constitutional violation was the norm, as it was in the cases of the Bakwena and Bangwaketse, the Tswana were never able to go beyond heredity to accommodate peaceful competition for political office (IEC, 2002). Evidently, succession rules were systematically violated in Bangwaketse and Bakwena political histories where competition and instability predominated for some time. There developed a political culture of internal strife and assassinations in Bangwaketse politics in which the long history of violation of the Tswana hereditary and regency systems included the ousting of Khutwane by his brother Khuto, the ousting of Segotshane by Sebego in 1842 and the uneasy existence of two rival Bagwaketse groups led by Gaseitsewe and Senthufe in 1850 (Nqconqco, 1977; IEC, 2002). The violent nature of these systematic violations prevented sustained peaceful competition for political office but sustained heredity in these ancient Tswana communities. Thus, the violation of the Tswana chieftaincy system was also unable to generate principles that advanced sustainable competition for political office.

The other observation is that the way in which the Tswana politically organised their societies, limited the chances of potential challengers and discouraged participatory succession politics (IEC, 2002). The *morafe* was organised in *mephato* (regiments) and only the king could create them. 'Every adult belonged to a *mophato...Mephato* (plural) were led by members of the royal family in order of seniority beginning with the heir apparent. A new *mophato* was created by the king when the heir was old enough to lead it' (Tlou, 1972: 110). Thus, leadership of *mephato* was hereditary and not open to participatory competition. In addition, the *mephato* were arranged in a hierarchy to ensure that there was no competition between them.

A migrant Tswana chief who settled with his people in an area that was already occupied by another Tswana group was expected to subject his leadership to that of the latter. In the case of leaders of migrant groups that were joining another Tswana state, the maxim was: *fa tlou e tlola noka, ke tloutswana* (when an elephant crosses a river, it becomes a little elephant) (Plaatje, 1916; Ngcongco, 1977: 178; IEC, 2002). The import of this proverb was to underline the point that the succession rules of the indigenous Tswana group took precedence over migrant Tswana groups. (Although the Bakgatla who settled in Bakwena territory violated this principle, sparking the 1875-1883 war which 'left Linchwe's Bakgatla in possession of thousands of Bakwena cattle, roughly 3,600 square metres of excellent grazing and the perennial waters of the Madikwe, Ngotwane and Limpopo rivers' (Morton 1998: 45)). Notwithstanding this violation, the effect of the proverb was to limit competition for leadership between two Tswana groups living in proximity to each other and to encourage submissiveness of the migrant chief.

SUCCESSION RULES IN MODERN BOTSWANA

This section reviews succession practices in modern democratic Botswana and seeks to establish whether or not they were guided by the traditional Tswana rules of succession. I disagree with prominent scholars who write that old Tswana political practices have died away and that only their symbolism remains. For instance, Thomas Tlou writes that, 'the title, *tau e tona* (great lion) used with reference to the president of the Republic of Botswana, derives from the skin traditionally donned by the new king' (Tlou, 1998: 23). But he wrongly concludes that because the president retained the traditional name, but not the skin symbolism, this means that Tswana values have died out. I also disagree with other scholars who write that 'the principles of succession and legitimacy were changed quite fundamentally, however, in the nationalist period beginning in 1946 and ending in 1966' (Crowder, Parson and Parsons, 1990: 21). Contrary to these positions, the argument in this chapter is that Tswana rules of succession remained strong in modern democratic Botswana, with little diversion.

Michael Crowder, Jack Parson and Neil Parsons (1990) have enumerated the changes in the principle of succession in the following manner. 'In the constitution the rules for succession to the highest office, that of president of the Republic of Botswana were fixed: but the rules contradicted the succession rules of the pre-colonial Tswana states...Generally, the president was elected by a majority of the elected members of the Botswana national assembly. In practice the leader of the majority party become president' (Crowder, Parson and Parsons, 1990: 22).

As a result, the argument is that the process of creating a supreme leadership by birth was simply replaced by the process of creating it by elected representatives. This was a positive development in the sense that the representatives of the national assembly 'elected' the president. But the intent and practice of limiting participation of the ordinary people was preserved. In addition, the limitation was extended to the chiefs. While chiefs are constitutionally required to have resigned their positions five years before they can stand for a constituency seat – part of the 1972 constitutional amendment - the House of Chiefs does not participate in electing the president.

Thus, the point is that the elected representatives replaced the royal family in the determination of the leader. Only elected representatives have the prerogative of deciding the leader of the country. So, the ancient Tswana constitutional practice of limiting political competition to a single institution - royalty in pre- and colonial times - has been continued by limiting political competition to a single institution - elected representatives. Thus, the gist of the ancient practice has continued. The only differences are that the chiefs who were the previous rulers in pre- and colonial times are now excluded from participating in determining the modern Botswana leader and are required to have resigned their chieftainship positions for the last five years before they can contest for political office. (Of course Ian Khama and Tawana Moremi III have violated this constitutional provision, so signalling their desire to change it). Thus, the similarities between traditional Tswana political practices and modern ones are still visible. Both excluded popular elections by the electorate and restricted political involvement to a single institution. In both systems, the population was reduced to the role of spectators regarding matters of electing the president. Now the chiefs are expected to be spectators too. It is in that light that some analysts talk of 'paternalist' (Holm and Molutsi, 1992) or 'elite' democracy in Botswana (Good, 2002).

The other point is that there was an element of automation in the way the elected representatives 'elected' the president. There is no formal election in which the elected representatives meet to elect the president. There is no caucusing or canvassing for votes from the elected legislators by different presidential candidates from the same party. Instead, the system is designed in such a way that during nomination time, every parliamentary candidate of a particular party signs a form indicating that his/her win is an automatic vote for the president or declares his/her allegiance to the party presidential candidate. Thus, every time a party candidate wins a parliamentary seat this automatically translates into a vote for the party presidential candidate. In summary, the president of the party that wins more parliamentary seats automatically becomes the president of the republic.

The above system of 'electing' the president superceded the system which existed up until 1972 by which the president stood for a constituency election. The previous system implied that the president would be appointed from among those who would have stood and won constituency elections. President Seretse Khama stood for a parliamentary seat only twice – in 1965 and 1969 - and won comfortably. But if the successor presidential candidate had lost his/her constituency election, what could have happened in that case? Such a scenario was very possible after Seretse Khama.

Vice President, Quett Masire stood and lost his constituency election in 1969 and 1974 to former Chief Bathoen Gaseitsiwe of the Bangwaketse who had resigned his position as chief and had been instantly elected as president of the opposition BNF. The fear in the BDP circle was that if Bathoen Gaseitsiwe defeated Vice President Masire he could still have won even if the latter had become the president of Botswana. Such a scenario would have sparked a political crisis for the ruling BDP and a constitutional crisis for the country. The Khama regime reacted to the 1969 Kanye constituency election contest between Chief Bathoen of the BNF and Vice President Quett Masire with a constitutional amendment. It ended constituency elections for the sitting and all future presidents and required chiefs to have resigned their positions for five years to qualify for parliamentary elections.

After the amendment was effected in 1972, Presidents Seretse Khama, Quett Masire and Festus Mogae, never stood for constituency elections. In contrast to other systems where either the president goes through primary elections and presidential elections as in the United States, or through presidential elections alone as in France and Zimbabwe, or where the prime minister goes through a constituency election as in the United Kingdom, the Botswana system is such that the president goes through no real election. This is because the electoral gains of the party automatically become the political gains of its presidential candidate. Thus, the Botswana president is inherited from the gains of the winning party.

Additional elements of hereditary politics were re-introduced into Botswana politics. Things were different before 1998 because parliament had a significant role in the presidential succession process.

'Succession to the presidency was covered in Section 35 of the constitution. If the office became vacant, the national assembly had to meet by the seventh day after such vacancy. Candidates for president had to be nominated by ten or more members of the national assembly prior to the assembly's sitting' (Crowder, Parson and Parsons, 1990: 24).

Through a set of constitutional provisions in 1998, empowering the president to appoint his vice president and for the latter to inherit the presidency, parliament unwillingly removed itself from presidential succession processes. At retirement or death or incapacitation of the president, the vice president automatically succeeds without the need to seek any approval from parliament. For instance President Sir Ketumile Masire retired in 1998, paving way for Vice President Festus Mogae who started a two-year term in 1999. Thus in modern Botswana, once the vice president is appointed by the president and approved by parliament s/he automatically succeeds if the president dies in office, retires or is incapacitated. Therefore once the vice president steps in to complete the term of his predecessor, he is automatically beyond the reach of parliament or anybody else.

After 1998, theoretically, the party selects the president once the two terms of the predecessor is complete. But as evidenced by the hostility of the supporters of automatic succession towards Ponatshego Kedikilwe (former chairman of the BDP) who was suspected of harbouring intentions for the presidency, anyone from the party leadership who challenges the president or his chosen successor is likely to face stiff resistance. For instance, Kedikilwe lost his chairmanship to Ian Khama at the BDP congress at Gantsi in July 2003. He also even lost the additional membership that he contested with twelve other people where he failed to be among the best five. Even then, President Mogae, who is constitutionally empowered to appoint five more additional members to the BDP central committee, left out Kedikilwe.

The supporters of automatic succession cut across parties and commonly view it in the light of the Tswana hereditary rules. They see it as upholding Tswana traditions of succession and could easily break away from the party if automatic succession is violated. If the challenger wins the day and becomes party president, as happened with the BNF in 2002 when Otsweletse Moupo successfully challenged and won against Vice President Peter Woto of the BNF, the supporters of automatic succession are likely to form a splinter party. This happened in the case of Koma, the out-going president of the BNF, and his supporters who formed the New Democratic Front (NDF) in early 2003.

In contrast, automatic succession is viewed by the supporters of the challenger and those autonomous NGOs, such as the Democracy Research Project (DRP) seeking to promote electoral democracy as a hindrance to a fully-fledged modern democracy. If the challenger wins the day, his or her supporters would see the hostile supporters of automatic succession as a group of undisciplined elements who mistakenly think they own the party and who should therefore be suppressed or expelled from the party. This is evidenced by the BNF suspensions that targeted former party leaders such as

Kenneth Koma and the expulsions of former senior leaders, which resulted in defections and in the creation of the NDF.

Together with the DRP and other NGOs who feel that the unity and integrity of the main opposition have to be preserved, defections and the formation of splinter parties have been opposed by some. But the point is that supporters of automatic succession are strongest in the ruling BDP and are a force to reckon with in the political system. This is evidenced by the strong resistance that faced the reformist government white paper seeking to abolish hereditary chieftainship and replace it with elected chieftainship. Hereditary chieftainship is the uppermost expression of Tswana political culture. Anybody who tampers with it, including the president or the BDP, is likely to meet stiff resistance from supporters of automatic succession.

It is possible to trace the continuities or discontinuities between the pre- and post-colonial Botswana political rules determining succession by comparing the offices of the president and the vice president. Two political factors distinguish them: (i) the vice president is appointed from sitting members of parliament. In contrast, the president is directly inherited from party electoral gains. Thus, the vice president is structurally a member of parliament and the president is strictly not a member. (ii) The sitting vice president stands for constituency elections and is expected to win a parliamentary seat. In contrast, the sitting president does not stand for parliamentary or presidential elections. He is not even voted in by the sitting members of parliament. Thus, the vice president is subjected to a limited democratic process but the president is above any real electoral process.

CANDIDACY IN PRESIDENTIAL, PARLIAMENTARY CONSTITUENCIES, AND COUNCIL WARDS

The argument here is that while leaders of political parties are free to stand in the indirect presidential race, other civic leaders such as business leaders, church leaders and chiefs are not. Party leaders are free to stand regardless of the remoteness of their chances of winning. Constitutionally, the leader of the party that wins most parliamentary seats automatically becomes the president of the republic. This means that for one to qualify as a presidential candidate, his/her organisation should have fielded parliamentary candidates. Taking the fielding of parliamentary candidates as the main criterion for one to qualify to be admitted as a presidential candidate is based on the assumption that only political party leaders stand a good chance of winning the support of the partisan elected parliamentarians, although this has never been put to a test.

In contrast, private individuals, civic leaders, business leaders and chiefs cannot stand for the absent/indirect presidential election. This is because none of them meet the requirement for the prior support of parliamentary candidates whose win is automatically counted as a vote for a preferred presidential candidate. Thus, the requirements for indirect presidential elections in Botswana exclude private candidates, civic leaders, business leaders and chiefs.

> In fact, Botswana opted for a multi political system that excluded large sections of institutionalised society from political contest. All other institutions in Botswana, except political parties, are required to be politically neutral and non-partisan. Section 62 of the Botswana constitution stipulates that no public servant, teacher in a state school, employee of a parastatal, or member of the House of Chiefs is eligible for election to the National Assembly. State schools place high school students in the same category of people denied active political participation' (IEC, 2002: 42)

There is no doubt that an electoral system that automatically excludes so many sectors of society from standing for the absent/indirect presidential elections is more than elitist. Such a system is discriminatory to the degree that it allows only party leaders to stand. Thus, party leadership has replaced royal families in the production of presidential candidates.

In the case of parliamentary constituencies and council wards, a system of direct elections is in place in which only party activists and private candidates may compete (Restrictions are imposed for civic leaders such as trade unionists and chiefs). Here, the candidate that polls the largest popular vote becomes the representative of the constituency or the ward respectively. The restrictions that govern the indirect presidential elections are not evident in parliamentary and council elections. But there are avoidances in the case of parliamentary and ward succession battles within parties.

Normally, political parties in Botswana avoid electoral clashes between senior politicians of the same party and seek to achieve smooth transfer of electoral gains from one candidate to his/her fellow party successor through retirement rather than through elections. Generally, when senior politicians of the same party contest in the Botswana political system, it is a clear sign that the party is experiencing factional problems and may be on the verge of splitting. (The BDP however has defied this prediction). For instance, when Mareledi Giddie and Michael Dingake met in the Gaborone Central Constituency and Councillor Ginger Ernest unseated Paul Rantao from the mayor-ship of Gaborone in 1993, it became very clear that the BNF was irreversibly factionalised and could experience a split - which it subsequently did in 1998 (Maundeni, 1998). Thus, avoidance is an important principle meant to sustain party coherence and limit internal party democracy.

In the more stable political parties such as the BDP it is not uncommon for incumbent constituency and ward party leaders to dominate their electoral area until death or retirement and even to choose their successor. This is evidenced by the fact that the average age for councillors is 49 and that of parliamentarians is slightly more. Thus, elements of hereditary politics still prevail in Botswana electoral politics as a stabiliser.

The exception is in Serowe South where cabinet ministers, Pelonomi Venson and Tebelelo Seretse, battled it out in the 1998 and 2003 primary elections. It is not clear whether the competition for position between Khama and Kedikilwe, and between Venson and Seretse will lead to new politics in the BDP or whether it is just an exception that will soon disappear through internal compromises. Could it be that the entry of women and soldiers in BDP politics would drive out the male fear of political competition or will their entry prove to be of no significance?

Generally, smooth transfer of power in the absence of electoral competition or heredity, was still possible because of three factors. Firstly, most Botswana political parties (except for the BNF that allows migrant candidates to compete wherever they want as shown in the above paragraph) encouraged avoidance of serious competition in a constituency or ward. That is, senior people of the same party hardly ever contest for a constituency or ward. Secondly, either the central committees of some political parties exercised strict controls over primary elections or the latter were restricted to party officials at different levels of the party organisation. This excluded ordinary card-carrying members as in the BDP before the recently introduced open primary elections. Thirdly, politically active youths were marginalised through lack of resources and the restrictive Tswana culture that relegates youths to the background. The marginalisation of youth allowed councillors and members of parliament to occupy their positions for extended periods of time without any serious challenge.

SUCCESSION RULES IN THE BDP AND BNF

Party national congresses, regional congresses and constituency conferences are the common avenues through which succession within political party structures are handled. Except for the Botswana Peoples Party (BPP) that has no recorded instance of electing the founding leadership of the party, all other main political parties elected their founding fathers. In the BPP, Motsamai Mpho invited Kgalemang Motsete to take over the leadership and both invited Philip Matante to be the vice president while Mpho played the role of secretary general. So, even when the BPP started experiencing leadership problems as the three leaders started fighting over party control, the party had no mechanism of resolving issues through an internal electoral process. The only conceivable option was a split, which occurred in 1963, eighteen months after the party's formation.

In contrast, the BDP and the BNF had elected their founding leaders thus developing mechanisms for resolving leadership disputes. In the case of the BDP, after electing the founding fathers into leadership positions, competition for the party presidency was placed under constitutional restrictions and the clause which authorised elections for that position 'as long as the party was in power' was waived. Although the clause was amended in 1998 as part of process of democratising the party for the 21st century, it has not yet been put to good use as no competition for the party presidency has occurred.

In the case of the BNF, all party positions in the central committee, including the president and the vice president, were open to elections every three years at congresses. Thus there were less constitutional restrictions regarding the filling of party positions in the BNF than in the BDP. Also, there was fierce competition rather than avoidance in the BNF. John Makgala has closely studied BNF congresses and shows that there was political explosion at every BNF congress that elected party officials. In 1970, the first BNF president, Daniel Kwele, resigned after the party engineered his replacement by the former Bangwaketse chief, Bathoen. The replacement was engineered because the BNF congress that was scheduled for Mahalapye, was abruptly moved to the unscheduled Kanye, Bathoen's ethnic capital and home. Many other members resigned with Kwele (Makgala, 2002). In 1985 after Bathoen retired from the BNF leadership, Dr Kenneth Koma and his group attempted to engineer the election of Wellie Seboni (a former minister in the BDP government who had defected to the BNF) to assume the vice presidency of the party. Amidst fighting between old and new members, the party leader suspended contestation for the position and the party went without a vice president until 1993 (Makgala, 2002).

In the lead up to the 1988 BNF congress, Lenyeletse Koma, Kenneth Koma's cousin, was expelled. After the 1988 congress, five 'dissidents' from the Kanye region, were expelled. 'Similar developments followed the 1993, 1997 and 2001 congresses' (Makgala, 2002: 13). After the Palapye congress of 1997, 11 former BNF members of parliament formed the Botswana Congress Party. After the Kanye congress of 2001, Dr Koma and his supporters formed the New Democratic Front that was registered in 2003.

The comparative conclusion that can be drawn is that there is more internal party democracy in the BNF than in the BDP. This is because all positions in the BNF have always been open to contest while the presidency has been closed to contest within the BDP. However, there have been more political problems and instability in the BNF where there is more internal party democracy than in the BDP where there is little internal party democracy. The introduction of internal party democracy in the BNF was not accompanied by the development of stable rules and procedures that could regulate competition and stabilise the party. All these exposed the party to long, drawn-out factional fighting, to splits and to self-weakening.

Comparatively, the BDP and the Botswana state have continued the core succession rules that were inherited from the pre-colonial Tswana states. In addition, the BDP '...was the party of a chief and much of its leadership was of royal descent, a feature of its leadership extending beyond the boundaries of the Bangwato state' (Parson, 1990: 102-3). The presidents of the BDP and of the Republic of Botswana have not been subjected to the electoral process and this is likely to continue for the foreseeable future.

CONCLUSION

Succession to high office in the Botswana presidency, in the Botswana Democratic Party, in the BNF and in the constituencies and wards, shows continuities with the ancient Tswana rules governing chieftaincy succession. The central aspect of the system is that the multitude (ordinary voters), are excluded from the process of filling a vacancy in the state presidency and in the BDP leadership. The tradition is strongly embedded in BDP politics to the extent that even when the succession rules were reformed to allow elections for the party presidency, no challenger emerged for the 2004 party presidential elections and no such election was held. The BNF and the Botswana Congress Party have diverged from the Tswana rules of succession and the cost to the former has been enormous in terms of party instability. But the divergence from the Tswana rules of succession by the BNF did not so much cause the instability as the failure to agree on the rules of the future congresses in advance. In preparation for the 2005 congresses, the BDP leadership was working on a compromise so that positions in its central committee would not be open for contest and nobody was emerging to challenge Khama for the chairmanship of the party. A compromise deal in the manner that Vice President Khama suggested would be a resuscitation of Tswana succession rules that ruled out competition for high office. At the time of completing this chapter, the BNF leadership was discussing cooperation for electoral gains with other parties and it was uncertain how this was going to affect succession rules and the filling of elected offices. However, supporters of automatic succession cut across the political parties even though they are more dominant in the BDP than the BNF and BCP.

REFERENCES

Crowder, M, J. Parson and N. Persons (1990) 'Legitimacy And Faction: Tswana Constitutionalism And Political Change' in

Good, K (2002) *The Liberal Model and Africa: Elites Against Democracy*, Houndmills: Palgrave.

Holm, J and P. Molutsi (1992) 'State-Society Relations In Botswana: Beginning of Liberalisation' in G. Hyden and M. Bratton (eds) *Governance In Africa*, Boulder and London: Lynne Rienner: 75-95.

IEC, (2002) *Voter Apathy Report*, Gaborone: Government Printer.

Makgala, J (2002) 'So Far So Good?: An Appraisal Of Dr Ng'ombe's 1998 Prophecy On The Fate Of The Botswana national Front', paper presented at a Department of History Seminar series, 12 November 2002, University of Botswana.

Maundeni, Z (1998) 'Majority Rule, Life Presidency and Factional Politics' in W. Edge and M. Lekorwe (eds) *Botswana: Politics And Society*, Pretoria: van Schaik Publishers: 378-396.

Maundeni, Z (2002) 'State Culture And Development In Botswana And Zimbabwe', *Journal of Modern African Studies*, 40, 1: 105-132.

Mgadla, P.T (1998) 'The Kgosi In A Traditional Tswana Setting' in W. Edge and M. Lekorwe (eds) *Botswana: Politics And Society*, Pretoria: van Schaik Publishers: 3-10.

Mgadla, P., and A.C Campbell (1989) 'Dikgotla, Dikgosi and the Protectorate Administration' in J. Holm and P. Molutsi (eds) *Democracy In Botswana*, Gaborone: The Botswana Society and Macmillan: 48-57.

Morton, F (1998) 'Land, Cattle And Ethnicity: The Creation of Linchwe's Bakgatla, 1875-1920' in W. Edge and M. Lekorwe (eds) *Botswana: Politics And Society*: 43-61.

Ngcongco, L (1977) 'Aspects of The History Of The Bangwaketse', PhD: Dalhousie University.

Ngcongco, L (1989) 'Tswana Political Tradition: How Democratic?' in J. Holm and P. Molutsi (eds) *Democracy In Botswana*, Gaborone: The Botswana Society and Macmillan: 42-47.

Parson, J. (1990) 'Succession, Legitimacy and Political Change In Botswana, 1956-1987' in J. Parson (ed) *Succession To High Office in Botswana*, Ohio: Ohio University Center for International Studies.

Platjee, S. T (1916) *Sechuana Proverbs, with Literal Translations and their English Equivalents*, London: Keagan Paul.

Tlou, T (1972) 'A Political History Of Northwestern Botswana To 1906', PhD., University of Wisconsin-Madison.

Tlou, T (1998) 'The Nature of Batswana States: Towards A Theory Of Batswana Traditional Government: The Batawana Case' in W. Edge and M. Lekorwe (eds) *Botswana: Politics And Society*, Pretoria: van Schaik Publishers: 11-31.

Tlou, T., N. Parsons and W. Henderson (1995) *Seretse Khama*, 1921-1980, Gaborone: The Botswana Society.

CHAPTER 6

VOTERS AND ELECTORAL PERFORMANCE OF POLITICAL PARTIES IN BOTSWANA

Mpho Molomo and Wilford Molefe

INTRODUCTION

Sir Seretse Khama (1970), the first president of the Republic of Botswana, described the country as 'a non-racial democracy' destined to be a 'model for southern Africa'. Studman (1993) described it as a 'shining example of democracy'[14]. Denavad (1995) described it as a 'frontrunner in democratic politics'. Taylor (2003) has described it as a 'rare bird' in Africa. We however share the views of scholars and politicians who have described Botswana differently. Good (1996) described it as 'an authoritarian liberal democratic state'. Chris Landsberg (2003) described it as 'an overrated democracy'[15]. Amidst all these categorisations it can be maintained that Botswana has, since independence in 1966 remained a functioning democracy. It has a unique record in southern Africa as a country that adhered to multi-party democracy when other countries opted for one party government. During this period, it has had regular free and fair elections in a free and conducive atmosphere. Based on a pragmatic foreign policy and prudent financial management, Botswana became an 'island of stability'[16] in a volatile region.

Despite this impeccable track record, Botswana presents an interesting paradox; although it exhibits features that characterise it as a functioning democracy, it is

---

14 This is informed by Khama's un-wavering commitment to democratic ideals and his personal circumstance of being incarcerated for marrying a white woman, Ruth Williams.

15 Statement made informally at the Centre for Policy Studies at a workshop planning the celebration of South Africa's 10th Anniversary of Democracy, Johannesburg, South Africa, 2003.

16 Wellie Seboni, a flamboyant politician referring to the strategic role that Botswana played in regional politics when the region was at crossroads described Botswana under the leadership of Seretse Khama, as 'an island of sanity in an ocean of political madness'. The region was polarised by a racial divide, the wars of liberation, and ideological battles characteristic of the cold war. For detail see Parsons, N., Henderson, W. and Tlou, T. *Seretse Khama 1921-1980* p. 322.

premised on a weak opposition, nascent civil society, and declining levels of electoral participation. This trajectory is manifested by a predominant party system in which one political party, the BDP, has since the independence election of 1965, won each and every election by a landslide victory. While constitutional and institutional performance is important for understanding the record of democratic performance in Botswana, it is equally important to understand the extent of citizen participation in the political process. Democracy is entrenched when people choose it as the most preferable form of government and support its sustenance in several ways, including voting.

This chapter seeks to understand the extent of electoral performance of political parties in Botswana. It starts with an analysis of the country's political and economic framework to set the context of understanding the interface between electoral performance and the consolidation of democracy. It departs from the basic premise that while elections are an essential part of democracy, they are not its sole determinants. It asks a number of substantive questions concerning the nature and extent of democracy in Botswana. First, it seeks to understand which political parties win elections, and why? Secondly, it asks whether or not political participation matters and whether low levels of political participation present challenges to political institutionalisation or democratic consolidation? Thirdly, it asks whether participation in civic organisations has an effect on political participation. In other words, do people who have a high measure of civic competence and political efficacy view politics differently? Are such people more inclined to support the ruling party or opposition parties? Fourthly, it seeks to establish whether economic growth or well-being is strongly correlated with democracy or does it have a spurious relationship? Are people motivated to vote in particular ways as a response to economic rewards and incentives? In another formulation, does relative deprivation lead people to be disinterested in politics or does it lead them to be alienated from government, and consequently vote for the opposition? Fifthly, it asks whether traditional voting trends of ethnic loyalty, family party and client-patron relationships are still applicable in influencing voter behaviour? To answer these questions, this chapter proceeds first by providing a contextual framework of understanding Botswana's politics.

CONTEXTUAL FRAMEWORK

Political participation is a broad concept that is anchored on the liberal democratic ideals. Dahl (1989:221) outlines it as a process where there are free and regular elections based on universal adult suffrage; where citizens have the right not only to vote in an election but also to run for political office. Democracy is consolidated when people choose it as the most preferable form of government and nurture it by participating in its activities. Pursuing the same point, Dalton (1996:40) points out that 'democracy should be a celebration of an involved public'. More specifically, the argument goes:

> Democracy requires an active citizenry because it is through discussion that, particular interest and involvement in political sphere, such as sport clubs, agricultural cooperatives, and philanthropic groups, promote interpersonal trust, fostering the capacity to work together and creating bonds for social life that are the basis for civil society and democracy.

It would be expected that since Botswana is a frontrunner of democratic politics in sub-Saharan Africa, it would be exemplary in citizen activism (Molutsi in **Chapter One** formulated other questions concerning Botswana's leadership in democracy). However, the comparison here is limited to electoral trends. Compared to other countries in the continent, and especially in the southern African region, it is noted that Botswana has low levels of political activism. Bratton, (1999:552) defines political participation as 'a multi-dimensional concept; involving far more than voting in elections, it includes election campaigning, collective action around policy issues, contacting political representatives, and direct action like protests and demonstrations'. As stated in Bratton (1999:550), political participation is shaped by the 'availability of political institutions that link citizens to the state'. The extent to which, Bratton adds, 'citizens become involved in the political process depends on their affiliation, through mass mobilisation campaigns, to agencies of voter registration, to political parties, and to voluntary associations'.

Voter apathy is understood to mean disinterest, alienation or non-participation in politics. Voter apathy is an important research question in Botswana because, since the independence election of 1965, there has been a marked decline in political participation with voter disengagement from politics. This trend has been a feature of Botswana politics, which led the Independent Electoral Commission (IEC) in 2002 to commission the Democracy Research Project (DRP) of the University of Botswana to investigate its causes. Some of the major recommendations of the Voter Apathy Report, were that, in order to motivate political activity, the IEC should mount an intensive voter education campaign before the elections. Perhaps more fundamentally, it was recommended that churches and other civic organisations should not only make announcements about voter registration and voting, but should also encourage their members to discuss and engage in politics.

The report noted that the church is one of the more developed and well-patronised organs of civil society in Botswana. But unlike other parts of the world, such as Latin America and Western Europe, where the church historically played overt political roles[17], in Botswana it has remained largely apolitical. For a long time it was only concerned with peoples' spiritual salvation leading to a total disregard for political freedoms and economic empowerment. As a response to a clarion call for more political activism by the church, Catholic Bishops (2004) in the run-up to the 2004 election in Botswana issued a pastoral letter on elections, which said: 'Get up, pick up your mat, and walk forward (cf: Mark 2:9)...election is another giant step forward on our long walk to freedom. However, there is a great danger for many of us to say, we have achieved our independence. Let us sit down on our mat and relax. Others may stretch out on the mat of disappointment, no longer interested in politics or in voting'[18]. The Bishops appealed to the youth and the unemployed to shape their destiny and future by exercising their democratic right to vote for a government of their choice. They also extolled leaders to be virtuous and to lead by example, and not use their position for self-enrichment. In addition, they preached a culture of tolerance and mutual respect for opposing political parties, urging them to 'listen to each other in order to find the way to a better life for all in [the] country which is tormented by HIV/AIDS, unemployment, poverty, and crime'.

The view is partly shared that in democratic theory the novelty of a vote and it alone, could approximate to the general will of the people. In a more substantive way, Mill as discussed in Duncan and Lukes (1966:159) contends that a vote:

> is a natural right, or a right deriving from the rendering of services; that powerful groups or interests must be absorbed into society rather than driven into violent action against established institutions; that the vote is necessary for self-protection; and that it, along with other forms of participation in the life of the nation, elevates those who possess it.

However, Berelson's views are shared in that, 'less than one-third of the electorate is really interested in politics, many vote without real involvement, open discussion and motives for participation are almost non-existent' (Duncan and Lukes,1966:161). Furthermore, it is common knowledge that the public is not well-informed about political issues. Moreover, even when they are well-informed, their knowledge serves

---

17 In Western Europe, Christian churches have traditionally supported Christian Democratic Parties.

18 The Pastoral letter was issued by Boniface Tshosa Setlalekgosi, Bishop of Gaborone and Frank Nabuasah, Bishop of Francistown. The letter was read in all catholic churches during the mass of 18 April 2004 and was also published in the media . See 'Pastoral letter on elections' *The Botswana Gazette*, 21 April 2004 p.9

to buttress already existing perceptions rather than sway their opinion to vote differently. At best, political information and election campaigns help to mobilise the undecided or free 'floaters' to take a stand rather than lead to a 'free decision'.

In making a further audit of democracy, Duncan and Lukes (1966:163) argue that, by and large, what we call democracy, is a 'system of decision-making in which leaders are more or less responsive' to the peoples' needs, it 'seems to operate with a relatively low level of citizen participation'. Therefore based on empirical evidence across the world, on the whole, even though it is desirable, it is 'inaccurate to say that one of the necessary conditions for democracy is extensive citizen participation'.

The literature also asserts that people's participation in the political process is necessary; Danevad (1995:384) quotes Bratton and Rothchild as having said: 'Governments do not regulate themselves; they must be checked and balanced by an active, articulate, and organised citizenry...when citizens regard state commands as legitimate, governmental effectiveness is more easily attained because it rests on bedrock of voluntary compliance.' By this, it is implied that democratic governance would be enhanced if civil society were vibrant and kept leaders under constant check to make them accountable to the people. However, in the case of Botswana, where civil society is weak, the state-society interface is limited. As discussed in Duncan and Lukes (1966: 167), Joseph Schumpeter, one of the leading theorists of the competitive theory of democracy has defined democratic theory as that 'institutional arrangement for arriving at political decisions and acquiring the power to decide by means of a competitive struggle for the people's vote'. A vote provides the electorate with the opportunity to change their leaders and enhances competition between candidates for political office. When there is no effective political competition between leaders, then the system ceases to be responsive to people's wishes.

Another view is the one propounded by Berelson that, instead of viewing voter apathy as a degeneration of the democratic process, it needs to be seen as a healthy sign in the political process. The argument continues that voter apathy 'helps the democratic system to function smoothly by facilitating change and reducing the impact of fanaticism, thus guarding against the danger of "total politics"'. Total politics implies embracing extra-legal methods, such as violence, to make a political point. In the normal course of things, the argument goes, people are complacent, and are only motivated to participate in politics if there is general discontent (Duncan and Lukes 1966:172). Thomas Dye and Harmon Zeigler (1993) referred to in the Voter Apathy Report (2002) argues that 'the masses are authoritarian, intolerant, anti-intellectual, atavistic, alienated, hateful, violent' and the political elite need not wake them out of their 'political indifference' without good reason.

Reference is often made to voting trends in Austria and Germany in the period between the two World Wars. During that period, both countries experienced a high voter turnout (Duncan and Lukes (1966:173). Following from these examples, it is evident that high political participation may not always be a 'sign of the health of democracy'. In some situations it can manifest serious political crisis. The basic contention is that political parties must aggregate diverse views but must do so in a manner that would not deviate from accepted norms. However, what is problematic is how much of disagreement or participation is considered optimal.

Following from the above logic, it could be argued that voter apathy may be reflected in a good light as showing the 'limitations of politics.' It is normal and common place that people may choose to ignore politics and life would still go on as usual. The honourable thing to do in democratic politics is to give people the political space and free will to 'interest or disinterest themselves' from politics. If people were compelled to vote, what guarantee do we have that they would not be compelled to do other things deemed socially significant? Nevertheless, as entailed in democratic theory, there is a normative interpretation that voting is a noble thing to do because through it, people exercise their democratic right to elect a government of their choice. Yet in the absence of concrete and conclusive evidence, that voter apathy sustains democracy, it appears reasonable to suggest that people 'ought to play [a part] in politics for their own good and for the good of society' (Duncan and Lukes, 1966:174-176).

VOTING TRENDS IN BOTSWANA

The challenge here is to explain the predominance of the BDP and the weakness of opposition parties. Over the years the BDP has been the only political party that has a national electoral appeal which won constituencies and wards across the country. It draws its electoral support predominantly from a rural base but continues to have a strong presence in urban areas. Although this is a changing feature, the BDP had a strong electoral presence in the Central, Kweneng, Ngamiland, Ghanzi, Kgalagadi and South East Districts. In 2004, as will be discussed in more detail later in the chapter, it won all the Francistown and Selibe Phikwe constituencies. In Gaborone, it won Gaborone North and presented a strong challenge in all the other Gaborone constituencies, especially Gaborone Central, which the Botswana Congress Party (BCP) won by a small margin of 91 votes.

The Botswana Peoples Party (BPP), which at independence was the main opposition party, has declined in terms of support. Except for the Kgatleng Constituency, which it won in 1965 and 1969, its support over the years was from a narrow ethnic base, amongst Bakalanga in Francistown and North East District constituencies. However, the BDP has since eroded the basis of its support to the extent of winning parliamentary seats in its traditional strongholds. The Botswana Independence Party (BIP), which was a splinter group from the BPP, was confined to the North West region but later joined with Freedom Party (FP) and later Botswana Alliance Movement (BAM). This was an attempt to broaden its base and to enhance its electoral appeal. Nevertheless, as will be seen in the trends projected below, its electoral fortunes have been marginal.

The BNF only came on to the political scene after the 1965 election and was only registered as a political party after Koma and his group failed to unite the warring factions of the BPP. It contested elections for the first time in 1969, and over the years began to project itself as the main opposition party. Its high point was in the 1994 election when it won 13 of the 40 parliamentary constituencies. However, its fortunes declined in 1999[19] as a result of the split it experienced and the formation of the BCP. During the 2004 election, the BNF made a major comeback by winning twelve seats and, perhaps more significantly, made decisive inroads into constituencies that are known to be BDP strongholds and won others outright. Except for the Kanye constituencies, which are its traditional strongholds, for the first time it won the rural constituencies of Kgalagadi North, Letlhakeng East, and Letlhakeng West. It also won the Ngwaketse West constituency, which for a long time was a marginal constituency, by a strong margin[20]. It also regained Kgatleng East from the BDP and won South East North Constituency. It would appear that the issues of poverty and unemployment, which the opposition articulated quite forcefully made an impact on election outcomes.

Figure 6.1 below shows the heart of voter behaviour and also depict trends of voter turnout. In broad outline, it is noted that except for 1965 and 1984 elections, which recorded voter turnout of more than 50 per cent of the eligible voters, all the other elections have been characterised by a low voter turnout. A number of factors explain voting trends in Botswana. First, there have been simplistic arguments that a low level of political participation is a result of limited knowledge about the Westminster parliamentary system that Botswana operates. It is argued that since the

---

19 In 1999, its seats dropped from 13 to 6 seats.

20 Ngwaketse West was a marginal constituency, which the BDP won by a margin of 10 votes during the 1999 election. During the 2004 election, the BNF won it by a 1 449 votes. Needless to say, this was a marginal constituency and there were other mitigating factors which could have tilted the scale in favour of the opposition. In the run-up to the election Debswana workers in the Jwaneng mine went on strike, and as a result several people lost their jobs.

majority of Batswana are rural and uneducated, they have not fully grasped the transition from rule by *dikgosi* to a republican form of government. Perhaps what may have clouded the matter further, the argument goes, especially in the Central District, was the knowledge that Seretse Khama, the first president of the Republic of Botswana was an heir to the Bagwato throne. Although he had abdicated, his election to president may have been misconstrued in some quarters to mean that, as president, he was now made a 'big chief'[21] for the whole country. The perception was that, as was the case with hereditary *bogosi* (chieftaincy), once elected to the position of prime minister in 1965, and subsequently made president, there was no need to renew his mandate. Nevertheless, in Botswana, dikgosi are civil servants, and as such, are expected to be non-partisan. The Chieftainship Act, the Tribal Land Act and Matimela Act have circumscribed the political role of *dikgosi*. Their involvement in politics is only incidental, and where they take overt political roles they are expected to resign their positions. Yet despite their peripheral role in politics, their political inclinations influence political outcomes. Plausible as this argument appears to be, it would make sense to attribute it to the Bangwato, and not other ethnic groups. Although Khama was popular in the whole country it would be presumptuous to suggest that his royal influence went beyond the Central District.

Secondly, it is argued that the pervasive low voter turnout illustrated in **Table 6.1** below is often attributed to complacency. Arising from the prudent financial management, relative absence of corruption and political stability that eludes other African countries, the BDP government has been credited as a success story. As a result, people may feel that the government is doing a good job; hence there is no need to replace it with another party. However, although this could be true of BDP supporters and sympathisers, it would certainly not be the case for opposition activists. The opposition sees itself as an alternative government and its natural course of action is to mobilise and unseat the BDP. So the complacency that is talked about should not affect the opposition vote. Perhaps the opposite of complacency, which is alienation, could be a factor in explaining low voter turnout (Parson, 1975:236). The predominance of the BDP may also give voters a feeling of resignation, that even if they vote, their vote would not make a difference. This scenario is exacerbated by the split and fracture of opposition parties, which divide the opposition vote to the advantage of the BDP.

To take each election in turn, it is likely that the high voter turnout in the 1965 election may be due to the fact that it was a historic election, which facilitated a transition from the colonial administration to an independent government. In this

---

21 This view was also popularised by opposition politicians, such as, Motsamai Mpho and Philip Matante.

election the voter turnout was 69 per cent. In the same election, the BDP won 28 of the 31 seats and their poll accounted for 80 per cent of the popular vote. The opposition BPP won 3 seats and 14 per cent of the popular vote, and the BIP, which did not win any seat, polled 5 per cent of the popular vote.

During the first few elections, including that of 1965, a factor that appears to explain the ruling party's large majority over opposition parties was that it contested all wards and constituencies, while opposition parties failed to field candidates in some of them. Where the opposition parties were able to field candidates, they did so with candidates who lacked credibility and had limited capacity to unseat incumbents. Moreover, the BDP not only had royal influence but was also founded by people who had been associated with the Legislative Council, the majority of whom were prominent people in their own areas. The opposition, which was headed by commoners (K.T Motsete, P. Matante and M. Mpho) in an era in which *bogosi* (chieftainship) was the only known legitimate form of government, were not taken seriously by an electorate that was essentially rural and uneducated. The BDP manifesto was founded on multi-racialism and support for *bogosi*. The opposition advocated radical politics, which projected a position that was anti-white and anti-*bogosi*, and was set on nationalising land occupied by white commercial farmers (Vengroff, 1976).

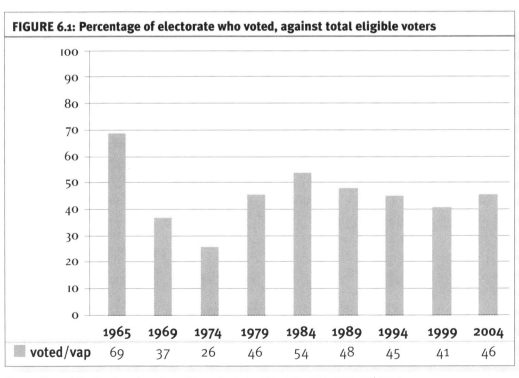

FIGURE 6.1: Percentage of electorate who voted, against total eligible voters

	1965	1969	1974	1979	1984	1989	1994	1999	2004
voted/vap	69	37	26	46	54	48	45	41	46

Source: General Election Reports, 1965, 1969, 1974, 1979, 1984, 1989, 1994, 1999, and 2004

Following the 1965 election an independence constitution was put in place, which provided for a unicameral legislature made up of a National Assembly comprising 31 elected members, 4 specially nominated by the president, the speaker and attorney-general. In addition to parliament, a second chamber comprising of a fifteen member House of Chiefs was created (this is now generating heated debates over the fact that it marginalises the non-Tswana ethnic groups). The House of Chiefs serves only in an advisory capacity with no legislative powers. It was perhaps the transition from traditional rule to a republican form of government that explains the sharp decline in voter turnout and party support in 1969. During that election, voter turnout dropped from 69 per cent to 37 per cent and the number of BDP seats also dropped from 28 to 24. The popular vote of the opposition increased from 20 per cent to 32 per cent. Perhaps the outcome of the 1969 election was a manifestation of 'tension arising from the traditional power structure [of *dikgosi*] being supplanted by a newly established central authority based on legal-rational principles' (Danevad 1995: 384). Based on the erosion of traditional authority, as reflected in the Chieftainship Act, the Tribal Land Act and Matimela Act, the cohesion that existed between *dikgosi* and the BDP experienced a noticeable rupture. The high point of this tension was when Kgosi Bathoen II of Bangwaketse resigned from *bogosi* to join the BNF, as Maundeni observed in Chapter Five. In what appeared to be an uneasy alliance between traditionalists and Marxists, Kanye and its outlying areas became the stronghold of the BNF and this legacy remains today.

The 1974 election was significant in many respects but most fundamentally, it marked the lowest ever turnout of voters in Botswana's political history. Only 26 per cent of the eligible voting population cast their vote. However, close analysis of this election reflects a complex picture. In this election, the BDP not only won 27 of the 32 seats in parliament but also increased its poll from 68 per cent of the previous election to 77 per cent. The opposition poll declined from 32 to 23 per cent. The 'rational choice' model can perhaps be used to explain BDP electoral victory in 1974. This model asserts that there is a strong correlation between government's ability to distribute economic goods, and voting behaviour (Ball, 1988:124). In the year preceding the 1974 election, the BDP government launched the Accelerated Rural Development Programme (ARDP), which was designed to provide visible rural development projects such as roads, schools and clinics. These programmes delivered tangible infrastructural developments that improved the lives of the rural poor. So, a strong win by the BDP could be associated with these developments. However, the record low decline of voter participation to 26 per cent remains largely unexplained.

In contrast to the 1974 election which was marked by a low voter turnout, the 1979 election was characterised by an improvement in voter participation. The proportions increased from a low of 26 per cent in 1974 to an increase of 46 per cent. The BDP proportion of the popular vote decreased slightly from 77 per cent to 75 per cent, and the poll of the opposition increased to 24 per cent. The 1984 election was also significant in that it was the only election since 1965 in which voter turnout was higher that 50 per cent: more precisely, it was 54 per cent. It also marked a continuing trend of decline of the BDP poll. BDP poll declined to 68 per cent, while that of the opposition increased to 32 per cent.

The 1984 election was also noteworthy for the fact that it was the first contested under the leadership of Quett Masire, who had for many years served as Seretse Khama's vice president. Prior to this election, it was believed that the BDP's overwhelming electoral dominance was a result of Khama's royal influence. Interestingly the BDP continued to dominate in terms of parliamentary seats won. Our conclusion is that the 1984 election marked a process of consolidating the democratic process. The BDP victory under Masire, was testimony to the fact that 'political order and legitimacy were increasingly grounded in the concept of elected representative parliamentary government' (Danevad, 1995: 390). However, it is noted that in this election, the BDP poll continued to decline and that of the opposition continued to increase.

There is also a view that changed economic circumstances had an effect on the 1989 elections. That election took place in the backdrop of a healthy balance of payments situation. The economy was doing well with an 'unparalleled economic growth', rate of about 12 per cent (Matsheka and Botlhomilwe, 2000:41). Nevertheless, the increased wealth changed the demographic features of Batswana. The trajectory that emerged, as a result of diamond revenues, led to increased access to education, job opportunities, urbanisation and possibilities of social advancement. More pressure was placed on government to provide citizen empowerment programmes[22] that were meant to enhance indigenous participation in the economy. The increased opportunities also led to increased demands on government. Economic prosperity also filtered through to the political sphere. It led to a more vigorous campaign for entry into politics, manifesting inter and intra party competition. During that election the BDP increased its seats from 28 to 31. Although the opposition seats declined, its poll of the popular vote increased to 34 per cent.

---

22 Programmes such as the Financial Assistance Policy, Arable Land Development Programme, and the Accelerated Rainfed Arable Programme were put in place to harness the various sectors of the economy.

It is important to emphasise that the 1994 election should be seen as a major milestone in Botswana politics and a consolidation of democracy. For the first time in the history of the country, an opposition party not only polled a significant share of the popular vote but those votes were also translated into seats. In that election, there was meaningful political competition at the polls in spite of the FPTP electoral system. The BNF won 13 of the 40 parliamentary seats and some ruling party ministers lost their seats. Despite this historic poll by the BNF, the election was characterised by a further decline in voter participation. Overall, only 45 per cent of the eligible voters cast their ballot. Disaggregating the poll further, the BDP poll declined to 54 per cent and that of the BNF rose to 27 per cent.

Against the rising tide of opposition popularity, the ruling party was beset by scandals in which high-ranking members of the party and government were implicated in acts of impropriety[23]. The continued decline of the BDP's popular vote suggested that, if nothing dramatic happened to enhance its electoral appeal, it would lose the 1999 election. Following this, the BDP commissioned a study to look into the factors accounting for the decline in their share of the poll. The Schlemmer (1997) Commission recommended that the party needed to inject new blood into its ranks, especially youth and women, and a leadership with 'sufficient dynamism' to carry the party forward. It was against this background that Ian Khama was brought to the helm of the BDP.

In 1999, the BDP went into the election under the leadership of Mogae and Khama, and in this election the percentage of votes cast continued to drop (41 per cent). However, the proportion of the BDP share of the popular vote remained the same (54 per cent), and that of the opposition increased to 41 per cent. The BNF entered the 1999 election as a fractured party following the disturbances at the Palapye Congress, where eleven of its Members of Parliament broke away and formed the BCP. The BNF, which had been an erstwhile official opposition, was reduced to two seats in parliament. Perhaps as a mark of loss of confidence on it by the electorate, during the 1999 election, it dropped from thirteen to six seats, and its share of the popular vote also dropped from 37 per cent to 24 per cent. The BCP accounted for eleven per cent of the votes cast, leaving five per cent for the BAM.

However the 2004 election mirrored the 1994 election in a number of ways. In these elections, the tussle was between two political parties, the BDP and BNF. In that election, the BDP won 44 of the 57 parliamentary seats, the BNF twelve seats and the

---

23 These included the 1991 Kgabo Report that investigated allegations of land impropriety in the peri-urban areas; the Christie report that investigated Botswana Housing Corporation activities, and the NDB scandal where it surfaced that the cash strapped organisation that at some stage repossessed tractors of defaulters at Barolong Farms was owed millions of Pula by a high ranking government official.

BCP one seat. While the BDP won 77 per cent of the seats, its share of the popular vote continued to decline, now accounting for 52 per cent. For the BNF, its share of the proportion of seats increased from 15 per cent (1999) to 21 per cent. In terms of the popular vote, its growth was only nominal, growing by one per cent from 25 per cent of 1999 to 26 per cent. However taking everything into account, the BNF's performance reflected a major comeback as it took place after another split had polarised it. Its erstwhile leader, Kenneth Koma, and a group which called itself the 'Party Line' broke away and formed the New Democratic Front (NDF)[24].

In the 2004 election, the party that reflected the highest growth of the popular vote, even though it did not translate into seats, was the BCP (perhaps reflecting the three party system that Molutsi discussed in Chapter Two). The BCP experienced a remarkable growth of five per cent from eleven per cent in 1999 to sixteen per cent in 2004. It accounted for the highest growth in the opposition vote. It had been expected that the BCP would retain the Okavango constituency, a marginal constituency which the BCP won by a margin of 82 votes[25] in 1999. During the 2004 election, fortunes changed and the BDP won the constituency by a margin of 256 votes. Nevertheless, the BCP redeemed itself by winning the highly contested seat of Gaborone Central by a margin of 91 votes[26], and showed strong signs of growth in several constituencies.

---

24 In the run-up to a Congress that was held in Kanye in 2001, the BNF was polarised in two main factions. In the struggle for succession, after Kenneth Koma stepped down as party president, two factions emerged; the Party Line and the Concerned Group. The 'Party Line' rallied behind Koma's anointed successor Peter Woto, and the 'Concerned Group' behind a fairly young Lotswaletse Moupo. At the Central Committee Elections in Kanye, the Concerned Group won all the positions. Instead of accepting the results, the Party Line broke-away to form the New Democratic Front.

25 In 1999 Okavango was contested by the BCP, BDP, BNF and BAM. In 2004 it was contested by BAM, BCP and BDP, and this time the other opposition fielded a PACT ticket fielding a BAM candidate.

26 After the election, the BDP lodged a protest and intimated that it would challenge the results in court but later withdrew the case.

Column	1	2	3	4	5	6
Year	Voting Age Population	Total Registered	Total voted	per cent of 2/1	per cent of 3/1	per cent of 3/2
1965	202 800	188 950	140 858	93	69	75
1969	205 200	140 428	76 858	68	37	55
1974	244 200	205 050	64 011	84	26	31
1979	290 033	230 231	134 496	79	46	58
1984	420 400	293 571	227 756	70	54	78
1989	522 900	367 069	250 487	70	48	68
1994	634 920	361 915	277 454	57	45	77
1999	867 000	459 662	354 466	53	41	77
2004	920 000	552 849	421 272	60	46	76
Average				70	46	66

TABLE 6.1: Voting Trends: 1965 - 2004

Source: Election Reports

Table 6.1 above, shows statistics of the total voting age population, which represents the total eligible number of voters in a given election year (column 1), the total number of registered voters (column 2), and the total number of electorates who actually cast their vote (column 3). Column 4 is a ratio of total registered voters to the total eligible voters. This ratio shows a declining trend, except in the 1974 elections, when the ratio rose from 68 per cent in 1969 to 84 per cent. During the 1999 election, the ratio was at its lowest (53 per cent). Column 5 gives the ratio of the total number of electors who voted to the total eligible population, and for our purposes we use this column to measure the extent of voter participation. Column 6 measures narrow aspect of voter participation, presenting only a ratio of those who voted against those who had registered to vote.

There is an observable trend in Botswana's politics in that since 1994 electoral competition has essentially manifested a two party system. The contest, although uneven, has been between the BDP and BNF. The BCP can be seen as the greatest setback for the BNF. This is because the growth of the BCP has largely been at the expense of the BNF, thereby giving the BDP a new lease of life. A close reading of the election results is that in at least twelve constituencies[27], there was a split vote between the BNF and BCP that advantaged the BDP. Since the BNF and BCP are appealing to the same voters, the two parties are basically competing against each other without the opposition as a whole making any headway. So far the BCP has grown at the expense of the BNF and the BNF has only made nominal gains since 1999. What this trend suggests is that unity of opposition parties is perhaps the surest way of the opposition to unseat the BDP from power.

27 These are Ngami, Okavango, Nkange, Selebi-Phikwe East, Selebi-Phikwe West, Kgatleng West, Gaborone North, South East South, Mogoditshane, Kweneng South, Francistown South and Ngwaketse South

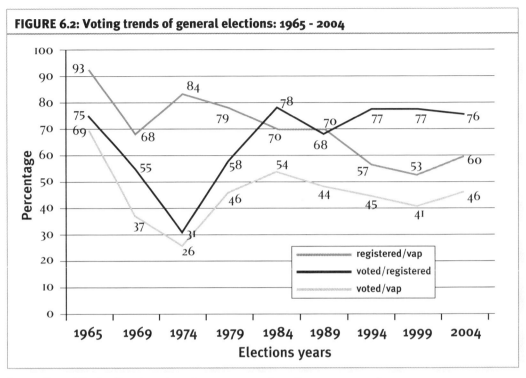

FIGURE 6.2: Voting trends of general elections: 1965 - 2004

Source: General Election Reports, 1965, 1969, 1974, 1979, 1984, 1989, 1994, 1999, and 2004

Figure 6.2 above presents a graphic picture of voting trends from 1965 to 2004 and these trends make a statement about the quality of Botswana's democracy. It demonstrates that the government of the day is a minority government. It was only in 1965 (69 per cent) and 1984 (54 per cent) that government was elected into power by a majority of the voting age population. In all the remaining election years, less that 50 per cent of the eligible voting population voted. However, since the constitution and the Electoral Law do not require that the majority of eligible voters should vote a government into power, then there is no cause for alarm. Nevertheless, the basic fact remains that for the years of 1969, 1974, 1969, 1989, 1994, 1999 and 2004, Batswana were ruled by a minority government.

With regard to voter registration, except for the 1974 elections when the proportion rose from 68 per cent in 1969 to 84 per cent, and in 2004 when it rose from 53 per cent to 60 per cent, there was a decline in the registration of voters. It is not immediately apparent why there was an increase in voter registration and the lowest voter turnout in 1974. However, the increase in voter turnout in 2004 can be attributed to the vigorous voter education campaign carried out by the IEC. The highest ever poll was in 1965 when 69 per cent voted and the 1974 election reflected the lowest over poll in the history of the Botswana general elections. Only 26 per cent of eligible voters cast their vote. In the 2004 election, 41 per cent of eligible voters cast their ballot.

Turning now to voting trends between political parties, we start from the basic premise that political parties are an effective link between the people and government and that a party that polls more seats and votes than others remains the preferred party to form a government. We agree with Parson (1976:234) that, judging by the voting trends wherein the BDP decisively won each and every election since independence, it is difficult to avoid the conclusion that the party is 'strong and popular'. Yet a close reading of the situation warrants further enquiry and analysis. As already shown, it was only in the 1965 election that the BDP won by a preponderance of 80 per cent of the popular vote. Starting with the 1969 election, except for 1974 where there was an increase in the BDP poll to almost the level of 1965 (77 per cent), there has been a marked decline in the number of people who cast their vote for the party. During the 2004 election, the party recorded the lowest level ever poll of the popular vote of 51 per cent. When the BDP poll is compared to that of the opposition poll, assuming they unite, then the 2009 election may see a change of government.

As outlined in **Table 6.3**, the BNF has seen a steady growth since 1979, although it stagnated in 1999 and 2004 as a result of the splits in the BCP and NDF respectively. During its years of growth, the BNF was narrowing the gap between its share of the popular vote and the BDP. During the 2004 election, there was another trend manifested by a growth of the BCP by five per cent, at the expense of the BNF, and a drop by two per cent of the BAM[28] poll. The opposition, except for the BCP, had contested the election under the banner of the PACT[29]. Our examination of the voting trends reflect that where the PACT fielded BAM candidates, it did not do so well compared to where it fielded BNF candidates. This trend reflects a further marginalisation of smaller parties. In our view these results show a clear trend of the bifurcation of the political system into a two party system. This demonstrates that the unity movement, when and if finally conceived, must be carefully thought through, and the BNF and its splinter groups need to be key players.

Figure 6.3 below presents a graphic picture of how political parties have performed since 1965. A clear trend has emerged that since 1974 the gap in terms of the popular vote between the BDP and BNF has been narrowing; there was a slight

---

28 BAM was registered as a political party following the merger of the Freedom Independence Party and United Action Party.

29 Representing BAM, BPP and BNF.

divergence in 1999 following the BNF split, and the 2004 election reflected the re-emergence of the trend. The BCP's growth shows that had there not been a split the difference between the BDP and the opposition would have narrowed further.

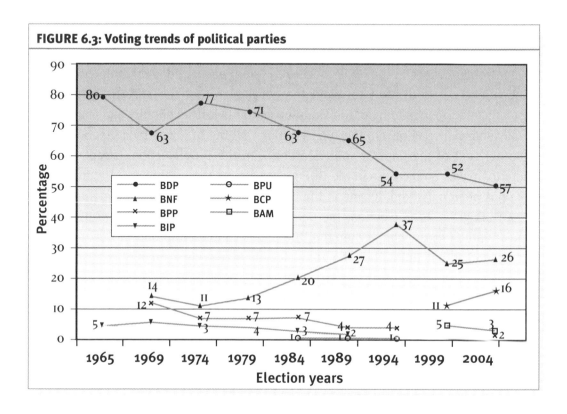

FIGURE 6.3: Voting trends of political parties

ELECTORAL TRENDS AT THE LOCAL LEVEL

At council level, even with the splitting of votes, opposition parties are eroding the basis of support for the ruling BDP. Although the opposition controls councils to the extent of having enough votes to elect Mayors and Council Chairpersons, the majority of councils are still controlled by the BDP. In all the election years, the proportion of council seats won by opposition parties has been minimal.

What can perhaps be seen as more significant is a comparison of voting trends (in **Table 6.2** and **Figure 6.4**) of the ruling party and opposition parties for parliament and council. At the parliamentary level, the opposition parties, especially the BNF, have over the years been closing the gap between their poll and that of the BDP. In contrast, the opposite prevails at council level where the gap between the BDP and opposition is wider than at parliamentary level, and has been narrowing at a smaller scale. It seems that what accounts for this trend is that the BDP, with a more elaborate party structure and funding, is able to reach all areas effectively.

TABLE 6.2: Party support (1965 - 2005) in local government elections

Number of seats

Party	1974	1979	1984	1989	1994	1999	2004
BDP	149	147	168	192	244	303	335
BNF	12	14	36	46	128	80	105
BIP/IFP	-	4	3	3	3	11	-
BPU	-	-	2	0	3	0	-
BPP	4	12	18	12	15	0	3
BCP	-	-	-	-	-	13	32
BAM	-	-	-	-	0	9	9
NDF	-	-	-	-	-	-	0
Total Seats	169	176	227	253	401	405	490

Percentage of Seats

Party	1974	1979	1984	1989	1994	1999	2004
BDP	88	83	74	76	61	75	69
BNF	7	8	16	18	32	20	21
BIP/IFP[30]	2	2	1	1	3	-	-
BPU	-	-	1	-	1	0	-
BPP	2	7	8	5	4	0	1
BCP[31]	-	-	-	-	-	3	7
BAM	-	-	-	-	-	2	2
NDF	-	-	-	-	-	-	0
Total percentage	99	100	100	100	100	100	100

Source: Election Reports

Table 6.2 and **Figure 6.3** above depict the percentage share of the political parties' council seats in all the constituencies and shows the proportion of council seats obtained by each political party during the elections. The proportion of seats obtained by the ruling BDP party has remained above the two-thirds of the seats, except for the 1994 elections when the BDP share dropped to 61 per cent, and that of

---

30 During the 1994 election, the Botswana Independence Party merged with the Freedom Party to form the Independence Freedom Party,

31 During the 1999 election the Independent Freedom Party merged with the United Action Party to form the Botswana Alliance Movement.

the BNF rose to 32 per cent. The performance of the BNF on the other hand has been improving steadily, except in the 1994 election when it experienced a split leading to the formation of the BCP. In 1999 and 2004, the BCP claimed three per cent and seven per cent of the council seats in the 1999 and 2004 elections, respectively. The distribution of council seats shows that only three political parties[32] manifest themselves as significant parties in the country.

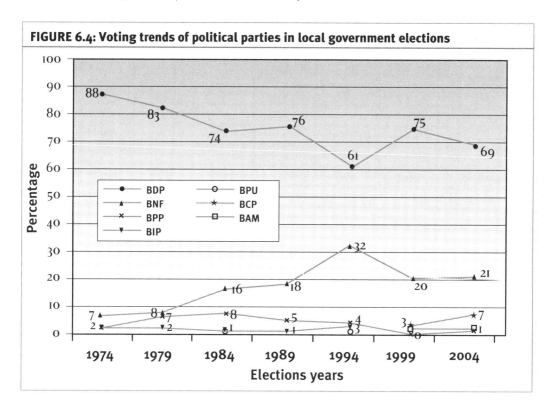

FIGURE 6.4: Voting trends of political parties in local government elections

Nevertheless, despite the preponderance of the BDP, opposition parties are beginning to make inroads into BDP strongholds. During the 2004 election, what puzzled[33] many was the fact that in the Serowe North West constituency in which Khama stood unopposed the opposition BNF won the Malatswai ward. Khama, in the Central District is seen as an icon of BDP's success. Nevertheless, an opposition win in a BDP stronghold shows a shift in the balance of forces and the trend of future electoral contests.

32 These are the BDP, BNF, and BCP.

33 Perhaps, the opposition win at Malatswai should not have come as a surprise because even during the 1999 election, the BDP won the ward against the BCP by a small margin of 72 votes compared to other wards in the constituency.

INDEPENDENT CANDIDATES

The 2004 election was different in many respects. Unlike previous elections in which independent candidates were not a significant factor in the 2004 election, for the first time in Botswana's political history, three independent candidates won council seats[34]. This development, in our view, shows the maturity and sophistication of voters that they are able to transcend party colours and to vote for a candidate they deem would best represent their interests. However, what seems to bedevil the concept of independent candidates is the perception of them as political opportunists. When candidates lose primary election on allegations of foul play they stand as independent candidates and, after winning the seats, they return[35] to their respective parties.

UNITY OF OPPOSITION PARTIES

In spite of the manifestation of political pluralism marked by the existence of several political parties, Botswana's democratic system is characterised by a weak opposition. It is a fact that a strong opposition is an indispensable part of a democracy as it should keep Government in check and accountable to the people. It appears that the fragmentation of opposition has meant that the BDP has enjoyed electoral dominance since independence. It has been unequivocally observed that opposition parties are generally weak due to inter-party faction fighting, internal splits, an unfavourable electoral system, and weak organisational capacity to promote alternative policies. The failure of opposition parties to unite and the propensity of their leadership to fight for positions has denied them the possibility of unseating the BDP from power.

The calls for unity of opposition parties are as old as electoral politics in Botswana. The BNF was formed in October 1965, eight months after the independence elections, not to contest the election, but essentially to reconcile the warring factions within the BPP. This could be viewed as the first failed attempt to unite the opposition parties. Under the banner of the nationalist politics which were influenced by the cold war ideological rivalry, the opposition perceived the BDP as a conservative neo-colonial party that would not deliver real independence. Having failed to unite the Matante and Motsete factions of the BPP, the BNF registered as a political party and added to the division within the opposition camp. Ironically, many of the opposition parties that exist in Botswana – BCP, United Socialist Party, Botswana Workers Front,

---

34 These were the Moshopha ward in the Central District, Seronga Ward in the North West District, and Mokatako ward in the Southern District.

35 Councillors Tebogo Ikaneng of Mokatako and Keekae Mokgathi have since rejoined the BDP and BNF, respectively.

NDF – are all splinter parties from the BNF. Thus, we observe that contrary to its banner of standing for unity, BNF is prone to fracture.

The predominance of the BDP at the polls, and the tendency of electoral outcomes to be a contest between two political parties suggest that the only hope for the opposition parties to unseat the BDP is to unite and contest the elections under the banner of one political party. This supposition is attested by the fact that in some constituencies, the combined poll of the opposition is greater than that of the BDP vote.

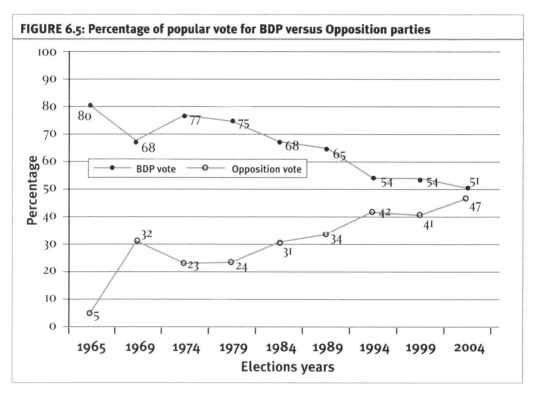

FIGURE 6.5: Percentage of popular vote for BDP versus Opposition parties

Figure 6.5 above shows a narrowing of the gap between the BDP poll and that of the combined opposition. In 1994, 1999, and 2004, the percentage differences were 12 per cent, 13 per cent, and 4 per cent, respectively. However, **Figure 6.6** tells a different story. The overall picture that emerges is that, unlike the percentage of the popular vote that shows a convergence of ruling party and opposition votes, with respect to seats, the BDP maintains a wide margin.

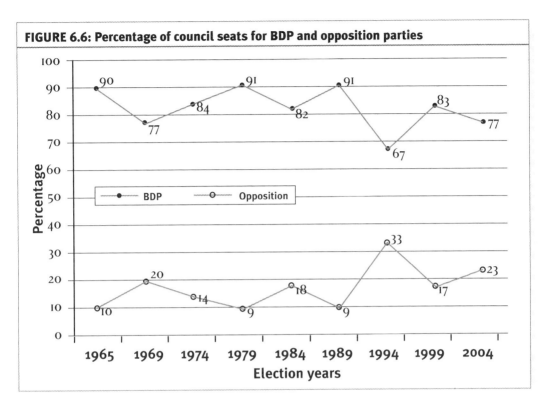

FIGURE 6.6: Percentage of council seats for BDP and opposition parties

It was only in 1994 that the BNF polled a significant share of the seats compared to the BDP. The BDP won 67 per cent of the seats while the BNF got 33 per cent. However, due to a split in the opposition the BDP increased its share of the seats in 1999. During the 2004 election, the proportion of the BDP's seats dropped by eight per cent, and that of the opposition increased by five per cent. **Figure 6.7** below compares the percentage of popular vote and percentage of seats between the BDP and opposition parties, showing an acute discord between popular vote and number of seats. What this trend suggests is that in 2009, assuming everything remains constant, it is highly likely that the combined opposition would poll more that the BDP, while the BDP would maintain a decisive win of the seats. If such a scenario were to emerge it would strengthen opposition allegations that the BDP rigs elections and that could throw the country into a political crisis, similar to what obtained in Lesotho in 1998.

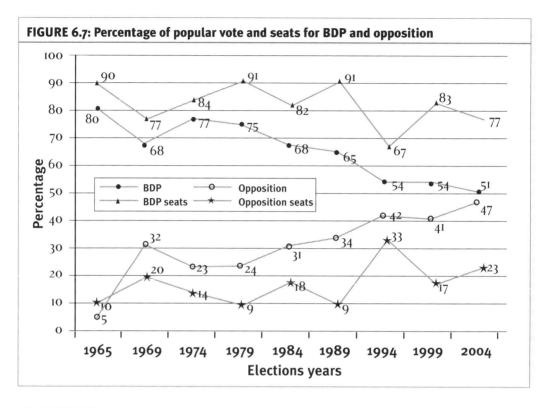

FIGURE 6.7: Percentage of popular vote and seats for BDP and opposition

SPLIT VOTE

Advocates of unity of opposition parties often take a simplistic view that a united opposition would dislodge the ruling BDP from power. Certainly, there are many factors that influence voting behaviour but it stands to reason that where the combined poll of opposition parties is greater than that of the ruling party, the outcome would be different in the wake of a united opposition. While there is no guarantee that when opposition parties are united people would vote them into power, the weight of the opposition vote is overwhelming. Assuming that everything remained constant, if the people who voted for opposition parties had voted for a combined opposition, then the election outcomes would have been different during certain election years.

When the percentages of the opposition vote for the 1989 elections are put together, the analysis shows that they could have won majorities in the constituency of Francistown (55 per cent), Kanye (54 per cent), Mochudi (51 per cent), Selibe Phikwe (51 per cent) and North East (51 per cent). Also for the 1999 parliamentary elections, our analysis shows that opposition parties recorded clear majorities when put together in some other constituencies[36]. In most of these constituencies, the break-up of the BNF in 1997 and the formation of the BCP split the opposition vote, giving the BDP a chance to win the election. In the 2004 election, at least 12 constituencies[37] had the combined poll of the opposition greater than that of the BDP. Of course this observation does not ignore the fact that the split between the BNF and BCP in 1999 and the one between the BNF and NDF in 2002 hardened negative attitudes. Given this state of affairs, negotiating unity would not be an easy project but the underlying fact is that it is a necessity. A lot of groundwork would have to be done, especially among the rank and file of the party, to ensure total understanding and ownership of the project. At least such talks could benefit from past mistakes. In 1998 when 11 BNF Members of Parliament broke away to form the BCP, they did so without full consultation of the party members, and they suffered a severe backlash in the 1999 election.

However, what is problematic is that arguments in favour of opposition unity often present a simplistic scenario, which does not spell out the agenda of a united opposition. It would appear that the agenda is to unseat the BDP without a coherent plan to implement once the BDP is out of power. What is most worrying is that the opposition has shown that it is prone to factional splits and leadership squabbles. Nevertheless, the BDP has its fair share of factionalism and if the opposition were to 'turn up the heat', it would gain measurable results.

CONCLUSION

What we see emerging from Botswana's political landscape is a predominant party system in which the ruling BDP dominates the poll by winning more seats, thereby enabling it to stay in government since independence in 1966. Yet, at the same time, while it maintains a high proportion of the seats in parliament, its share of the popular vote is declining and that of the opposition is rising. However, despite this trend, there is a growing bifurcation of the political system which appears to be creating space for just two political parties. As a result it appears that the only feasible way for the opposition to unseat the BDP from power is to unite and contest the elections as a united opposition.

---

36 Kgatleng West 54 per cent, Kgatleng East 60 per cent, Ngwaketse West 53 per cent, Gaborone Central 52 per cent, Francistown West 52 per cent and Selibe Phikwe 52.

37 Ngami 54 per cent, Okavango 52 per cent, Francistown South 55 per cent, Nkange 52 per cent, Selibe Phikwe East 59 per cent, Selibe Phikwe West 58 per cent, Kgatleng West 62 per cent, Gaborone North 59 per cent, South East south 59 per cent, Mogoditshane 61 per cent, Kweneng South 51 per cent and Ngwaketse South 51 per cent.

Our overall conclusion is that in the 2009 election Botswana will be at crossroads. Given the trends that are prevalent now and which have been building over time, the BDP will lose the election in terms of the popular vote but win it in terms of seats to form government. Amidst long standing allegations that it rigs elections in its favour, such an occurrence could foment a major upheaval. What is clear is that the discord that we are observing is a result of the 'winner takes all' electoral system, which was the cause of the disturbances in Lesotho in 1998. Perhaps reforming the electoral system in Botswana could avert the likelihood of that scenario.

TABLE 6.3: Voting trends of political parties: 1965 - 2004									
	1965	1969	1974	1979	1984	1989	1994	1999	2004
BDP	113 168	52 518	49 047	101 098	154 863	162 277	151 031	192 598	213 308
BNF	-	10 410	7 358	17 480	46 550	67 513	102 862	87 457	107 451
BIP	6 491	4 601	3 086	5 657	7 288	6 209	-	-	-
BPU	-	-	-	-	3 036	2 186	3 016	-	-
BPP Matante	19 964	9 329	4 199	9 983	14 961	10 891	11 586	-	7 886
BPP Motsete	377	-	-	-	-	-	-	-	-
BCP	-	-	-	-	-	-	-	40 096	68 556
BAM	-	-	-	-	-	-	-	15 806	11 716
IFP							7 653		-
UDF							783		-
LLB							235		-
BLP						48	23		-
MELS								22	121
NDF									3237
Indep.	789		321	278	1 058			1 004	104
Rejected								17 483	8 893
TOTAL	140 789 9	76 858 8	64 011 1	134 496 6	227 756 6	249 124 4	277 189 9	354 466 6	42 1272 2

Source: Election Reports

REFERENCES

Almond, G and Powell, B (1966) *Comparative Politics: A Developmental Approach* Boston: Little Brown and Company, 1966.

Almond, G. and Verba, S (1966) *The Civic Culture* Boston: Little Brown and Company

Afrobarometer Website WWW.Afrobarometer.org

Ball, A.R. (1988) *Modern Politics and Government* London: Macmillan,.

Baregu, M. and Landsberg, C. (2003) *From Cape to Congo: Southern Africa's Evolving Security Challenges* London: Lynne Rienner Publishers.

Berlson, B, Lazarsfeld, P. and McPhee, W. (1954) *Voting: a Study of Opnion Formation in a Presidential Campaign* Chicago: Chicago University Press.

Bratton, M. (1999) 'Political Participation in a New Democracy: InstitutionalConsiderations in Zambia', *Comparative Political Studies* 32, 5 pp. 549-588.

Bill, J.A. and Hardgrove, R. L. Jr. (1973) *Comparative Politics: The Quest for Theory* Columbus: Charles E Merrill Publishing Co.

Central Statistics Office, 1991 Population and Housing Census: Population Projections 1991-2021, Gaborone: Government Printer, 1997.

Dahl, R (1961) *Who Governs?* New Haven: Yale University Press.

Dahl, R (1989) *Democracy and its Critics* New Haven: Yale University Press.

Diamond, L. (1999) *Developing Democracy: Toward Consolidation*. Baltimore: JohnHopkins University Press.

Dalton, R. (1996) *Citizen Politics* New Jersey: Chatham House Publishers,

Danevad, A. (1995) 'Responsiveness in Botswana Politics: Do Elections Matter?' *Journal of Modern African Studies* Vol. 33:3.

Democracy Research Project, (2002) *Voter Apathy Report*, Gaborone.

Diamond, L. (1996) 'Is the Third Wave Over' *Journal of Democracy* 7, 3 pp.20-37

_____ *Developing Democracy: Toward Consolidation*. Baltimore: John Hopkins University Press.

_____(1994) 'Rethinking Civil society: Toward Democratic Consolidation', *Journal of Democracy* 5,3 pp. 4-17.

Duncan. G and Lukes, S. (1966) 'The New Democracy,' *Political Studies* vol. Xi: 2.

Duverger, M. (1954) Political Parties: *Their Organisation and Activity in the Modern State*, Cambridge: University Printing House.

Dye, T and Ziegler H (1993) *The Irony of Democracy: An Uncommon Introduction to American Politics,* 9th Edition. Belmont, California: Wadsworth.

Edge, W. and Lekorwe, M.H (1998) *Politics and society in Botswana*, Pretoria, J.L. Van Schaik.

Government of Botswana, (1992) *National Migration Study: Patterns, Causes and Consequences*, Gaborone: Government Printer,.

Gerhart, G. (1979) *Black Power in South Africa: The Evolution of an Ideology*, Berkeley: University of California Press

Good, K. (1993) 'At the End of the Ladder: Radical Inequalities in Botswana', *Journal of Modern African Studies*, 31, 2

_____ (1996) 'Authoritarian Liberalism: Defining Characteristic of Botswana', *Journal of Contemporary African Politics*, Vol. 14:1.

_____ (1999) 'Enduring Elite Democracy in Botswana', *Democratisation* Vol. 6:1

Holm, J. (1987) 'Elections in Botswana: Institutionalization of a New System of Legitimacy', in Hayward, F. (ed.) *Elections in Independent Africa* Boulder, West View Press.

Holm, J. and Molutsi, P. (ed) (1989) *Democracy in Botswana* Gaborone: Macmillan Botswana Publishing Company.

Karan. A. (1998) *Women in Parliament: Beyond Numbers*, Stockholm, International Idea Hand Book Series.

Khama, S. (1970) Botswana: *Developing a Democracy in Southern Africa. An Address at the Dag Hammersjold Centre*, Uppsala, Sweden.

Mattes, R. and M. Bratton. 2003 'Learning about Democracy in Africa: Awareness, Performance and Experience", *Centre for Social Science Research Working Paper No. 48* University of Cape Town pp1-42.

Matsheka, T and Botlhomilwe, Z.(2000) 'Economic Conditions and Election outcomes in Botswana: Is the relationship Spurious', *Pula: Botswana Journal of African Studies* Vol. 14:1

Marcuse, H. (1964) *One dimensional Man: Studies in the Ideology of Advanced Industrial society*, Boston, Beacon Press.

Michels, R. (1959) Political Parties: *A Sociological Study of Oligarchical Tendencies of Modern Democracy* New York: Dover Publication.

Mogae, F. G. (1984) *Report to the Minister of Public Service and Information on the General Election, 1984*, Gaborone: Government Printer.

Mogae, F. (2002) *State of the Nation Address*, Gaborone, November.

Mokopakgosi, B.T and Molomo, M.G. (Ed) (1991) *Multi-Party Democracy in Botswana,* Harare: Sapes Books.

Mokopakgosi, B.T and Molomo, M.G. (2000) 'Democracy in the Face of a Weak Opposition, *Pula: Botswana Journal of African Studies* Vol. 14: 1.

Molomo, M.G. and Somolekae, G. (2000) 'Sustainable Electoral Democracy in Botswana' a paper presented at an International IDEA Conference on *Toward Sustainable Democratic Institutions in Southern Africa*, Gaborone 8-10 May 2000.

Molomo, M.G (1998) 'The political Implications of the 4 October 1997 Referendum for Botswana', *Democratisation* Vol. 5:4 (1998).

Molomo, M. G. (2000) 'Understanding Government and Opposition parties in Botswana', *Commonwealth and Comparative Politics* Vol. 38:1.

Molomo, M.G. (2003) 'Political Parties and democratic Governance in Botswana,' (Ed) Mohamed Salih *African Political Parties: Evolution, Institutionalization and Governance*, London Pluto Press.

Molutsi, P. and J. Holm (1990) 'Developing Democracy When Civil Society is Weak', *African Affairs*, 89 pp323-340.

Mosca, G. (1939)*The Ruling Class* Translated by Hannah D. Kahn New York, McGraw-Hill.

Mpabanga, D.(2000) Declining Voter Participation in Botswana: Trends and Patterns', *Pula: Botswana Journal of African Studies* Vol. 14:1

Mmegi/AI, Election Marred by State Sponsored Violence, *Mmegi* October, 2002.

Mmono, N. *Report to the Minister of Presidential Affairs and Public Administration on the General Election*, 1989 Gaborone: Government Printer (1989) and (1994).

Norris, P. (2002) *Democratic Phoenix: Reinventing Political Activism*. Cambridge University Press.

Otlhogile, B. and Molutsi, P. (Eds.) *Consolidating Democracy: The Electoral Process Under Scrutiny* Report of the Workshop on Electoral Law and Administration of Elections in Botswana held on 19-20th February, Gaborone, 1993.

Osei-Hwedie, B. (1998) 'The Role of ethnicity in Multi-Party Politics in Malawi and Zambia,' *Journal of contemporary African Studies*, Vol. 16:2

Pareto, V. (1935) *The Mind and Society* Translated by Andrew Bongiorus and Arthur Livingston, New York, Hartcourt, Brace and co.

Parson, J. (1976) 'A Note on the 1974 General Election in Botswana,' in (ed) D.L. Cohen and Jack Parson *Politics and Society in Botswana* Gaborone.

Parsons, N., Henderson, W. Tlou, T. (1995) *Seretse Khama* 1921-1980 Braamfontein: Macmillan.

Przeworski, A. (1992) 'Neoliberal Fallacy', *Journal of Democracy* 3,3 pp45-59.

Putnam, R. (1993) *Making Democracy Work: Civic Traditions in Modern Italy* Princeton: Princeton University Press.

------------ (1995) 'Bowling Alone: America's Declining Social Capital', *Journal of Democracy*, 6 pp65-78.

Schumpeter, J. (1950) *Capitalism Socialism and Democracy* 3rd Ed. New York: Harper and Row

Schlemmer, L. et. al (1997) *Present Realities and Strategies for the Future: Training Workshop for the Botswana Democratic Party.*

Stedman, S. (ed.) (1993) *Botswana: Political Economy of Democratic Development* Boulder, Colorado: Lynne Rienner Press.

Seeletso, G. (1999) *Report to the Vice President and Minister of Presidential Affairs and Public Administration on the General Election*, Gaborone: Government Printer 1999, 2004.

Sithole, M .(2000) 'Zimbabwe: The Erosion of Authoritarianism and Prospects for Democracy,' in (ed.) York Bradshaw and Stephen Ndegwa, *The Uncertain Promise of Southern Africa*, Bloomington, Indiana University Press,

Somolekae, G. (1999) *An Evaluation of the Performance of the Independent Electoral Commission (IEC) in Botswana's 1999 Election*, Gaborone, Democracy Research Project.

Steenkamp, P. L. *Report to the Minister of Public Service and Information on the General Election*, (1974) and (1979), Gaborone Government Printer.

Taylor, I (2003) 'As Good as it Gets? Botswana's "Democratic Development"' in ed. Henning Melber *Limits to Liberation in Southern Africa: The unfinished Business of Democratic Consolidation* Cape Town: HSRC Press pp72-92.

Vengroff R. (1976) 'Central Local Linkages: The Party system' in (Ed) D.L. Cohen and Jack Paron *Politics and Society in Botswana*, Gaborone.

Winstanley, G. (1965)*The Bechuanaland General election 1965: Ballot Envelopes and Voting Counters*

Winstanley, G. (1969) *Report to the Minister of Health, Labour and Home Affairs on the General Elections*

Zaffiro, J.(2000) 'Broadcasting Reform and Democratisation in Botswana', *Africa Today* Vol. (2000).

Newspapers

The Botswana Gazette

The Botswana Guardian

The Midweek Sun

Mmegi wa Dikgang

Daily News

CHAPTER 7

ORGANISATION OF POLITICAL PARTIES

Mogopodi Lekorwe

INTRODUCTION

Botswana is one of the few African countries which has been able to sustain multi-party democracy through its political parties. This chapter analyses how the parties are organised. First, it looks at the functions of political parties in a democratic polity and at the reasons for the delay in the formation of political parties in Botswana. Secondly, it discusses the structure of political parties, briefly covering the election of party presidents, and focusing on their powers and how the parties conduct their congresses. It concentrates on two political parties, namely, the BDP and the BN. This selection is based on the share of the national vote in the general election of 1999. Thirdly, it discusses internal democracy within the two parties, relying on the study carried out by the Democracy Research Project (DRP) in 1989.

THE ROLE OF POLITICAL PARTIES

In a liberal democracy such as Botswana, political parties perform a variety of important functions which keep the political system together and working. First, they perform an 'inputting' function where citizens get their needs and wishes known by the government. Without political parties, individuals would stand alone and there would be a strong chance of being ignored by government. By working through political parties they can make an impact on some political decisions. Secondly, political parties aggregate interests of different groups. They help tame and calm interest group conflicts by aggregating their separate interests into a large organisation. Through political parties, interest groups moderate their demands, cooperate and work for the good of the party. Thirdly, political parties help to integrate different groups into the political system. As they welcome new groups into their ranks and give them a say in politics, groups are given both a pragmatic and a psychological stake in supporting the overall political system.

Fourthly, political parties perform the function of political socialisation in society. As they integrate groups into the society, they also teach their members how to play the political game. They are expected to provide political education to their supporters to sharpen their understanding and appreciation of democratic ideals. They also do this through introducing citizens to candidates, teaching them to speak in public, to conduct meetings and to reach compromises. Thus, they build among them a deep sense of legitimacy for the system as a whole. Fifthly, political parties enhance democracy by mobilising citizens to vote. Parties whip up voter interest through their campaigns. Political parties exist mainly to take control of state apparatus. Thus the party which wins gets government jobs and assumes state power in order to shift policy to its way of thinking. The factors determining whether a party wins the election depend, among other things, on resources, such as financial and human, and an effective party structure. The nature and character of the party structure is usually defined by the party constitution.

Compared to other African countries, political parties in Botswana emerged quite late. Their history begins in the late 1950s and early 1960s. Several reasons account for this late development. In many countries the cause of the liberation struggle developed as a response to colonisation. To a large extent, the intensity of exploitation determined the complexion and the rate of national formation and maturation of political parties. The nature and character of colonisation in Botswana was milder compared to other countries. In part this was due to the absence of large scale alienation policies that were present in countries such as Kenya, Zimbabwe and South Africa. Consequently, this caused the delay in the birth of the middle class which was the catalyst for the formation of nationalist movements (NengweKhulu, 1979). The 1960s witnessed the emergence of national consciousness as this coincided with the wave of decolonisation and the granting of independence to colonies in Africa. Indeed some scholars have argued that the colonial government provided the impetus for political mobilisation in some countries such as Botswana (Weinstein & Grootpeter, 1979). In the southern African region, the 1960s was a crucial period for the formation of nationalist movements to fight against the forces of oppression and exploitation, particularly in South Africa. The two main nationalist movements, the African National Congress (ANC) and the Pan African Congress (PAC), were outlawed, forcing their leaders to flee to neighbouring countries, particularly Botswana, Lesotho and Swaziland.

In Botswana the outcome of the influx of the exiles from South Africa, particularly in the aftermath of Sharpeville, formed the basis for the formation of the earliest nationalist movements. This contention is supported by the fact that two of the founding members of the first serious political parties in Botswana, P.G. Matante and Motsamai Mpho had been political activists in South Africa. They were active members of the PAC and ANC respectively. Migrant workers also played an important role as they were active in black-nationalist politics in South Africa. When these people returned to their home countries they continued with this role, hence they formed the nuclear of the working class and were the major driving force behind the formation of political parties. This view is however, rejected by Jack Parson (1984) who argued that hostel conditions in South Africa, and the fact that whilst back in Botswana these people retreated to their customary rural existence, could not have given rise to any form of political consciousness among the migrant workers. Moreover, the policies adopted by the colonial administration of granting independence to the colonies contributed to the formation of political parties. In addition to these factors, Batswana saw their independence as inevitable as many of the countries in west and east Africa became independent and this led to the formation of political parties in the country.

THE BOTSWANA DEMOCRATIC PARTY (BDP)

The BDP was formed in 1962 by Seretse Khama with some other Legislative Council Members. These were mainly men of professional or traditional status in their ethnic groups. The three top most positions went to Seretse Khama – President, Tsoebebe – Vice President and Ketumile Masire – Treasurer. The formation of the BDP was encouraged by the colonial administration which was anxious that a suitable national leader be identified to whom the mantle of power could be handed over. Seretse Khama who personified the party's emerging position of combining traditional legitimacy and peasant support with modern education was the obvious choice (Parson, 1984).

The constitution of the BDP provides for a mass-based structure. It has an elaborate structure working upwards from the party cell, sub-wards, wards, sub-branches, constituency branches, a regional organisation, the National Congress, up to a National Council and a Central Committee. The discussion now focuses on the election of the Central Committee and the party president. Article 28 of the BDP constitution stipulates composition of the Central Committee. It consists of eighteen members as follows: the President; the Chairperson; the Secretary General; the Deputy Secretary General; the Treasurer; the Deputy Treasurer; ten ordinary members of the party; Chairpersons of the Women's and Youth Wings. The Central Committee meets when convened by the President of the Party, or at the requisition of at least one third of its members. It controls the day to day affairs of the party with power to determine the policy within the framework of decisions taken by the National Council and / or National Congress. It is also responsible for and has the power to make regulations for the effective running and administration of the party.

Members of the Central Committee are elected at the 'party national congress', every two years with the exception of the party president. The congress elects position holders in the Central Committee and five additional members. The party president has the prerogative of appointing five other additional members to the Central Committee. Apart from the clauses prescribing who is eligible for election as a member of the Central Committee, there are no other guidelines with regard to the five members to be appointed by the party president. In practice, however, the president can use this clause to do the balancing act. The then President Masire used the clause in 1993 to bring Merafhe and others into the Central Committee after they had lost elections.

The BDP constitution provides the manner in which the party president is elected. Article 29 of the BDP constitution gives two options, election of the president when the party is in power and when it is not in power. In the first option, the party president is elected by a secret ballot at a national congress of the party called by the Central Committee during every general election year (this has never happened). In the second option, that is, when the party is not in power, the party president shall be elected at every congress of the party (BDP constitution, Article 29(e). This has also never happened as the party has been in power since independence). But in principle the criteria determining who could be elected into the position of party president is based on the constitution of the country. Under the Botswana constitution, to be eligible for election as president, one has to satisfy three main conditions: be a citizen of Botswana by birth or descent, have attained the age of 30 and be eligible to be elected as a member of the National Assembly (Constitution of Botswana, Section 33). These conditions mean that those who acquired their citizenship by naturalisation do not qualify to contest for the presidency of the country. By implication the BDP constitution embraces these sentiments. The BDP constitution goes further to state that any person aspiring to be a presidential candidate should be of 'good standing in the party' (Article 29(i), (ii)).

The BDP constitution departs from the Botswana constitution with respect to succession in a situation where a vacancy arises in the presidency. In the case of the BDP when the party is in power the vice president automatically becomes the state and party president. This clause was used when Masire stepped down and Mogae became the president. But if a vacancy occurs when the party is not in power, the party chairperson acts as the president until the next congress (Article 29(c),(d). This is because the BDP party constitution has no position of vice president.

POWERS AND FUNCTIONS OF THE BDP PRESIDENT

The president of the BDP, who also becomes the State President when the party is in power, has powers and functions defined by the party constitution under Article 34. He/she is the principal spokesperson of the party on national and international affairs; convenes and presides over Central Committee meetings; gives instruction on any matter to any official of the party and empowers any member of the party to exercise any powers or specific function for and on behalf of the party or Central Committee as may be valid and lawful. He or she has the power in exceptional circumstances, as specified in the disciplinary rules of the party, to suspend any member of the party for a stipulated number of days for unacceptable behaviour pending action by the Disciplinary Committee.

From the foregoing, it can be argued that the extent to which the party president wields power is derived from the constitution and also depends on the character of the individual. The test case was the release of the Kgabo report which implicated two government ministers - the late Peter Mmusi and Daniel Kwelagobe in illegal land dealings. The Kgabo report marked the beginning of open clashes between Mmusi and Kwelagobe and their supporters on the one hand and those who supported the report's findings on the other. The two government ministers resigned their positions in cabinet and took the matter to court to clear their names. The then President Masire pleaded with them to withdraw the case from the courts but all his efforts were in vain. The two ministers made some demands to Masire in order for them to withdraw their case from the courts. They said they could only withdraw the case if Masire denounced parliament, the cabinet, the Kgabo report and the White paper on it. Masire however, stood his ground and said he would rather resign his position as president than concede to the demands of the two men. The Central Committee then had no choice but to suspend them from their party positions in mid 1992.

Although the president presides over the Central Committee, the constitution does not give him/her powers of finality on any issues that may be discussed. This means the Central Committee may hold different views and may even vote against his/her wishes. However, the president can use his/her position to get certain things to his/her favour. Three cases are used to demonstrate how Mogae exercised his powers. First, is the Kabo Morwaeng case where there were serious differences between those within the party who sought to prevent him from standing in the primary elections citing the reason that he was a new member, and those who wanted him to. It was apparent that the party was factionalised over the issue. The secretary–general led a faction against what came to be known as the Ian Khama-Mogae faction. The central issue was the manner in which Morwaeng was admitted into the party. Kwelagobe used the party constitution, Article 8(e) to argue that Morwaeng had to wait for a period of twelve months before he could be allowed to contest the elections in the party. It is alleged that Kwelagobe told Mogae that he did not have supreme powers over the party. But Mogae insisted that this issue be referred to the BDP legal advisers who in the end ruled in Morwaeng's favour which confirmed the Khama-Mogae faction's position. Mogae and Khama also went further to appoint a Commission of Inquiry to probe Kwelagobe's alleged abuse of power in Molepolole. This was done without the secretary-general's knowledge or that of the party chairman – Kedikilwe (*Gazette*, 18 June, 2003).

Secondly, Mogae also broke tradition by publicly declaring his support for Khama against Kedikilwe for party chairmanship. A number of people in the party, including some analysts, felt that Mogae was, in a way, declaring his factionalism. But he rebuffed that by saying institutional positions should not be personalised. It is clear that Mogae believed that Khama's move was a positive one to improve internal democracy in the party. At the BDP women's congress Mogae said 'to contest for a party position entails no enmity towards the incumbent' (*Monitor*, 3-9 June, 2003). When the then deputy secretary–general of the BDP, Ms Pelonomi Venson, wrote to the party structures requesting them to start discussing the issue of setting up a vice presidency in order to prevent Khama from contesting the chairmanship of the party, Mogae again showed his resolve and distaste for this issue by writing a letter to reprimand Venson for bringing back this issue with the party structures without his knowledge. These three cases demonstrate that the party president can indeed flex his muscles if the need arises.

ORGANISATION OF BDP CONGRESSES

The BDP National Congress is the supreme national policy-making body of the party. It meets ordinarily every two years, otherwise an extraordinary congress can be convened by the party president or upon requisition by the majority of the members of the National Council (NC). The NC is the body entrusted with reviewing the implementation of party policies as they are determined by the BDP National Congress

(Article 27, BDP constitution). The BDP National Congress performs very important functions for the party. It elects the party president as well as members of the Central Committee by secret ballot. It formulates and reviews party policies and programmes, amends, approves and adopts the party constitution and also defines, orientates and approves general policies and plans for national development. Once the national congress has adopted policies and programmes, these are binding upon all members, and are obligatory for all members to implement. Any change can only be effected by the national congress. The programme agreed upon at these congresses, forms the basis of the national development plan as the BDP has been the party in government since independence. The success and failure of government policies can easily be claimed or denied by the ruling party, in this case the BDP. A clear demonstration of the difficulty of drawing the dividing line between government and the party has been shown by the president. At the special congress of the party, April 2004, during the launch of the BDP manifesto, President Mogae stated that the BDP government continues to make strides in its declared war against HIV/AIDS (*Mmegi*, 27 April 2004). He recounted BDP's successes in terms of health services, that is, the number of clinics and health posts constructed in different parts of the country, the number of villages electrified as well as roads constructed.

It is at such national congresses that resolutions are adopted which influence the functioning of government. For example at the 28th Congress of the BDP, it was resolved that government should set up a commission to review the activities of local government. Following this resolution, the president set up a local government commission in 2001. As part of the congress agenda, the BDP usually invites other political parties from neighbouring countries such as the African National Congress, Chamachamapinduzi, Frelimo, Lesotho Congress Party, MPLA, SWAPO, UDF – Malawi and ZANU PF. An interesting phenomenon is that it seems the invitation is extended to those in power irrespective of political ideology. Thus it appears the key is to support each other to retain power.

THE BOTSWANA NATIONAL FRONT (BNF)

The BNF was founded shortly after the 1965 elections. Following these elections, there were some people who were unhappy about BDP policies. A meeting was called in Mochudi by Kenneth Koma who had just returned from the University of Moscow with a doctoral degree. Koma had a socialist view of the problems in the then Bechuanaland. The first interim president of the party was Ridwell Molomo, who was shortly replaced by Daniel Kwele. Koma preferred to be the secretary for external affairs. Although Koma did not become the party president until later, he personified the party and was the author of most of its literature, which was complicated and contained Marxist terminology. The language used was often above the heads of most of the people in a country where the majority of the people were illiterate (Gossett, 1986). As Makgala put it, Koma built himself a formidable personality cult marked by personal rule and its attendant sycophancy in the BNF (Makgala, 2003).

From its establishment the party represented a combination of traditionalism and a type of socialist rhetoric. Its main task was to organise a national democratic struggle led by the radical section of the middle class in the long term interest of the peasants (Parson, 1984). The tactics the party employed were to align temporarily with the corrupt feudal elements, which were the chiefs. This strategy in some way paid dividends because Bathoen Gaseitsiwe, unhappy with the way the BDP government treated the chiefs, resigned his chieftainship and went into politics. He became the party president in 1970 until 1977 when Koma took over. He brought with him an electoral base which was largely ethnic. Through him the BNF did well in the South region of the country. On two occasions the vice president of Botswana lost the elections to Gaseitsiwe.

The BNF constitution has not undergone drastic changes since the formation of the party. The operating constitution was adopted in 2002 at the Francistown Special Congress. It stipulates that the basic aim of the organisation is 'establishing a democratic state guided by the principles of a social democratic programme' (BNF Constitution: preamble). The specific objects of the Front are: a) To mobilise all patriotic and democratic forces into a dynamic political force; b) To struggle against international capital and to eliminate all forms of neo-colonialism in Botswana and to align with all progressive and democratic forces the world over; c) To contribute by word and deed to the consolidation of the national unity of different communities in Botswana and to struggle for genuine equality of all ethnic communities in Botswana; d) To struggle against all forms of discrimination, exploitation and oppression; e) To conscientise Batswana about the socio-economic and political problems confronting the country; f) To promote and strengthen more democratic organisations such as trade unions, women's and student organisations and; g) To struggle for genuine democratic, economic independence and social justice, human rights and peace.

Thus, the party constitution describes the BNF as a progressive, popular democratic movement which embraces diverse political and ideological tendencies unified by its social democratic programme. To achieve its mass democratic character, mass organisations are encouraged and allowed to affiliate to the party as group members. The BNF, unlike the other political parties, has two types of membership. It has individual membership and group membership. To qualify for individual membership, individuals must apply orally or in writing to the secretary of the appropriate or nearest ward, or to any member of the party authorised to receive such applications. Group membership is open to any organisation or programme which has not less than 50 and 100 members respectively. Such an organisation has to accept in writing the principles, policy constitution, programme, rules and regulations of the BNF and to abide by its decisions.

The BNF Constitution details out the organisational structure from the lowest levels which are the cell and ward, to the highest levels which are the constituency structure, regional structure, national conference and the Central Committee. Article 12.1 provides a detailed composition of the Central Committee of the party as follows: President; Vice-President; Secretary General; Deputy Secretary General; Treasurer; National Chairperson; National Organising Secretary; Political Education Secretary; Publicity and Information Secretary; International Affairs Secretary; Electoral Affairs Secretary; Public Education Secretary; Labour Affairs Secretary; Economic Affairs Secretary; Local Government Secretary; Land, Housing and Environmental Secretary; Health and Welfare Secretary; Affirmative Action Secretary; Sports and Culture Secretary; Religious and Interdenominational Secretary; National Affairs Secretary; BNF Youth League President; BNF Women's League President; a representative of the Parliamentary caucus; a representative of the Regional Chairperson.

Apart from this long listing, which in many respects resembles names of different ministries should the party come into power, the BNF Constitution specifically states that 30 per cent shall be women. In practice however, it has not been easy to meet this criteria. The Central Committee has powers among which is included, the power to expel any member of the party on the recommendations from his/her respective ward or constituency or on its own initiative, the powers to suspend any member for misconduct or violation of the policy of the party. These powers were used by the BNF Central Committee when they expelled Peter Woto and suspended Koma from the party. The BNF executive is composed of the President, Vice-President, Secretary General, Deputy Secretary General, Treasurer and the National Chairperson.

The BNF constitution does not go into details to describe who qualifies to be the president of the party. It only states that any member qualifies to be a candidate for party presidency provided that one is a citizen of Botswana and has been a member of the party for at least five years. Presumably within those five years, one would have been active enough to know the policies and the structures of the party. The president of the BNF is expected to be the principal spokesperson on national and international affairs and is expected to preside over Central Committee meetings and convene meetings of the Central Committee and the executive committee.

The constitution stipulates the power bestowed upon the president of the party. Article 19.3.1 of the BNF Constitution gives the president the power to take any action in the interest of the party pending convocation to any relevant body or organ of the party in cases of emergency. He or she also has the power to appoint an ad-hoc committee to advise the BNF on any matter whatsoever. In addition he or she can give instructions on any matter to any official of the BNF, or empower any member of the BNF to exercise any powers or specific functions for and on behalf of the BNF in the Central Committee. Among other things, group members have the right to participate in all the activities of the party including congresses, conferences, workshops, study groups, public rallies and public demonstrations.

Factional fighting in the BNF often provokes fierce debates in the party's congresses. Its factional fighting came to the fore after the party won only three parliamentary seats rather than the fourteen that it had predicted (Maundeni, 1998). Every BNF congress has been preceded by serious problems where there are either resignations or expulsions before or after such meetings. In 1970 following the Kanye Congress, the party suffered a number of resignations due to the sudden change of venue without properly informing party functionaries. In 1988, one of the Central Committee members, Lenyeletse Koma was expelled because, among other things he had alleged that he wrote speeches for the party leader and president, Dr Koma (*Guardian*, 9 Sept 1988).

The 1993 Mahalapye Congress also followed the same trend. It was held to elect a new Central Committee and after the meeting a number of people resigned from the party citing unhappiness with the way the congress was conducted. The BNF entered the 1997 Ledumang Congress amid serious polarisation in the party. There were two factions, one which perceived itself as progressive and was led by Michael Dingake and the other faction which perceived itself as conservative and was led by Klaas Motshidisi. The two factions traded accusations and counter accusations of opportunism.

The Ledumang Congress was to be a major event as it was convened to elect the leadership to take the party into the 1999 elections. The group led by Dingake won the Central Committee elections. The old guard within the party protested claiming that Central Committee elections had been rigged as an attempt to do away with left wing elements in the party. This group named itself the 'Concerned Group' (CG). Many members of the party saw this as extreme because there were no complaints filed during the congress (*Mmegi,* 22-28 May 1998). Following the Ledumang Congress, the CG served the BNF president with a petition threatening to take the party to court over the results of the elections. The president and the vice-president held different views regarding the way forward in this matter. It was clear that Koma was sympathetic to the CG and sought to prevent a court case, while the vice-president, Dingake was willing to go to court. The latter was also willing to allow the CG to exercise its democratic right under the constitution to convene an extra-ordinary congress for purposes of a re-run of the elections. But the BNF president pretended to be neutral while there was an acrimonious tussle between the vice-president and the Central Committee on the one hand, and the CG on the other hand. In the process Koma, whose pretended neutrality waned, toured the country with some members of the CG where he denounced the party Central Committee. Obviously the CG used rough tactics to win Koma's support including the allegation that Dingake wanted to take the party from him.

The BNF held a Special Congress in Palapye in 1998. This later came to be known as the 'Battle of Palapye' in the local media, but was convened among other things to amend certain sections of the party constitution. The attempt to do this had failed several times. Two provisions in the constitution were particularly controversial. The first was the minimum probation period of three years that a new member had to wait before they could stand for any party position and the second was the multi-organisational character of the BNF. It was important that these issues were addressed in order for it to be seen that the party constitution was progressive. However, rivalry intensified as the date for the congress drew nearer. The differences between the factions were never resolved and reached a climax during the congress. Accusations and counter accusations continued with factions fighting to win Koma's sympathy. At this point, Koma's behaviour clearly indicated that he was leaning more towards the CG than to the Central Committee. Following mayhem and a fracas at the congress, the Central Committee suspended Koma from the party presidency through a motion tabled by the Mahalapye constituency and seconded by Gaborone West constituency. However, constitutionally the congress had no powers to suspend the president. Dr Koma in turn invoked Article 12.1.6 of the constitution to dissolve the Central Committee. This position was later upheld by the High Court which ruled that Koma was within his rights to dissolve the Central Committee, though technically the issues had not been sufficiently argued before the judge to enable him to give his final determination on the actual powers of the president.

The 2001 Kanye Congress was held to elect a new Central Committee and, more importantly, to replace Dr Koma as he had finally agreed to retire. The BNF entered this congress with two factions, the one faction which was reformist consisting mainly of CG members and the other one favoured by Koma, which came to be known as the 'Party Line' (PL). This time Moupo of the CG faction was one presidential candidate and Peter Woto of the PL was the other. Moupo's CG campaigned vigorously whilst the PL faction basked in the name of Koma. Moupo's CG swept the board and, as with other BNF elections, the PL faction protested the results with Koma's backing. Members of the PL continued to refer to Koma as the president of the party despite the fact that Moupo had been elected to replace him. However, the newly elected Central Committee was committed to instilling discipline in the party and the secretary general, Akanyang Magama threatened action against those who disobeyed observance of party constitution. Finally the Central Committee expelled Peter Woto and a few others from the party. Later, Koma was also suspended from the party for six months. The rivalry between the CG and the PL never abated until the latter eventually decided to register a new political party in the name of the New Democratic Front (NDF) under the leadership of Dick Bayford.

PRIMARY ELECTIONS

Primary elections originated and evolved in the United States of America at the turn of the century – between 1903 and 1920 (Ginsberg, B and Stone, A 1986:120). They came into being as a result of intra-party rivalries and party factions perceiving themselves more appealing to the voters than others. In addition, primary elections were seen as a way of curbing corruption, reducing control of the party by the top leadership and satisfying dissenting voices within the party. Gradually, it became evident that parties with primaries were more stable and popular compared to those without them (ibid p.120). The idea of primary elections has since found meaning in some of those countries that propagate and emulate western systems of liberal democratic government. Generally, primary elections are meant, inter-alia, to relieve party leadership of the process of nominating candidates for office within the party. In this way the people exercise the right to nominate candidates for office in the constituency, wards or councils and this strengthens the liberal democratic system. Another significant feature of the primaries is that they give dissenting candidates a chance to officially fight for positions within the party. In this way the party membership has a chance to choose the most preferred candidate themselves.

Since their introduction into the political parties in Botswana, primary elections have attracted a lot of controversy to the extent that some of the splits within the BDP and BNF have been attributed to them (Molomo, 2000). This section focuses on the conduct of the primaries within the BDP and BNF. To understand the current system, this is done from a historical perspective using the research findings of the Democracy Research Project (DRP) on the 1989 primaries of the two parties. The purpose is to attempt to analyse and narrate as accurately as possible what took place in those primary elections. The section considers the origins and significance of primary elections and their introduction into the Botswana electoral politics by the two parties and then examines the changes introduced by these parties in the conduct of these elections, particularly the new BDP system known as 'Bulela Ditswe'.

Primary elections are just two decades old in Botswana. Introduced by the Botswana Democratic Party (BDP) in 1984, they are an important mechanism for political parties to select candidates for general elections. However, the holding of primaries by individual parties is not required by the constitution of the country. This means that candidates whose parties do not hold primary elections have equal standing in terms of the general elections. Some parties, such as the Botswana People's Party (BPP), Botswana Unity Movement (BUM), New Democratic Front (NDF) and MELS, do not hold primary elections, but the BDP, BNF and BCP do. Primary elections seem to be a feature of large parties. The BDP started holding primaries because of the increase in the number of party candidates aspiring for office within the party. Also, there had been an increase in the number of educated people, some of whom had been in the civil service, showing interest in standing for political office. In the run up to the 2004 elections, the BDP had a number of highly educated people amongst their candidates who had been approved to contest for the primaries.

Prior to 1984, due to perceived shortages of educated and trained professionals in the ruling BDP, there was no fierce competition for positions and no need for primaries. The president of the BDP was therefore at liberty to pick someone to represent a particular constituency (Gazette, December 2003). With an increase in the number of candidates in the 1980's, however, the BDP decided to institute primary elections so that the people could nominate candidates of their choice[38]. Primaries thus were seen as the most democratic way of selecting candidates and also prevented the party leadership from imposing candidates of their choice. However, it should be noted that the Central Committee of the BDP had the ultimate power to endorse or reject a candidate taking into account the calibre and ability of the candidate to serve the party and the nation.

---

38 Interview with BDP political officer at Tsholetsa House, 24 July 1980

The experience of the 1989 primaries in Botswana is interesting particularly as exemplified by the two parties, the BDP and the BNF. The parties' access to resources tends to be central to the success or failure of their primaries. This is particularly so in the case of opposition parties which lack the resources available to the ruling BDP. What follows is a historical account of the experience of the 1989 primaries held by the BDP and the BNF.

The BDP like other registered societies in the country is guided by a constitution which is approved by its general membership. Article 37 of the BDP's Constitution empowered the Central Committee of the party to put in place rules and regulations governing party primaries.

> 'Whenever a general election for Parliament and local government or by-election is about to take place, the Central Committee is charged with the responsibility of arranging for such elections. This responsibility includes fixing the period during which constituency as well as ward meetings would be held for purposes of selecting aspirant candidates, fixing the date by which names of nominees should be sent to the Central Committee, and for communicating such information to the Chairman and Secretary of the concerned Branch Executive Committee'.

The BDP constitution also prescribed the method of selection.

> 'The branch executive in consultation with the Central Committee is responsible for convening the branch congress for the conduct of parliamentary nomination and the ward congress for council elections. The ward congress is attended by the ward committee, the Member of Parliament for the area and six delegates from each cell, Kgotla or village, depending on the circumstances of a particular area'.

The BDP Central Committee commissioned two of its members to be present at the branch and ward congress as returning officers who were not entitled to vote. If a returning officer wanted to stand for elections in that branch or ward, he/she had to inform the Central Committee and would then be excused from conducting elections in that branch or ward. Voting proceedings were read out by returning officers who called for nominations from the floor. Each nominee had to be supported by at least one member present in the congress. The rules also required that nominations must be more than one but certainly not more than six. It was also possible for candidates to be nominated in absentia provided the returning officers had obtained their consent in writing. To ensure that all members exercised their democratic right without fear, all voting was by secret ballot. At the close of nominations, returning officers collected ballot papers and placed them in a container which was sealed in the presence of the voters, and sent to the Central Committee.

In accordance with the BDP constitution, an aspiring candidate wishing to stand for BDP primaries had to meet certain requirements. At the date of holding primary elections an aspirant candidate should have been a member of the BDP for a period of not less than twelve months. However, the Central Committee has the power to waive this clause if it deems it necessary. The regulations contain a provision that the Central Committee can nominate a candidate if the rules and regulations are unworkable due to some reasons, which however are not specified. To date the BDP has not invoked this clause.

Although members of the BDP chose, by way of primary elections, who their party candidates were to be in the general elections, the Central Committee, in accordance with Article (41) of the constitution, had the final say in the selection of all candidates wishing to stand for elections. However, candidates could appeal to the Central Committee within fourteen days if they were not satisfied about the conduct of the election. In such cases, the decision of the Central Committee is binding and the candidate cannot appeal to any superior organ within the party. The organisation and conduct of the primary elections were largely dependent on the above rules and regulations.

The 1989 primary elections were the second to be held by the BDP since 1984. Comparatively the BDP's primaries, due to its previous experience, were somewhat better organised than those of the BNF which was holding primaries for the first time. In accordance with Article 37 of the BDP constitution, the Central Committee issued rules and regulations governing primaries which, among other things, state that: 'Whenever a general election for Parliament and local government or by-election as the case may be is imminent the Central Committee shall fix the period for the primary elections'.[39] In pursuance of the above, the BDP conducted primary elections in 1989 in all 34 constituencies. For the purpose of these primaries, constituencies were divided into two groups – the southern and the northern parts. The primaries were held over two weekends in March, starting with the southern part and followed by the northern part. Also in keeping with the rules each constituency was assigned a team of returning

39 Clause 2 of the old Rules and Regulations of BDP governing primary elections

officers by the Central Committee. Depending on the size of the constituency, as many as three teams were assigned to a constituency. For example, large constituencies such as Maun/Chobe, Kgalagadi, Ghanzi were each assigned three teams. On arrival in the constituency where elections were being conducted, constituency chairman or regional organiser welcomed the returning officers and explained their purpose before handing over the exercise to them.

Once the proceedings were handed over to them, returning officers were responsible for the proper conduct of primary elections. To ensure that things went smoothly, they often took time explaining to the delegates the constitutional provisions pertaining to the primaries. Returning officers invariably went into the details of who was eligible to vote as well as the qualifications of candidates. Although this appeared tedious, it did not seemingly bore delegates as most of them appeared not to know the rules and what was expected of them. The primaries started with parliamentary nominations and were then followed by local government elections for different wards.

There was close adherence to religion in almost all the primaries. All proceedings started with a prayer and were then followed by party songs. Although primaries are a party affair, not all members are eligible to vote. It was only the delegates and those who held certain positions within the party who voted. To this end, efforts were made to ensure that proper delegates voted. The result of this was that voting often started later than scheduled. Those who were eligible to vote in parliamentary elections were: the Committee of Eighteen; Councillors; Members of Parliament; two Youth Wing representatives; two Women's Wing representatives; Ward delegates

For local government elections, the following were eligible to vote in BDP primary elections: Ward Committee members; Member of Parliament (where there was one); Councillor(s) for the ward and delegates from each cell. These formed the basis of the electoral-college which was set up by the Central Committee which had powers to endorse or reject the winning candidate. The elections were characterised by the absence of formal campaigning and speech-making. The candidates neither published any manifestoes nor raised any issues at this stage. Probably the assumption was that the issues they had to address coincided with the party programme. The consequences of not allowing candidates to express themselves by way of campaigning robbed delegates of an element that should be considered important for public speakers such as politicians. It appears that, at this stage, the character of the individual was considered more important than the issues. Party primaries were therefore more personality oriented than issue oriented.

BEHIND THE SCENE CAMPAIGNS DURING BDP PRIMARIES

The fact that there was no formal campaign does not exclude the possibility of some candidates engaging in behind-the-scenes campaigns. At times there were indications of some form of private campaigning and lobbying having taken place.[40] Some candidates felt that the absence of formal campaigning in the primaries was a constraint particularly for specially nominated councillors who wanted to stand for elections. Those who shared wards with incumbents were disadvantaged because they had very little interaction with the people in the ward. Their residence in the ward did not improve their chances because they had not been elected by the people. This was not an issue where the specially nominated councillor had good relations with the incumbent and he/she would have had a chance to interact with the electorate. But in wards where there was no good relationship, as was the case in some wards, voters were not afforded an opportunity to make a proper judgment on the abilities of such an individual.

The question of who voted is important because it addressed a host of issues pertaining to participation in the primaries. Such issues include educational background, gender and social status as well as political consciousness. The implications of some of these issues are important because they reflect the level at which delegates understood the purpose of participating in the primaries. Quite clearly the assumption was that all party members should have the right to determine who the party candidate would be. However, to the contrary, as Holm points out: 'The rules governing the primaries can enhance or reduce equality of the votes by including or excluding them from participating in selecting their party's candidate' (Holm, J 1989:193). Since only a certain section of party membership voted, these voters could systematically misrepresent the wishes of total party membership. Only registered members of the party were expected to take part in the primaries, but proof of party membership was not always successful. Party rules were silent on the age of those who could participate in the primaries. Hence even those who were seemingly under 21 voted even though they did not qualify to vote in the general elections. Statistics show that the majority of those who voted were women, a picture which is also reflected in the general elections. This gender aspect is interesting because the lower one went into the party hierarchy, the more women prevailed, but very few of them were offering themselves as candidates. Women dominated the fund raising activities of the party as well as the choirs. It appears that although the women are more active in the party, men monopolise the leadership positions. Perhaps this has a lot to say about the culture of

40 Some candidates admitted having done house-to-house campaigns

Batswana where women are not expected to lead but are relegated to the background.

The results of the ballots were not announced immediately because counting of the ballot papers was carried out by the Central Committee at the party's headquarters. This was in accordance with party rules and this also gave the Central Committee the opportunity to exercise its prerogative of determining who the party candidate would be, even if such a candidate did not get the majority of the votes. This practice was viewed unfavourably by some party members who felt that it reduced the value of their vote. The prevalence of the Central Committee's decision created some problems in Kanye where Mr Mogwe, the then Minister of Mineral Resources and Water Affairs, was alleged to have lost to Mr Mothusi Batsile in the primaries and the committee seemed to prefer the former. Some members showed such concern about this matter that the party leader, Dr Quett Masire and Minister of Works, Transport and Communication, Mr Butale, had to attend a meeting in Kanye to explain this decision of the Central Committee to the people. In the end the issue was resolved by Dr Masire who emphasised that the decision of the Central Committee was in line with the party constitution which had been approved through the democratic process. It is however important to note that this dissatisfaction did not lead to such serious factionalism within the party as to induce members to resign and join other parties or to contest elections as independent candidates.

BNF PRIMARIES

The BNF has rules and regulations governing the conduct of primary elections. For council and parliamentary candidates primary elections were to be held at ward level by the general membership of the party. Anyone wishing to stand for council elections indicated this in writing to the ward committee, the name of whose membership should be made known to the general membership of the party. So the BNF primaries were more participatory than those of the BDP. The BNF ward committee is entrusted with the responsibility of calling a meeting to announce the names of the candidates to the general membership. Anyone wishing to stand for parliamentary elections had to indicate that intention by writing to the constituency committee which is entrusted with the task of making the names known in the constituency through various ward committees.

The supervision of council candidates was conducted by the constituency committee or the executive committee of the constituency. Members participating in primary elections were registered in the same wards in which they voted during the general elections. Parliamentary candidates were supervised by members of the National Committee or the Central Committee. Voting was by secret ballot or any other fair way preferred by the general membership. Proceedings of the primaries were recorded. The results of primary elections which were announced within the constituency were forwarded to the Secretariat through the secretary general, along with the names of contestants, numbers of those present, and the number of votes cast for each candidate. Finally, the Central Committee satisfied itself of the manner in which elections were conducted and had the final powers to approve or reject the outcome (BNF primary rules and regulations).

The BNF electoral officers explained the rules and regulations of the primary elections to the general membership. Among the electoral officers was the supervisor of the elections who saw to it that the election process was properly organised. After the rules had been clearly read out to the party membership, the audience was given the chance to choose between open and secret ballot system of voting. In the majority of cases observed, the BNF voters chose the open system and the results of the election were made known to the general party members immediately. There appeared to have been no imposition of candidates by the Central Committee in the BNF primaries because those who stood for office had already been scrutinised by the Central Committee. However, the Central Committee still reserved the right to approve or reject candidates despite their support from the general membership of the party.

Religion, or adherence to the Christian faith, appeared to be a common feature of the BNF primary elections as well. This probably helped to allay any fears that the BNF would discourage freedom of religion if and when it assumed power. Another feature of the conduct of BNF primary elections was disregard for time. None of the primaries meetings that I observed started on time. Sometimes members, and at other times officials did not appear to know about venues, dates and times of primary elections.

All BNF primary election meetings had chairpersons and electoral officers. In some cases the chairperson took time to explain to the electorate the significance of primary elections. Chairpersons introduced electoral officers and, in a few cases, the supervisor of primary elections, to the general membership of the party and made a roll call of the wards concerned. Electoral officers explained to party members the two methods of voting and asked them to choose either the open or the secret ballot. It was also explained to the electorate that candidates had, as a policy, to submit applications to the Central Committee.

In some cases the candidates were given a chance to make speeches before the voting process started. The speeches reflected commitment to the party and the aim of the speakers to make a serious challenge to the rival BDP. Some of the BNF primary elections were interesting. In one instance, for example, the names of the candidates were written on a board in their presence. Voting was done by open ballot, the voters raising their hands in support of the candidates of their choice. In another instance, two movable boards with inscriptions +1 and 1 were provided. The two candidates were asked to stand before the audience with their respective blackboards. Party members were then asked to vote for the candidate of their choice by showing their support for either +1 or 1.

Also noticeable was the preponderance of women participants in the primary elections. In Woodhall Ward (Lobatse) for example, 63 people attended, and of this number 37 were women and 26 men. In Peleng (Lobatse) there were 70 people, 46 of whom were women and 24 men. The overwhelming number of women in this process underscores the way in which women actively participate in political activities at the lowest level, much more than their male counterparts.

In the BNF primary elections there appeared to be no clear cut system of screening outsiders. The supporters of the party appeared to trust each other, probably because of the conspicuous absence of people from outside the district. It was also not clear if some of the BNF supporters were below the age of 21. Actually the BNF rules and regulations, like those of the BDP were silent on the question of age. As is often the case with elections, those who lost blamed the Central Committee of the BNF arguing that the results had been unfair and the committee had in fact decided on the winner well in advance. However, in no case have such been charges supported by valid evidence. One provision which seemed to be missing was the absence of a policy or regulations(s) to enable losing candidates to appeal to the Central Committee against the outcome of the results.

Although all BNF primaries were characterised by singing, feasting and drinking were conspicuously absent from their primaries save for the sale of basic foods meant to raise funds for the party.

There was a dearth of information relating to what went on behind the scenes. Clearly, speculation was rife that the Central Committee had called respective candidates to brief them on campaign strategies and on thorny issues that they should raise not only to appeal to the voters, but also to challenge rival parties. The behind-the-scenes campaigns appeared more pronounced with BNF primaries in Kanye than elsewhere. It appeared that the central and constituency committees had agreed among themselves as to who the candidates were to be. It also became apparent that the electorate had been prepared to vote for one candidate and not the other. The incumbent MP for the area was challenged for the position (as per arrangement) and on losing the election he broke away to form a splinter party. Thus, the BNF used a different method from the BDP, to vet who they wanted as a candidate.

The question of who voted in general and for the BNF in particular was an interesting one because it revealed many issues such as gender, educational background, social standing and, in some cases, the political background of voters. The implications of some of these issues were important because they showed the degree to which the party members had been politicised and the extent to which some sections of society took part in the exercise simply to protect their interests, be they gender related, economic, educational or otherwise. A quick glance at the voting age of the BNF revealed that most voters were middle-aged. Out of a total of 89 recorded cases for example, 30 per cent were aged between forty-one and fifty, 25 per cent between twenty-one and thirty, 11 per cent between fifty-one and sixty, and 34 per cent between sixty-one and seventy. Clearly then the age of most BNF supporters fell between the ages of twenty and fifty which means that majority support of the BNF as a political party came from the youth and middle aged.

Rather surprisingly statistics indicated 58 per cent of the recorded 89 were males and 42 per cent females. This indicated that men outnumbered women in their support for the BNF or at least showed that BNF men responded more positively to the call by their party to vote in the primaries. This was the opposite of the trend as women had been in the majority in the case of the BDP. Statistics also indicated that 73 per cent of the BNF voters were born within the constituency in which they voted and 27 per cent from outside of it, indicating that the party had a solid local base. From the experiences of the 1989 primaries for the BDP and BNF, it is clear that certain issues had to be addressed in order to improve the situation. Mainly the issues had to do with age, campaigning and voter eligibility. Of the two parties the BDP has introduced some drastic changes in the conduct of their primaries. A brief discussion on the BDP rules follows.

THE LATEST BDP PRIMARY ELECTION RULES: 'BULELA DITSWE'

The BDP reviewed its primary election rules following the litany of problems experienced both before and after the electoral process. Pre-primary problems included among others the manipulation of electoral colleges in an attempt to aid the interests of some candidates. These problems were also evidenced by the number of appeals and petitions following the primary elections particularly those preceding the 1999 national election. The appeals concerned the following areas: un-constitutional formation of electoral colleges, un-procedural selection of delegates, buying of votes, inequalities due to canvassing efforts by outgoing incumbents and ineptitude of presiding officers. These appeals were responded to but in the majority of cases it was found that the grounds for such appeals were insufficient and they were ignored. This however does not imply that the appeals had no substance. Indeed some were dismissed because of failure to follow the laid down procedures. With regard to post-primaries, problems included the following: weakness of the operating party structures, lack of understanding of procedures and regulations of the party, denying some members the opportunity to participate at key events of the party, creation of 'no go areas' and personalisation of wards and constituencies in particular by incumbents.

These problems and many others compelled the party to review its electoral system. Two approaches were suggested to address the problem. One was to expand the electoral college to include committee members of structures of the party right from cell committees to branch committees. This was a simple modification of the electoral college system. The most widely favoured approach was the unrestricted franchise for all card-carrying members of the party to vote in a ward or constituency. It was felt that if the electoral college had no restrictions, then it would be less vulnerable to manipulation. In addition, the advocates of this approach argued that in a democratic society, all members have a fundamental right to a say in the selection of those who will represent them in the general election. The party adopted this model in 2001 for the 2004 general elections. This new system dispensed with the electoral college replacing it with a new open contest one where voters decide who the candidate will be without the Central Committee having powers to reject the winning candidate. This system was first tested in a by-election in the Lentswe-le-Tau constituency in 2002.

With the introduction of the open membership voting system a number of key features have been introduced. The system is run like a mini election which has high administrative costs. The party therefore established a primary election fund in order to finance the administration and associated costs of the primary elections. At present a candidate in a primary election for a council seat pays a non-refundable fee of P500.00 whilst the parliamentary candidate pays P1000.00. There is also a strict vetting process by the Central Committee whose decision is final and cannot be challenged. The Central Committee considers amongst other issues the following: the prospective candidate's integrity, personality, commitment to the party, ability to represent the party and the public if elected, and all other qualifications and disqualifications under the electoral law of Botswana (BDP Primary Election regulations 3(d)). The criterion used here can be very controversial and the Central Committee is not obliged to state the reason for rejecting a candidature. For example, the Central Committee has used its powers to reject Kgosi Tawana's candidature in the primary elections.

Once the candidates have been approved, it becomes the responsibility of regional committees to introduce them to the BDP electorates. The branch committees are expected to facilitate equal access to campaign opportunities for all candidates. The Central Committee, the Women's Wing and Youth Wings are also expected to support the candidates by providing voter education before the primaries and providing candidates with support during the campaigns after the primaries.

Unlike in the electoral college system, the counting of the ballots and announcing of the results is carried out at the place of the primary election and on the same date as the election. Delegates to the primary election are registered members in good standing, in a particular cell, sub-ward, ward, sub-branch or branch. As in the general elections, polling stations are open from 06.00hrs - 18.00hrs with the right of extension of two hours. With respect to campaigning, the rules state that 'there shall be no campaigning within a radius of 100 meters of the premises of a primary election' (Clause 12 (b)). Campaigning here includes chanting any candidate's name and displaying a candidate's insignia, emblem or image and doing any act that is calculated to influence delegates. This addresses campaigning rules at the time of voting which may be easy to control as these rules apply to the general elections as well. The difficulty however, is how to control campaigning prior to the voting day. This has happened in some areas (Francistown) for example where it is understood one potential candidate had already printed T-shirts even before the official launch of the candidates. Indeed, the BDP leadership complained about some candidates who had started canvassing for support even before they were formerly allowed to do so. This situation became so serious that President Mogae cautioned members about the effects of such developments in the party. He voiced his displeasure at a BDP conference in Gaborone saying, 'its effect is the creation of mistrust, enmity and suspicion within the ranks of the leadership and those affected' (*Monitor*, 8-14 April 2003).

In an attempt to smooth the process, the party has come up with code of conduct for candidates in the primary elections. This includes the following;

- candidates shall conduct themselves in a manner consistent with the demand of the electoral act
- candidates shall not use rallies to castigate competitors
- candidates are free to determine the content and style of their campaign provided that their choice does not cause injury to other competitors or the party
- pre and post primary celebrations of any kind are prohibited, and
- candidates who have not won primary elections are duty bound to support the winning candidate.

Those who have won primary elections are duty bound to create an atmosphere conducive to party unity and accommodate losing candidates.

CONCLUSION

This chapter has discussed several issues pertaining to the organisation of political parties in Botswana. It has demonstrated that political parties are important in any political system as they aggregate the interests of citizens. As the constitution of Botswana provides for and guarantees freedom of association, citizens can freely choose any political party or movement that they believe can better represent their interests. Indeed in the last few years Botswana has witnessed the mushrooming of political parties. This normally happens in the run up to general elections as politicking intensifies.

What is critical however, is whether the growth in numbers reflects any added value to the electorate. For a party to be able to discharge its mandate it is important that it is generally appealing to the electorate and has credible leadership as well as a functioning organisational structure. It has been shown that opposition parties tend to experience more internal problems than the ruling party. The BDP which has been the ruling party since independence in 1966 enjoys the advantages of incumbency.

This chapter has also looked at internal democracy within the parties and observed that the BDP and the BNF were the first to introduce the system of primary elections in Botswana. This was due to the fact that the two parties had an increase in the number of those who wanted to contest the elections. The experiences of the BDP and of the BNF in the 1989 primary elections have been used to provide the historical context which led to the establishment of the current systems. Reforms were introduced to address some of the earlier difficulties experienced, but it is clear that there are still serious problems to be dealt with in order to have an improved system.

Both parties have been brought before the courts of law concerning the outcome of their primary elections. Although there is an attempt by the two parties to align their processes of primary elections to national elections, serious problems remain especially the lack of resources, both financial and human, needed to administer the system.

More research has to be carried out to identify the root causes of the problems. These are issues that the Democracy Research Project (DRP) may want to pursue following the 2004 general elections.

SELECTED REFERENCES

Roskin, M.G et al (2000) *Political Science: An Introduction*. 7th edition New Jersey: Prentice Hall

Botswana Democratic Party Constitution

Botswana National Front Constitution

Edge, W & Lekorwe, M editors (1998) *Botswana: Politics and Society*. Pretoria: J.L van Schaik Publishers.

Gazette, 18th June 2003.

Ginsberg, B and Stone, A (1986) *Do Elections Matter?* New York M.E Sharpe Inc..

Gossett, C.W (1986) *The Civil Service in Botswana: Personnel policies in Comparative Perspectives*. Stanford University.

Holm, J (1989) 'Elections and Democracy in Botswana' Holm, J and Molutsi, P (eds) *Democracy in Botswana*. Gaborone. Macmillan.

Makgala, C.J (2003) 'So far So Good': Dr. Ngoma's 1998 Prophecy on the fate of the BNF' *Pula: Botswana Journal of African Studies*, Vol. 17 no 1.

Maundeni, Z (1998) 'Majority rule, Life presidency and factional politics' in Edge, W & Lekorwe, M op cit.

Molomo, MG & Mokopakgosi, B.T. Editors (1991) *Multi-Party Democracy in Botswana*. SAPES. Harare.

Mmegi Monitor 3 - 9 June 2003

Mmegi, 27 April 2004.

Molomo, M.G (2000) 'Understanding government and Opposition Parties in Botswana' *Commonwealth and Comparative Politics*, Vol 38:1.

Molomo, M.G (1998) 'The Political Implications of the October 4, 1997 Referendum for Botswana' *Democratization*, Vol. 5:4.

Nengwekhulu, R (1979) 'Some findings on the Origins of Political Parties in Botswana' *Pula: Botswana Journal of African Studies* Vol. 1:2

Parson, J (1984) *Botswana: Liberal Democracy and the Labor Reserve in Southern Africa*. Boulder. Colorado, Lynne Rienner Press.

Weinstein, W and Grootpeter, J (973) *The Pattern of African Decolonisation: A new Interpretation*. Syracuse N.Y.

CHAPTER 8

FUNDING OF POLITICAL PARTIES: LEVELLING THE POLITICAL PLAYING FIELD

Mpho Molomo and David Sebudubudu

INTRODUCTION

This chapter looks at the funding of political parties as a crucial aspect of modern democratic theory. Joseph (2000: 12) argues that democratic theory is concerned with the process by which ordinary citizens exert a relatively high degree of control over their leaders. It is argued that citizens must be vigilant and must advocate for, and understand, their rights and responsibilities. Based on these maxims, we hold that democracy will remain an aspiration, which people should continually strive to realise. It is therefore incumbent on any democracy constantly to review, reformulate and improve its procedures with the aim of widening the frontiers of democracy. In this regard the funding of political parties is of critical importance. The need to fund political parties arises from the fact that they are important players in the democratisation process, and for them to discharge their mandate effectively they must be well resourced. There is also the view that democracy is a 'rare bird' in Africa, and where it exists, it should be nurtured and strengthened. We maintain that democracy has become the most treasured birthright in the free world and we suggest that the funding of political parties is one way of preserving and strengthening it.

It is acknowledged that political parties played an important function in leading the crusade to attain political independence. We reiterate that political parties aggregate diverse interests in society and develop them into coherent demands and platforms which are then filtered into the political system. In a more direct way, political parties develop policies and manifestos, which become their blueprints or social contracts and, once elected into power, become their programme of action. They serve as a platform for political mobilisation, recruitment and voter education, and provide the electorate with choices as to who should wield political power. As mobilisation agents, political parties are central to the whole project of political participation and electioneering. In a democracy, as provided for in the constitution, political parties renew their mandate through elections every five years.

This chapter examines the politics of funding political parties, which is a highly contentious subject in Botswana. First it unravels the relationship between funding and the entrenchment of a dominant party. Secondly it argues that reform of the funding of parties in Botswana is essential if the country is to retain its reputation as a liberal democracy. It is also noted that although Botswana's democracy has been widely documented no studies have specifically addressed the issue of party funding. The chapter assumes the basic premise that democratisation is about choice and political competition and that meaningful choice and competition can only take place in a situation where the political playing field is level and political parties are evenly resourced to compete fairly. Political parties can reach the electorate on an equal basis, only if they are sufficiently resourced.

As the world moves towards greater democratisation, we identify funding of political parties as one of the key factors in promoting open systems. We argue that better-resourced parties are well positioned to promote some of the key tenets of liberal democracy, transparency and accountability, as well as to ensure political equality in electoral contests. It is commonplace that election campaigns depend, to a large extent, on the resources at the disposal of political parties. Yet political parties across the political spectrum are often under-resourced. Political party activity relies heavily on volunteers, but political parties need to have a core staff that works to support the implementation of its vision and strategies at all times. They need offices and permanent staff, all of which require resources. A successful campaign, especially in a country like Botswana, which is diverse and large with difficult terrain, needs reliable campaign vehicles. Moreover, campaigns need money to buy advertising time and space and all other necessary equipments.

In Botswana, political parties do not have equal access to funding opportunities. The ruling BDP has access to more sources of funding than any other party in the country. Given that public funding of political parties is one way of investing in democracy, we advocate for its provision. Nevertheless, it is clear that as a political ideal, the funding of political parties remains a contested concept. In this chapter we engage in the various debates relating to funding of political parties, and begin by setting the context for understanding these debates in the Botswana setting.

CONTEXTUAL FRAMEWORK

It is acknowledged that in a region characterised by mixed political fortunes, Botswana has remained a functioning democracy since independence in 1966. Over the years, it has held regular 'free and fair' elections in a stable political atmosphere. Despite this impeccable track record, Botswana's political process has been characterised by a predominant party system in which the BDP has won each and every election by a landslide victory. To date, nine general elections have been held, with the most recent in October 2004. The preponderance of the BDP at the polls has often been explained in simplistic terms, that its success is simply a result of its popularity. Whilst this may well be so, there are other important factors that need to be taken into account in explaining the popularity of the BDP. Its electoral strength is, among other things, a manifestation of deep-seated structural problems in Botswana's polity and electoral system. Key, among these factors, is the uneven political playing field caused by disparities in financial resources.

Based on these realities, we argue for the need for political party funding. Nevertheless, it should be pointed out that funding of political parties is not the only factor that ensures electoral success. Other factors such as organisational capacity play an equally important role in electoral contests. But it is clear that organisational capacity cannot be divorced from adequate funding because 'campaign contributions seem to determine political outcomes more than voting' (Cox 1998:57 quoting Ketting Foundation).

THE ELECTORAL LAW AND PARTY FUNDING

The law in Botswana does not adequately provide for disclosures of funds. As a result, the ruling and opposition parties have traded accusations and counter accusations that the other party benefited from undisclosed sources of funding. What is perhaps more disturbing is that the law in Botswana covers a very narrow aspect of campaign financing, which deals mainly with disclosure of election expenses by candidates and not political parties. Candidates are compelled by law to disclose expenses incurred immediately after the writ of elections has been issued but this is not stringently enforced. Despite it being a requirement that politicians should declare their election expenses, they do not always do so. What accounts for this laxity, in our view, is the fact that they are not reimbursed and hence have little incentive to account for the expenses. However, to ensure a level political playing field, a strict code of financial regulation is desirable.

It is also observed that in Botswana, the law on election expenses is inadequate. It does not address the concerns that Ewing (1992) identified regarding the requirements for political equality and participation. There is therefore a need for legislation that provides for disclosure of sources of election expenses and that regulates how such money should be spent during election campaigns. As previously stated, the law in Botswana does not provide for funding of political parties but only deals with election expenses and the maximum amount of money to be spent by each candidate, without spelling out the source of such funds. Section 78 (1) of the Electoral Act defines 'election expenses' as, 'all monies expended or expenses incurred on account of, or in respect of, the conduct or management of that election by the candidate or on his behalf or in his interests and for the purposes of this subsection, money shall be deemed to have been expended or expenses incurred in respect of the conduct or management of an election if expended or incurred after the issue of a writ in relation to that election'

Sections, 82 and 85 of the Electoral Act deal with disclosure of expenditure and return of election expenses. Section 82(1) reads 'all money provided by an association or group of persons or any person for the election expenses of a candidate, whether as a gift, loan, advance or deposit, shall be…fully disclosed'. Furthermore, Section 85 (1) states that within 90 days after the result of any election has been declared every candidate at that election shall render to the returning officer a true return of all expenses pertaining to the election. Section 79 of the Electoral Act states that campaign expenditure or expenses of any candidate shall not exceed P50, 000.00.

In the light of the above it is considered that Botswana needs to revise the Electoral Act and introduce a law on party funding by the government. Such a law should also set the limits on the amount that political parties could spend on their campaigns. The current Electoral Act only specifies the level of election expenses per candidate but even this law is not strictly adhered to. There is also a need for a law that forces parties to disclose their sources of funding. Otherwise, issues of national security and interest are likely to be compromised. Moreover, there is a danger that political parties might be able to buy votes.

According to the Electoral Act, each candidate is only allowed a maximum of P50, 000.00, as election expenses. During the 1999 election, the BDP received P2.4 million from sources that the BDP treasurer called 'friends and the business community' (*The Botswana Guardian*, 23 July 1999). At the minimum, assuming that the BDP had other sources of funding, e.g. from revenues it gets from renting part of its headquarters, Tsholetsa House, and membership subscriptions, the P3.4 million divided by the number of constituencies means the BDP had an excess of P80, ooo to spend in each constituency! Until recently, some government departments such as the Wildlife and National Parks rented part of the building. It appears the ruling party does not seem to be concerned about conflict of interest in renting out office space to government departments, for profit, whilst being the governing party.

WHY PARTY FUNDING?

As Africa is moving towards democratisation, funding of political parties has been identified as one of the key factors in promoting open systems. The same principle should apply to Botswana because better-resourced parties are necessary in promoting key tenets of liberal democracies, transparency and accountability. Since it is no longer possible to practise direct democracy, as was the case with the ancient Greek city-states, democracy now takes the form of representative government in which the electorate exercise their democratic right of free choice. However, such a right can only be meaningfully exercised if the electorate is educated to make informed choices and political parties are better positioned to provide alternative programmes and candidates. Where political parties do not have adequate resources to train their people, democracy often remains hollow. The funding of political parties allows them to maintain a certain level of political visibility, and to compete effectively in the political arena. To be effective, political parties need funds to finance their campaigns, to print campaign material, use billboards, distribute fliers, as well as to advertise in the electronic and print media. Although it depends on the formula agreed to dispense such resources, funding of political parties, by and large, ensures equitable distribution of resources.

In a number of countries it has been observed that opposition parties have performed poorly in elections partly because they are not adequately resourced. Botswana is not an exception. Selolwane (2002:68) acknowledges the 'resource capacity' as one of the factors responsible for opposition party's failure to provide the electorate with an alternative to BDP rule. Botswana, the oldest multi-party democracy in Africa, has been described by many as the model of democracy in Africa but is likely to regress given the fact that it is lagging behind in some critical areas that facilitate democratic discourse.

Arguments in favour of political party funding are that political parties need funds in order to be able to articulate their ideology, programmes and policies to the people. In a difficult terrain such as Botswana where most of the rural areas are in heavy sand, such areas are only accessible by four-wheel drive vehicles. The opposition parties that do not have funds are not able to canvass for political support effectively in these areas. Effective electoral campaigns are contingent upon the availability of financial resources and these resources are essential for organisational and strategic planning, manpower training and transportation.

There have been calls by opposition parties and academics to discuss the need for political party funding but this suggestion has not been widely debated by all the stakeholders. The ruling party, perhaps as a beneficiary of the status quo, remains adamant that it is not necessary. Addressing a press conference, President Festus Mogae said his government would consider the funding of political parties in an attempt to strengthen democracy. However he noted, 'the issue has to be debated first to find out the right way of going about it.' The president feared that this would increase the 'likelihood of fragmentation of opposition parties' hoping to 'make 'money' out of the process. (*Mmegi*, 12-18 November 1999). According to Burnell (1998:7) 'the prospect of public funding could persuade a range of civic associations to attempt to transform themselves into parties.' This argument however is contested because if the public funding of political parties was established then a policy and formula would have to be developed to regulate the disbursement of such funds. In countries where public funding of political parties is in use, 'the principles of proportionality and equity' guide the way public funds are allocated to individual parties (National Democratic Institute for International Affairs, 1998).

There are some who claim that state funding of political parties stifles political initiative. Assuming that state funding would undermine the link between political parties and its mass membership. The opponents of state funding argue that parties which receive state, private or foreign funding have the propensity to develop 'powerful centralised bureaucracies at the expense of grassroots efforts, individual members and organisational sub-units' (Fenandez, 1994:114). Most parties in Africa survive on membership subscriptions, and as such, recognise their members as an important resource that should never be taken for granted.

It is acknowledged that public funding of political parties must come from taxes and that there is always an opportunity cost in public spending. Public expenditure must always be prioritised to service critical sectors of the economy. In the light of competing demands for government funds such as for fighting HIV/AIDS, unemployment and poverty, the question has been asked as to whether it is not a luxury to finance political parties? The scepticism goes further to assert that political parties are often self-seeking and candidates often seek political office not to service the common good but for their own personal gain. As a result, investing in democracy is accorded a low priority.

Yet the experiences of other countries demonstrate that economic development is untenable in an unstable and fragile political environment. The need for political party financing can never be over-emphasised. Democracy is a fragile process that should never be taken for granted and must constantly be nurtured to facilitate its consolidation. It needs to be seen as a public good to be protected in the national interest.

As argued by Good (1999:50) political competition between unevenly matched political parties only guarantees inequalities. Manifesting the need for equality in the political sphere and the recognition that without equal political participation, the scope of democracy is limited, Ewing (1992:17) identifies levels of political equality. He observes that each and every political party or candidate represents a particular vision of the world and, for it to be known, there is need for funding to ensure effective propagation of the view and campaign. No matter how good a campaign message is, if it is not communicated and disseminated to the people, it will never make a political difference. All political parties must have access to the media and other forms of communication such as the internet, to reach out to the electorate.

Although financing political parties could not completely level the playing field it would enable opposition parties to reach more areas of the country and a larger proportion of the electorate. Andren (1970:54) notes that political party funding accounts for a 'fair and open competition and access to the electorate'. Also, Nassmacher, who is cited in Fenandez (1994:113), argues that open political activity is as crucial for modern society as is free social welfare. Both are done for the public good and are therefore worthy of public support. Levelling the political playing field suggests that the political parties and candidates must have equal chances of reaching out to the electorate. In Botswana, the law guarantees unfettered access of parties and candidates to the electorate, but such access remains an empty promise, if some parties are disproportionately more resourced than others.

Much as the political system provides an enabling environment for the discourse of political activity, political competition is still limited in Botswana because opposition parties do not have adequate resources to engage in competitive campaigning. Political parties should be the primary drivers of the democratisation process, yet their scope of influence, especially opposition parties, is limited because they are under-resourced. The incumbent political party, the BDP, on the other hand, enjoys major advantages by virtue of being in power. It is able to take advantage of state resources and, through political patronage, rewards party activists and supporters. Compared to the opposition parties, which are poor and demoralised, it enjoys political visibility, which puts it ahead of opposition contenders.

Democracy as an interactive process is based on constant interaction between representatives and the electorate. Such interaction may be face to face, through house-to-house campaigns or through the freedom square, but it also takes place through the electronic and print media. The media provides a platform for political participation and accountability. It keeps political debates alive in a free, independent and critical manner between political parties and the electorate. Yet opposition parties complain that government monopolises the official media. Moreover, they are unable to utilise the private media due to unavailability of resources.

Political parties, through their voter education programmes, enhance democracy by creating a forum for the flow of information and ideas about the political process. Through their campaign process they can act as agents for political mobilisation, education and change. Political campaigns institutionalise the development of democratic norms and values, and instil a culture of openness and tolerance of opposing political views. Through them, voters gain a comprehensive understanding of the political process in general and, more specifically, the election management process. Yet political parties cannot effectively embark on this process, if they are not empowered with resources.

The funding of political parties is of critical importance to ensure necessary competition in the electoral process. The National Democratic Institute for International Affairs (1998:6) states that:

> in order to carry out their democratic functions effectively, political parties must be supported by financial and other resources. Such resources include funds to operate the basic infrastructure of political party institutions, as well as a wide variety of resources that support the ability of parties to communicate with the population.

In support of this view, Ware (1998:242) argues that, 'well financed parties can provide linkage with mass electorates; a wholly publicly-funded system would prevent the distortion of party priorities in the direction of fund raising, and even partly publicly funded systems might reduce the inequalities in resources between parties and candidates'. Adequately funded parties help ensure political equality in electoral contests.

The functions that political parties are expected to perform require funding. Ewing (1987) identified three critical functions of political parties in the electoral process as organisation, representation and governance. First on organisation, Burnell (1998:6) identified other factors that are equally important in electoral contests. These range from 'charisma' to a shrewd political acumen, 'party discipline and organisational competence', good sense of judgement for 'policy positions that look credible to voters' and, perhaps, a 'degree of luck'. Although these features are equally important in themselves, they are driven by money. Secondly, on representative government, John Stuart Mill (referred to in Duncan and Lukes, 1996:158) said, 'nothing less can be ultimately desirable than the admission of all to a share in the sovereign power of the state'. However, for the populace to have a share in the sovereign power of the state, they must take part. in a meaningful and equal way, in the political process. Political parties are the cornerstones of representative government. Without them, democracy withers and decays. Therefore, for them to discharge their mandate effectively, they must be well funded. Thirdly, on democratic governance, Botswana's democratic process is measured against international practice, which includes, the constitutional provisions of established democratic norms based on observance of civil liberties such as the freedom of speech, freedom of association and assembly, regular elections and the rule of law.

The political context regulating the activities of political parties and the conduct of elections needs to provide for an open, accountable and transparent political process that is acceptable to the broad spectrum of society. Such a framework needs to provide an enabling environment for political and civil society actors to operate without any inhibitions. In the liberal democratic process, political parties play an important role in aggregating diverse interests and formulating them into coherent programmes for political action. They enhance democracy by creating a forum for the flow of information about the political process. In propagating their political views, political parties, both ruling and opposition, act as agents for political change and education. They contribute to this process in three specific ways. First, they undertake to maintain or change government through the ballot box. Secondly, political parties facilitate the understanding of concepts of democratic governance and relationships within government. Thirdly, they educate the electorate on the responsibilities of elected officials and public accountability. By way of institutionalising the development of democratic norms and values, they instil a culture of openness and tolerance of opposing political views. In similar vein, in the process of mobilising for political choice and competition, voters gain a comprehensive understanding of the electoral and election management systems. Only political parties that are well resourced could achieve this.

MODALITIES OF POLITICAL PARTY FUNDING

According to the National Democratic Institute for International Affairs (1998:6) in most democracies, political parties receive funding from both private and public resources. However, the balance between the two differs significantly. Political parties in Israel receive the bulk of their support (approximately 85 per cent) from the public treasury. In contrast, political parties in the United States receive a majority of their funds from private resources. The exception is the presidential campaign which is financed primarily through public funds.

A comparative study conducted by the National Democratic Institute for International Affairs (1998:8) found out that public funding systems have been implemented for a variety of reasons. Some systems focus support on the elections while others on party organisation, and others on both. For those that focus on political parties, funds are disbursed up-front or parties are reimbursed expenses incurred during the electoral process. A second major objective for public funding is to provide political parties with the necessary 'resources to participate in parliamentary politics'.

In South Africa, political parties are funded in proportion to the number of representatives they have in the National Assembly. For parties to qualify for state funding prior to elections, they have to 'gather at least 10 000 signatures from five of South Africa's nine provinces, or register at least two per cent support nationwide in an independently conducted poll. In the case of parties only contesting provincial elections, 3 000 signatures' are required (Southhall and Wood 1998:210). In Namibia too, parties are funded in terms of the number of representatives they have in the National Assembly 'and [funding] is maintained between elections to enable parties to man local offices and staff' (Lodge, 2000:146). State funding is good for democracy because it ensures that parties are well resourced, and are able to contest elections more closely.

In southern Africa, the predominant party system is a characteristic feature of multi-party politics. Whilst the state of affairs is a reflection of the level of support for some political parties, it is also a statement about the level of resources available to political parties. Ruling parties, by and large, enjoy advantages as a result of being in power. Although Botswana is one of the oldest democracies in Africa, it has so far failed to adopt best practices that nurture democracy. It is one of the few countries in southern Africa (Swaziland, Zambia, Mauritius and Lesotho), which has not yet embraced public or state funding of political parties.

Manifesting its liberal democratic tendencies, funding of political parties in Botswana is left to market forces. Yet even market driven economies, such as that of the United States, have public funding of presidential campaigns. Political parties in Botswana raise funds in a number of ways. These include, general membership fees, organising party concerts, selling party documents such as manifestos and, where possible, securing funds from private donors. Important as they are in funding political parties, these sources are not reliable and sustainable, especially in a country like Botswana with a small and sparsely distributed population. Moreover, in a country where the majority of the politically active population are lowly paid and unemployed, funding political parties on membership subscriptions is unsustainable.

In a country such as Botswana where voter apathy is high, 39 per cent, there is a need for a well-articulated and coherent voter education and mobilisation campaign to ensure that all corners of the country are covered. Political campaigns are generally expensive especially in a country the size of Botswana. Therefore, there is a need for political parties to employ various strategies so that they can reach the electorate. Voter apathy suggests that there is a need for political parties to go beyond conventional methods of reaching the electorate such as addressing public rallies.

Only well-resourced parties can afford the costs of advertising in the print media and radio stations; only well-resourced parties are able to print posters, hire billboards, buy advertising space in local newspapers and on private radio stations, send letters to voters and conduct house-to-house campaigns. Without doubt, all of these strategies promote the image of political parties. As noted above, the party in power, the BDP enjoys the advantage of incumbency. Opposition parties accuse the ruling party of monopolising the use government resources, such as, the government controlled media and kgotla (village assembly) to address meetings. The kgotla is a forum for selling public policies to the people and soliciting their views. In a country such as Botswana, where the ruling party dominates, platforms such as the kgotla work primarily to the benefit of the BDP. Although the opposition is not barred from using these resources, the chances of them doing so are limited as not many of them are in council and parliament.

The evidence above suggests that, in terms of reaching the electorate, the BDP has an upper hand. It is the only party that manages to field candidates for all parliamentary and council elections throughout the country. Other parties find it very difficult to reach all four corners of the country because they do not have their own party transport and largely depend on vehicles of individual loyal members.

Political party funding raises the question of which aspects of political activity to finance? There is a broad array of political party activity that may be financed. These include establishing constituency offices, transportation, research, voter education, stationary, telephone and fax bills, advertisements, printed materials and accommodation, subsistence and salaries for staff. Political party financing, if it is not controlled, could be problematic because it could lead to 'buying votes' as well as compromising the independence of political parties and subsequently the sovereignty of the country.

Another contested issue concerns the criteria that could be used in funding political parties. Should this facility be accorded to every political party or should it be restricted only to registered ones? Furthermore, should finances be dispensed in accordance with the number of registered members or the number of votes they polled in the previous elections? Under this framework, there could also be what is often referred to as 'incentive funding'. As the name suggests, it could reward political parties that have performed well and also those that include groups that have been traditionally excluded from mainstream politics. For example, it could mean allocating more funds to a political party that returned more women, youth and minorities into council or parliament. Furthermore, it could be argued that funding parties that are not in council and/or parliament would actually help to broaden the political base. Conversely, it could also be argued that supporting political parties in proportion to their popular support would entrench existing power imbalances. Nevertheless, if these imbalances reflect the will of the people, why should this be perceived as a problem? But such a dispensation could create difficulties by excluding newly-formed parties and those that do not have representation in council or parliament.

The third material question is what form political party funding should take? Basically there are four types of political party funding that this chapter seeks to explore. These are public, private, foreign funding and the funding of political parties through the creation of a democracy fund.

PUBLIC FUNDING

According to Fernandez (1994:112), public financing of political parties, candidates and political campaigns is now a widespread phenomenon practised in at least 30 countries around the world. In southern Africa, it is practised in Malawi, Mozambique, Namibia, Seychelles, South Africa, Tanzania and Zimbabwe.

State or public funding of political parties can have adverse implications for democratic discourse. It could result in state interference and public and bureaucratic interference in the affairs of political parties. That is, political parties would have to account for such monies. However, this would largely depend on the model of funding that is in use. In the case of Botswana the public is not that vocal but bureaucratic intervention cannot be ruled out. According to Ware (1998:243), public funding of political parties 'may be a device for squeezing small parties and contribute to parties becoming more remote from their members…' as they would 'put much less effort into building a membership base.' This would be working against one of the aims of political parties, that is, that of establishing 'links with mass electorates'. Therefore, there is a need to strike a balance between party funding and its implications.

In Germany, for example, 'the law stipulates that public funding may not constitute more than 50 per cent of a political party's funding.' This is to ensure that parties are accountable to the private sources of support. However, systems that rely on private funding must also cope with the possibility that private contributions may exert inappropriate influence on the political systems (National Democratic Institute for International Affairs, 1998:9). This clearly shows that when introducing a law on party funding there is a need to strike a balance between national interests and the role-played by political parties. With respect to 'anonymous donors', this is not allowed in a number of countries such as the United States of America and Canada. Secret donations not only compromise the values of democracy, but may also encourage corruption.

PRIVATE FUNDING

Private funding of political parties makes available critical resources needed for canvassing of political support. Private financiers often represent special interests, with a particular vision of the world. The dangers of private funding of political campaigns are that it often compromises the integrity and accountability of government. When elections are won, donors may expect special favours as a result of their donations, and the interests of the ordinary voters may be compromised. Arising from these realities is the imperative that a strict financial disclosure of all donations be made during a campaign.

EXTERNAL FUNDING

In the era of globalisation, where the politics of the nation-state have implications for international commerce and trade, it is argued that external actors have a stake in national politics. However, where funds from foreign governments or foundations are involved to define the political agenda, it is necessary to be vigilant to ensure that the sovereignty of the state is not compromised (Fernandez, 1994: 106). The law in Botswana does not stop political parties from securing external funding nor does it regulate external funding. The BNF in 1994 secured funding from an undisclosed source, believed to be a sympathetic foreign political party and this, perhaps, explains its performance at the polls in that election year. Similarly, the BDP, in 1999, received an external donation (P2.4 million from an anonymous foreign donor). In fact, the BDP has in previous elections benefited from external financing (Otlhogile, 1991:26).

There are some inherent dangers in external funding. For instance, there may be conditions attached to such donations. Donors prefer to keep their donations a secret because they are never sure which party will win the elections. According to Burnell (1998:15), donors 'fear unforeseen consequences as a result of being drawn into a country's domestic political arena. The backers incur political embarrassment if they become identified with successful political contenders who then stray from democratic practice' and 'those seeking particular gains could suffer as a result of unwittingly backing losers and alienating the winners'. However, it is generally believed that parties that are organisationally sound and 'espouse liberal policies' attract funding from external donors. Moreover, following the demise of communist states, political and economic liberalism has gained hegemonic influence and parties that articulate such policies stand a better chance of receiving foreign funding.

DEMOCRACY FUND

One way of avoiding a partisan appeal to political party funding, and of ensuring that no one political party enjoys unfair advantage because it is well connected to business, the country needs to consider setting up a democracy fund. Such a fund may benefit from subventions made by government, donations from individuals, corporations and foreign governments. These funds can be allocated to political parties based on a formula agreed upon by all stakeholders and may be disbursed by a supposedly neutral body like the Independent Electoral Commission (IEC).

CONCLUSION

Free political competition assumed in democratic governance cannot exist among unevenly matched political parties. By any standard, the freedom and fairness of an election is measured, among other variables, by the ability of political parties to compete equally for political support. State funding of political parties is therefore a crucial way of levelling the political playing field. We have measured the fairness of elections by the ability of all political parties to canvas for political support and proposed the creation of a democracy fund, which would be a pool of resources from all those who wish to support and nurture democracy. Such a fund would avoid partisan funding and would adhere to ethical standards of disbursing funds. It is suggested that funds could be allocated to political parties, based on a formula agreed upon by all stakeholders and administered by a neutral body like the IEC.

REFERENCES

Alexander, H. (1989) 'Money and politics: Rethinking a Conceptual Framework', in *Comparative Political Finance in the 1980s*, Cambridge University Press

Almond, G and Powell, B. (1966)*Comparative Politics: A Developmental Approach* Boston: Little Brown and Company.

Andren, N. 'Partisan Motivations and Concern for System Legitimacy in Scandinavian Deliberations of Public Subsidies' in Heidenheimer, A. J. (ed) *Comparative Political Finance* Lexington, MA: D C Heath.

Botswana Congress Party, (1999) *Democratic and Development Programme: Programme and Statement of Principles*, Gaborone,.

Botswana Democratic Party, Election Manifestoes, 1984, 1989, 1994, 1999, Gaborone.

Botswana Democratic Party,(2002) *Botswana Democratic Party Primary Election Rules and Regulations*, March 2002.

Botswana National Front, (1994) *Election Manifesto of the Botswana National Front*, Gaborone, Party Secretariat

Burnell, P (1998) 'Introduction: money and politics in emerging democracies' in Burnell, P and Aware, A (eds) *Funding Democratisation*, Manchester: Manchester University Press.

Cox, A (1998) 'Ethics, Campaign Finance, and Democracy', Article, Alert, March/April 1998.

Danevad, A. (1995) 'Responsiveness in Botswana Politics: Do Elections Matter?' *Journal of Modern African Studies* Vol. 33:3.

Du Toit, P. (1995) *State Building and Democracy in Southern African: Botswana, Zimbabwe and South Africa*, Washington DC: United States Institute for Peace.

Duncan. G and Lukes, S. (1966) 'The New Democracy,' *Political Studies* Vol. Xi:2 .

Edge, W. and Lekorwe, M. (1998) *Botswana: Politics and Society* Pretoria: J. L. Van Schaik Publishers.

Ewing, K (1987) *The Funding of Political parties in Britain*, Cambridge; Cambridge University Press.

Ewing, K, D (1992) *Money, Politics, and Law; A Study of Electoral Campaign Finance Reform in Canada* Oxford; Clarendon Press.

Fernandez, L, (1994) *The Legal Regulation of Campaign Financing, in Free and Fair Elections* (ed) Steytler, N., Murphy, J. De Vos, P and Rwelamira, M, Cape Town: Juta and Co, Ltd (1994).

IDEA, (2000) Towards Sustainable Democratic Institutions in Southern Africa, International IDEA Conference, Gaborone, Botswana 8-10 May 2000

Joseph, R (1999) (ed) *State, Conflict and democracy in Africa*, London: Lynne Rienner Publishers .

Lekorwe, M (1989) 'The Kgotla and the freedom square: one-way or two-way communication?' in Holm, J and Molutsi, P (eds) *Democracy in Botswana*, Gaborone: Macmillan Botswana Publishing Company (Pty) Ltd.

Lodge, T (2000) 'How Political Parties Finance Electoral Campaigning in *Southern Africa*' in *Southern African Elections Forum, Conference Report*, Windhoek: 11 – 14 June 2000.

Mmegi/The Reporter, Gaborone, 13-19 August 1999.

Mmegi/The Reporter, Gaborone, 17-23 September 1999

Mmegi/The Reporter, Gaborone, 12-18 November 1999

Molutsi, P (1991) 'Political Parties and Democracy in Botswana' in Molomo, M. G and Mokopakgosi, B. T (eds) *Multi-Party Democracy in Botswana*, Harare; Bardwells.

Otlhogile, B (1991) How Free and Fair ? in Molomo, M. G and Mokopakgosi, B. T (eds) *Multi-Party Democracy in*

Botswana, Harare; Bardwells.

The Botswana Guardian, Gaborone, 23 July 1999.

The Botswana Guardian, Gaborone, 22 October 1999.

The National Democratic Institute for International Affairs (1998), *The Public Funding of Political Parties; An International Comparative Study*, United States Agency for Development / South Africa.

Republic of Botswana, (1969) *Report on the General Elections*, Gaborone, Government Printer.

Republic of Botswana (1974) *Report to the Minister of State on the General Elections*, Gaborone, Government Printer.

Republic of Botswana (1979) *Report to the Minister of Public Service and Information on the General Election*, Gaborone, Government Printer.

Republic of Botswana, (1984) *Report to the Minister of Public Service and Information on the General Elections*, Gaborone, Government Printer.

Republic of Botswana, (1989) *Report to the Minister of Presidential Affairs and Public Administration on the General Elections*, Gaborone, Government Printer.

Republic of Botswana, (1994) *Report to the Minister of Presidential Affairs and Public Administration on the General Elections*, Gaborone Government Printer.

Republic of Botswana (1968) Electoral Act Chapter 02:07, Gaborone: Government Printer.

Schikonye, L. 'The Functioning and Funding of Political Parties (in the SADC region)' a paper presented an International IDEA-SADC Conference: 'Towards Sustainable Democratic Institutions in Southern Africa' in http://www.idea.int/ideas_work/22_s_africa/elections_5_botswana.htm.

Selolwane, D. O (2002) 'Monopoly Politikos: How Botswana's Opposition Parties Have Helped Sustain One-Party Dominance' in *African Sociological Review*, 6,1.

Schlemmer, L. et.al (1997) *Present Realities and Strategies for the Future*: Training Workshop for the Botswana Democratic Party.

Stedman, S. (ed.) (1993) *Botswana: Political Economy of Democratic Development* Boulder, Colorado: Lynne Rienner Press.

Southhall, R and Wood, G (1998) 'Political party funding in Southern Africa' in Burnell, P and Aware, A (eds) *Funding Democratisation*, Manchester; Manchester University Press.

Wiseman, J (1998) 'The slow evolution of the party system in Botswana` in *Journal of Asian and African Studies*, Vol. 33, No.3.

Ware, A (1998) 'Conclusion' in Burnell, P and Aware, A (eds) *Funding Democratisation*, Manchester; Manchester University Press.

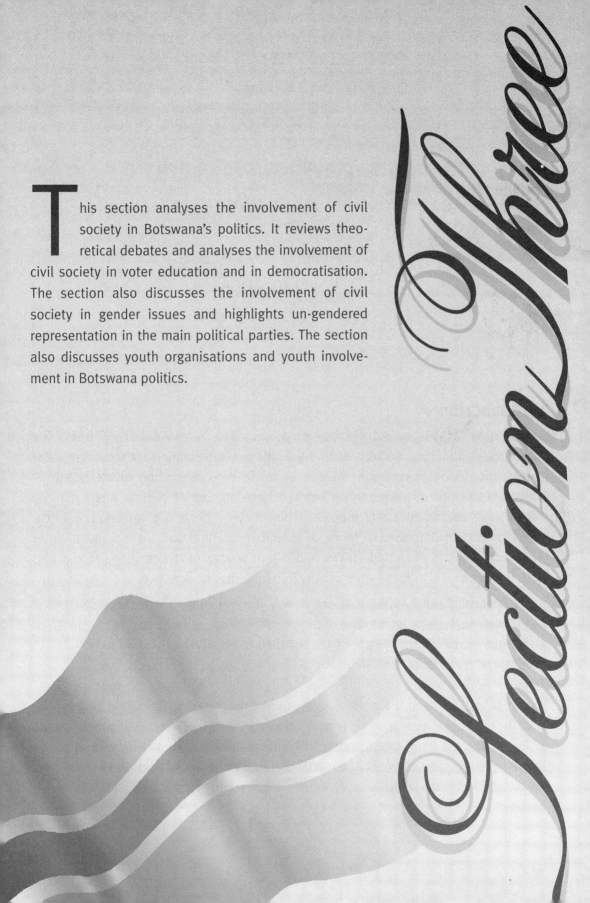

This section analyses the involvement of civil society in Botswana's politics. It reviews theoretical debates and analyses the involvement of civil society in voter education and in democratisation. The section also discusses the involvement of civil society in gender issues and highlights un-gendered representation in the main political parties. The section also discusses youth organisations and youth involvement in Botswana politics.

Section Three

CHAPTER 9

CIVIL SOCIETY AND VOTER EDUCATION IN BOTSWANA: 1965-2004

Adam Mfundisi

INTRODUCTION

This chapter focuses on voter education as provided by civil society. The IEC, the government and civil society each have the responsibility to encourage voter participation and spearhead voter education. In my opinion the future health of Botswana's democratic governance lies in a large number of eligible voters actively taking part in the election process. This chapter therefore analyses political developments in Botswana in terms of voter participation and the amount of voter education that has been undertaken in different phases of the election process. But first, it is necessary to place voter apathy into historical perspective.

Political disenchantment is not a new phenomenon. Since the first General Election in 1965 a sizable number of the population has either been disfranchised or chose not to vote. From 1965 to 1998, eighteen to twenty year-olds were not able to participate in elections, thus depriving a relatively large proportion of the population from developing a civic duty and responsibility to their country. In the 1999 elections, young people between the ages of eighteen and twenty were allowed to vote for the first time, but the level of their participation was disappointing. Few young people bothered to cast their vote contrary to high expectations from many quarters who viewed the eighteen to twenty year-olds as more enlightened and progressive than other sections of the electorate. Generally, voter apathy cuts across all demographic groups.

VOTER PARTICIPATION AND DISENGAGEMENT FROM THE POLITICAL PROCESS

Voter turnout at elections is used as a yardstick of people's participation in the political process. It is argued that a strong democratic government is dependent on the participation of citizens in structures, institutions and operations of communities and government. A 2002 IEC report on Voter Apathy in Botswana has concluded that there was a high level of voter apathy. Declining voter participation in civil society activities and government is a worrying phenomenon. There is a growing need to engage apathetic and disempowered groups of voters to ensure higher participation in the electoral process. There is a view that voter turnout at elections is an indication of the ability of government, the electoral management body and civil society to motivate eligible voters to register and cast valid ballots.

Table 9.1 Voter turnout at Botswana general elections 1965 - 2004				
Year	Voting population	Registered voters	Votes cast	% vote/eligibility
1965	243 365	188 950	140 789	58 %
1969	267 647	156 428	85 879	32 %
1974	309 810	236 483	73 897	24 %
1979	362,515	243 483	142 245	39 %
1984	416 996	293 571	227 756	55 %
1989	507 569	367 069	250 487	49 %
1994	609 000	370 356	281 931	46 %
1999	800 000	459 251	330 779	41 %
2004	900 000±	552 849	421 272	47 %

Source: Modified from Report to the Vice President and Minister of Presidential Affairs & Public Administration on the General Elections 1999. Appendix L

Table 9.1 shows voter turnouts at Botswana's General Elections since 1965. In the first election, slightly over half of those eligible voted. This dropped to 32 per cent in 1969 and to 24 per cent in 1974. Since then voting patterns have been fluctuating over the years, with the lowest turnout of 24 per cent in 1974.

To take the voting age population instead of registered voters, only 41 per cent of the potential voters voted in 1999 general elections and in subsequent by-elections fewer registered voters were attracted to the polls. In 2001, in a referendum that in part requested electorates to agree or disagree with the extension of the retirement age of judges, only 2.6 per cent of registered voters showed up at the polls. The shrinking numbers of people exercising their democratic right to vote is a cause of concern to the government, the Independent Electoral Commission (IEC) and to the democratic fraternity at large. Elections are an important barometer for ensuring popular participation in a representative democracy. By exercising their right to vote, citizens are giving legitimacy and credibility to the electoral process. When citizens disengage from the electoral process, representative democracy might be under threat.

Despite many years of agitation to lower the voting age from twenty-one to eighteen, the 1999 general election has shown that young voters exhibit the worst apathy of all. After the voting age was lowered in 1997, less than five per cent of eighteen to twenty year-olds turned out to cast their ballots in the 1999 general election.

REASONS AND CAUSES OF VOTER APATHY AND ALIENATION

There is little consensus about the reasons and causes of voter apathy in Botswana. But voter apathy is analysed against the background of illiteracy, socio-economic factors, absence of democracy during the colonial era, lack of voter education, lack of civic education and unaccountable politicians. This approach provides a number of explanations for political apathy and alienation of voters. First, historical circumstances militate against massive voter turnout at elections. As the DRP pointed out in the Voter Apathy Report, political activism is largely a post-colonial activity. During the colonial period there was no culture of competitive elections for leaders, as chiefs were not elected but were a product of inheritance. Secondly, the electoral system excludes the highest office of governance – the presidency - from direct elections. This seems to de-motivate a large section of the population from being actively involved in elections. From the 2002 DRP research, it is clear that the majority of the Botswana population supported direct elections to the office of president. As the Botswana Constitution gives the president wide and extensive executive powers, it is imperative for there to be direct competition for the position to enhance democracy and good governance.

Thirdly, it seems that voters disengage from the political process because of the apparent domination by one party for more than 40 years of democratic rule. The BDP has been in power since the first democratic elections in 1965. Un-balanced competition is a disincentive to voters as the outcome is certain. The BDP has massive resources that come from big business in the country. In 1999 it received a huge donation from a covert source outside the country. (Some commentators have alleged that the source of the money is De Beers Mining Company, owner of all diamond mining in the country.) The political playing field is very uneven and exacerbated by the BDP government's reluctance to adopt the idea of state funding of political parties in Botswana. In addition, the poor state of our opposition political parties adds to the woes of the electorate. Fragmentation of opposition parties in Botswana has led to continued domination by the ruling BDP, leading to cynicism and disappointment of a substantial proportion of the population. The opportunity to effect a change of representatives at both national and local government levels has been an incentive for many to take part in elections, for example in the 1990s, in Kenya, Malawi, South Africa and Zambia.

The weaknesses of political parties in Botswana must be taken into account in any analysis of voter disengagement in the political process. Political parties in Botswana have displayed a high degree of authoritarianism in leadership, structures and procedures (Neocosmos, 2002). Political leaders' behaviour, attitudes, and activities have led people to perceive them as untrustworthy as they make promises that are not fulfilled. Hence potential voters shun the elections because of lack of confidence in political leaders and institutions. Another accusation levelled against politicians and government institutions is that they serve their own interests at the expense of public interest. The ascendance to political office in Botswana is perceived as one way to enrichment and self-aggrandisement. Additionally, political parties often field uninspiring candidates who fail ultimately to stimulate voters' interest or excitement. Weak candidates who are unable to attract more supporters are another obstacle to the participation of a large number of voters. Campaigns of political parties are often abusive, negative and rarely based on substantive issues.

Another reason for voter apathy in Botswana relates to the electoral law that limits the time the polls are opened on Election Day – 6.30 a.m. to 7.00 p.m. In towns and big villages, some potential voters work long hours and commute long distances to work, hence they may not have adequate time to cast their ballots. There is thus clearly a need to reform the electoral system and parliamentary institutions in order to restore confidence and integrity in the political system in the country and motivate more citizens to take part in elections. Under Botswana's 'First-past-the-post' electoral system, election outcomes do not accurately reflect voter preferences except in a two-person race. In the 1999 general election in Botswana, the ruling BDP received 54 per cent of the votes, which was translated into 83 per cent of parliamentary seats, while the Botswana National Party (BNF) had 25 per cent of the vote but only 15 per cent of the seats. Furthermore, the Botswana Congress Party (BCP) got 11 per cent of total votes but received 2 per cent of parliamentary seats. This type of system distorts the interests and aspirations of voters, hence some may disengage from the political process. Distortions from the 'First–past-the-post' electoral system reduce voter choices, hence some may feel their votes will be wasted because they are casting a vote for a losing candidate.

THE IMPORTANCE OF VOTER EDUCATION – EFFORTS BY GOVERNMENT AND CIVIL SOCIETY

The seriousness of national voter apathy can no longer be ignored. The Botswana government has an increasing obligation to improve voter turnout in elections because the legitimacy of the government is derived from substantial citizen participation in political activities. The government has entrusted the Independent Electoral Commission with voter education with the goal of arresting political apathy and the alienation of voters from the electoral process. Due to the mammoth task envisaged in the process of voter and political education, the IEC has turned to civic society organisations for assistance. Voter education is a new phenomenon in Botswana. Before the 1999 election, there was little emphasis on this area. More attention was devoted to public information on registration and voting process. Many Batswana are disengaging not only from voting but also from civic activities. Community service is no longer a cherished endeavour for many people.

The point is that low voter turnout and civic disengagement need to be addressed as a matter of urgency. Botswana has long been described by many commentators as a shining example of democracy, good governance and prudent financial management. In sustaining this reputation, the importance of voter education in particular and civic education in general can not be over-emphasised. The outcome of any election has an impact on all the people in the county, not only in terms of taxation but also in terms of policies and programmes in key areas such as education, health, security, social welfare, environment and transport. It should be emphasised that improving voter participation in elections will not be easy, or attained at once or solved overnight. It will require a broad based approach and innovative strategies as the reasons for voter apathy are many and varied. There is need for deeper understanding of the contributing factors and the analysis of possible solutions. Declining voter turnout is a serious issue, but most of the causes of voter apathy and alienation are not easy to reverse. However, the central point is that voter education must be the main antidote to voter apathy and voter disengagement from the political process.

ASSESSMENT AND EFFORTS

It has been said that, 'A free society must rely on the knowledge, skills, and virtue of its citizens and those they elect to public office', (Centre for Civic Education). After the 1965 election, there was apparent lack of investment in preparing eligible voters to register and cast their ballots. It was wrongly assumed that democracy was self-perpetuating. But it is now recognised that the government and other stakeholders should be committed to financing programmes that educate citizens about their rights and responsibilities. Voter awareness is important to motivate as many eligible voters as possible to be ready, willing and able to participate in the political process governing the country. The legitimacy of the government in power as well as the integrity of the electoral process is at stake if many people shun elections. In addition, representative democracy and accountability of government officials could be compromised if less people go to the polls to elect representatives. This will invariably lead to declining engagement of citizens with government and its agencies leading to people simply being spectators in policy-making in the country.

The other point is that elections should allow all eligible voters, irrespective of gender, race, socio-economic status and political affiliation to vote on an equal basis. In order to make informed decisions however, voters should be aware of the purpose of elections, their voting rights and obligations, range of electoral procedures and options. In effect, if electorate is ignorant of the election process, voter apathy becomes pronounced, large numbers of spoilt ballots become the norm, lack of confidence creeps in and the integrity of the electoral process becomes questionable. In the end, the results of the elections are in doubt and the stability of a country might be in danger.

STAKEHOLDERS IN VOTER EDUCATION: THE ROLE OF CIVIL SOCIETY ORGANISATIONS

Though the IEC has the legal responsibility for and authority over voter education, civil society organisations can play a significant role too. There is an increasing need for policy dialogue between the government, the IEC and civil society on the issue of voter education. The mobilisation of civil society organisations in election year is crucial for voter education activities. These organisations have the capacity, skills, resources and voluntary ethos to be able to reach diverse groups in society. The IEC should ensure the engagement and participation of civil society in the formulation, implementation and monitoring of strategies for educational development. Civil society organisations include, campaign networks, teacher organisations, student representative bodies, religious organisations, political parties, youth organisations, women's organisations, trade unions, professional bodies, and social movements. All these bodies are closer to the grassroots, and hence are able to transmit effective information to the population scattered across the whole country.

It is important to emphasise that a strong and vibrant civil society engaged in a diverse range of public activities is essential for a healthy democracy, allowing Botswana society to articulate their concerns to all levels of government. Civil society organisations can ensure public accountability by government and its agencies to the population. In addition, they can increase voter awareness in elections as well as keeping political parties focused on the socio-economic and political concerns of citizens. It is clear that civil society in Botswana is weak and few Batswana participate in political activities. There is a particularly notable drop in membership of political parties as well as civic organisations. Therefore, it can be said that if many people start to leave political life, the basis of representative democracy is under serious threat.

Various groups of civil society may be mobilised country-wide to disseminate electoral information to reach far and wide to the whole population of the country. Some of these organisations pursue special interests that can conduct voter education and mobilise their own constituencies. Examples of these groups may include youth voters, women voters, rural voters, disabled voters and minorities.

YOUTH VOTER EDUCATION PROGRAMME

The political indifference of youth is a worrying phenomenon in Botswana as will be shown in detail in another chapter. The fact that Botswana has a predominantly young population means that there is an urgent need to engage as many young people as possible in the political process for the future of the country. These young men and women are the future leaders of the country who should be encouraged to participate actively in the election process. The IEC should strive to reach the youth as they constitute a substantial number of eligible voters and are mostly affected by the socio-economic and political decisions made by the government. It should collaborate with the Botswana National Youth Council (BNYC) to motivate young voters to participate actively in the election process of the country to lend legitimacy to the elections. The BNYC (*The Reporter, Mmegi Wa Dikgang,* 2003) has conducted a series of Leadership Development Workshops throughout the country aimed at empowering those young people who were interested in standing for political offices in the 2004 general election. This is one way of encouraging the youth to participate in the electoral process as voters as well as candidates.

The development of information technology provides a valuable opportunity to engage the youth in the political process. The influence of the internet on the younger generation is profound. The IEC may use this mode of communication as a means to promote political debate and exchange of information and ideas on the election process. The electoral management body has designed a website but it has not been used to arouse the political interests of the youth. In addition, Botswana has a number of popular music stars that are highly influential to young people. The electoral management body should use these public entertainers as ambassadors to arouse the interests of young people.

Lastly, it is argued that civic education in primary and secondary curricula must be introduced to enhance political education from an early age. Our young people should understand how our democracy operates and know their political rights and responsibilities as citizens. A democratic nation must place emphasis on the knowledge, skills and virtue of its voting population and those they elect to public office, whether at national or local levels of governance. Schools should develop curricular programmes on civic education and government. The IEC has embarked on a project to assist schools prepared to develop such programmes.

THE ROLE OF THE MEDIA IN VOTER EDUCATION

Botswana, like most countries of the world, does not have laws governing the conduct of the media during elections. The media has an effect upon both the presentation and the outcomes of political canvassing. News reporting can be an asset and at the same time a liability to the electoral process. The media can be an effective channel for information and educational messages to a large audience. Media strategies may embrace radio programmes, television stations, newspapers, magazines and the internet. The media modes of communication do however have their own weaknesses. For example in a society that is rural, illiterate, unemployed and suffers acute poverty and deprivation, the media may not be so effective as a disseminator of election materials to the voters. Yet voter education programmes rely strongly on printed materials, for example: badges, posters, stickers, booklets, banners, comic and picture stories and numerous clothing items. Furthermore, educational methods such as creating information centres and innovative advertisements in places such as billboards, sports facilities and sides of buses, taxis and trains, should be used. Music concerts, plays, dance, street theatres and other forms of artistic and cultural activities should be employed to promote democracy, civic responsibility and voter education.

Kessel (2000:61-62) has rightly pointed out that, 'Media play role as informers, educators and entertainers of the public. Mass media provide information on public policy issues and provide a platform for discussion. Media help empower their audience by making them aware of their civil and political rights and by explaining how and why these rights should be exercised.' The media, whether public or private, has a role to play in the dissemination of electoral information about political parties, candidates, policies and the electoral process of a country. This enables the voter to make an informed choice when casting a valid ballot at election time.

The public broadcasting media was, until the 1990s, a state monopoly and could not be employed for purposes of voter education. Radio Botswana has long been the mouthpiece of government and, by extension, ruling party machinery. The Radio Botswana station has the capacity to reach people who could not otherwise be reached physically by the electoral body and its officials. It plays a critical role in disseminating information to a large audience in most parts of the country. However, Radio Botswana is controlled by the government of the day and is used as a propaganda tool by the ruling party, Botswana Democratic Party (BDP). In the 1990s there was a proliferation of private radio stations in Botswana, mostly concentrated in Gaborone. Their coverage is limited to Gaborone and surrounding villages. In the countryside, the government-controlled Radio Botswana still dominates the political landscape. Nevertheless, some of these privately owned radio stations have programmes that cover civil and political issues but they have tended to concentrate extensively on advertisements because of financial interests or considerations.

With regard to the print media, the government newspaper, *The Daily News*, was the sole paper available to disseminate information to the public until the 1980s. It is a daily paper that is distributed freely. It has extensive coverage, unlike independent newspapers that are accessed at a price. Private newspapers mushroomed in the 1980s, for example, *The Reporter*, *Mmegi Wa Dikgang*, and *The Botswana Guardian*.

As part of the public information programme, the IEC necessarily has to involve the private press, media and wire services. Different media houses should be paid to take an active role in informing and motivating people to participate actively in the political process. They should empower the mass media to make voters aware of relevant issues and problems, consequences and costs of present and past policies and alternatives for the future. Educating voters about their inalienable rights and obligations in a representative democracy is an essential component of building a viable and vibrant civil society.

As noted earlier, the mass media has its own weaknesses, for example, its inability to reach all parts of the country and its emphasis on negative and sometimes biased reporting. In Botswana, the media has done a disservice to the large sections of society through various actions and omissions. News reporting has tended to concentrate on negative campaigns and has often ignored the pertinent issues which underlie the elections. The media coverage of elections in the country has always been mild, thereby contributing to voter alienation and voter apathy. The government-owned media should be required by law to give a fair coverage and equitable access to all competing political parties.

The other important civil society organisations that can have a profound impact on voter education are the religious institutions which have a large following in Botswana. Religious groups have played a large part in voter education in different countries of the world, for example in the United States of America, the United Kingdom, South Africa and Zimbabwe. However, in Botswana, there has been slow participation of religious groups in voter education although the government has not discouraged these spiritual bodies from participation in non-partisan voter education amongst their denominations. It is critical for these bodies to participate in elections in order to impact positively on the future of communities and the nation at large.

It is debatable whether political party organisations should be viewed as part of the civil society. Some perceive political parties as being outside the realm of civil society because their aim is to seize political power, but some define civil society in broader terms to include these political organisations. However, it is clear that political parties are indispensable in conducting voter education as they have the most interest in the political contest. They can explain to people why they should vote, what the procedures of voting are, the importance of the secrecy of the ballot and the general security of elections. Political campaigns attract a lot of attention and political parties have the motivation to urge followers to cast valid ballots as they have close contact with the voting population. Nevertheless, the ability of political parties to conduct voter education is dependent on the availability of resources, human as well as financial. In a country such as Botswana, political parties do not have adequate resources to carry out the mammoth task expected of them. Moreover, political parties are not financed by the state, but have to fend for themselves. They are likely to be more concerned with carrying out programmes that attract more votes for them. They may even be selective, concentrating on constituencies that are deemed most likely to be supportive. Therefore, voter education should ideally be undertaken by non-partisan, civil society organisations.

It is clear from this that there are many opportunities and challenges facing government, political parties, the Independent Electoral Commission and civil society in relation to combating the voter apathy that is injurious to democracy and good governance. Poverty and deprivation in the midst of plenty has to be addressed by both the government and civil society if voter alienation is to be tackled. A state of helplessness and dependency on the handouts by government and NGOs has to be addressed as a matter of urgency, as has the gap between the haves and the have-nots in society that has been widening for decades. In this era of information technology, all necessary means have to be employed to attract voters to register and to vote in the elections. The internet should be used extensively to mobilise the youth and the educated on the importance of elections in a democracy like that in Botswana. The IEC website should include electoral information to be accessed by voters to enable them to make informed choice.

It is recommended that the government, the IEC, and civil society organisations should endeavour to inculcate in the general population a civic education culture in order to foster democratic values and ethics in the country. Voter education should be supplemented and complemented by other interventions in the body polity. All these strategies should ensure large scale participation by citizens in the electoral process. Voter education programmes should take into consideration the unique characteristics of the local population, e.g. language, custom, tradition, beliefs, literacy, economic and social status. The media such as TV and radio stations, newspapers and magazines should be used extensively to encourage voter participation. Additionally, there is need for posting of voting equipment at civic gatherings, local churches, mosques, and synagogues, post offices, stadia, library, and government offices.

REGISTRATION OF VOTERS

Potential voters can be targeted through specially designed information and education campaigns that include advertisements, pamphlets, radio and television programmes, public rallies and information displays at public places. Registration facilities can be provided in places frequented by members of the public, for example, clinics, schools, public fora (Kgotla) and post offices. Registration reforms have to be undertaken to make it easier for potential voters to enlist to qualify to vote in elections. All barriers to registration have to be eliminated or reduced to ensure wide spread participation by eligible voters.

VOTER AND CIVIC EDUCATION

There is a need for continuous voter and civic education in the periods between general elections in order to cultivate awareness among the general population on the role of democratic participation in every facet of their lives. Voter education targets eligible voters by giving them information on electoral laws, electioneering, registration requirements, rights and obligations, voting process, counting and the announcements of results. Civic education, on the other hand deals with broader issues of civility, loyalty, patriotism, rights and obligations of citizens.

CONCLUSION AND RECOMMENDATIONS

In identifying alternative explanations to voter apathy, it has been noted that some of the factors to voter apathy are socio-economic, legal, political, and demographic. It is also noted that to arrest the situation requires a broad based approach that encompasses many variables. All stakeholders in the voter education programmes should be involved in the formulation, implementation, and evaluation of the policy. Voter education is not a panacea for the ills of voter participation in the electoral process. The socio-economic, cultural, and political context varies from time to time and methods must be adapted accordingly. An approach that suits one situation may be doomed to failure in another. Therefore, there are various strategies and methodologies that can be employed by government, IEC, civil society, and many other actors to overcome low voter turnout.

A range of recommendations has been made for effective voter education in Botswana involving all the stakeholders in society. The IEC should issue accreditation to all civil society groups involved in voter education to enable it to monitor and maintain uniformity as well as a high standard of voter awareness. Furthermore, where feasible, the election management body should provide the necessary funding and logistical support to organisations undertaking voter education. The IEC together with stakeholders must develop innovative techniques in their voter education programmes especially in this era of technological revolution.

Electoral and political reforms are critical for the health of Botswana's democracy so revered by many in the developing countries. These electoral and political reforms should aim to make elections more competitive, as well as political institutions more responsive and relevant to citizens' needs and aspirations. Popular trust in political institutions such as the legislative and executive branches of government and electoral process in the country may lead to more citizens taking an interest in elections.

Finally, the introduction of civic education into the national curriculum of primary and secondary schools is long overdue in Botswana. There is a need to build the civic responsibilities of the population from an early age in order to enhance long term popular participation in the political process. In addition to civic education, voter education programmes would contribute to specific issues pertaining to the electoral process. There should be thorough implementation and evaluation of voter education programmes. Moreover, adequate planning and funding for voter education activities is important to realise voter awareness and voter participation in the electoral process.

REFERENCES

Holm, J. & Molutsi, P. (eds) (1988) *Democracy in Botswana, The Proceedings of a Symposium held in Gaborone*, 1 – 5 August 1988: Macmillan Botswana (Pty), Ltd, Gaborone

IEC, *Civic and Voter Education Curriculum: The Road to 2004 General Elections*

IEC, News Letter vol. 2 2002

IEC, (2002) *Voter Apathy Report: an abridged version*, Gaborone, IEC.

IEC, (1999) *Report to His Honour the Vice President and Minister of Presidential Affairs and Public Administration on the general elections 1999*, Government Printer: Gaborone

Kessel, I. (2000) 'Stability or Democracy: on the Role of Monitors, Media and Miracles'. in J. Abbink and G. Hesseling (eds) *Election Observation and Democracy in Africa*, Basingstoke: Macmillan

Neo Cosmos, M. (2002) 'The Politics of National Elections in Botswana, Lesotho and Swaziland' in M. Cowen and L. Laako (eds) *Multiparty Elections in Africa*, New York: Palgrave

NGOs and Civil Society: Realities and Distortions (http://laetusinpraesens.org/docs/ngocivil.php)

The Botswana Reporter (Mmegi Wa Dikgang) newspaper, Opinion, 23-29 May 2003

Reynolds, A. (1999) *Electoral Systems and Democratisation in Southern Africa*, Oxford: Oxford University Press

Soiri, I. 2000 'SWAPO Wins, Apathy Rules: The Namibian 1998 Local Authority Election, in Cowen, M & Laakso, L. *Multiparty Elections in Africa*, Oxford: James Curry

CHAPTER 10

CIVIL SOCIETY AND DEMOCRACY IN BOTSWANA

Zibani Maundeni

INTRODUCTION

The central focus in this chapter is to assess the extent to which civic organisations in Botswana were involved in the democratisation process, broadly defined to mean reducing the dominance of government officials in the development process and increasing the participation of civic players. The argument is that the non-partisan character of Botswana's civic organisations has not prevented them from participating actively in democratising the public space. What follows is a literature review and an analysis of the involvement of individual civic organisations in the democratisation process.

The literature on civil society in Botswana is disappointingly limited. The first serious scholar to write about civil society in Botswana was John Holm (1989). His initial concern was with economic interest groups and their interaction with the state. The second work by John Holm and Patrick Molutsi was on state-civil society relations (1992). It was not until the holding of a 'civil society conference' which was organised by the Democracy Research Project (DRP) in 1995 and the production of a Conference Proceedings Report in 1996 that more articles appeared on civil society in Botswana.

It appears that the only substantive research on civil society that exists is based on three surveys conducted by the DRP, in 1987, 1991 and 1994, respectively. The latest article by former DRP coordinators, Holm, Molutsi and Somolekae in 1996, have concentrated on assessing organisational development, or lack of it, for civil society. It sought to answer three relevant questions, in order of importance: (a) what types of organisational development are required to create a civil society in a democratising African state? (b) What was the effect of political democracy on the emergence of a civil society? and (c) What was the possible impact of a nascent civil society on democratic practice?

The three former coordinators of the DRP observed that Botswana operated a paternalistic democracy characterised by a weak civil society that lobbied the bureaucracy rather than the politicians and was hesitant to engage in partisan politics (Holm, Molutsi and Somolekae, 1996). They argued that organisational development, characterised by continuous organisation, permanence of office and partisanship, was a necessary ingredient to a dynamic civil society. 'When this type of institutionalisation exists, even authoritarian regimes, such as the one in apartheid South Africa, give grudging recognition to civil society' (Holm, Molutsi and Somolekae, 1996: 43-4). However, the authors noted the absence of the ingredients that strengthened civil society in Botswana. They observed that civil society in Botswana was characterised by ad hoc ways of organising or 'adhocracy'.

> 'The existence of almost any group is not certain. Many groups can best be characterised as ad hoc. They have spurts of activity to address particular problems. Committees meet, leaders publish a newsletter, supporters turnout in sizeable numbers for group events. Then, the organisation goes into decline. Top leaders do not even show up to make reports. Committees never meet. Grass roots involvement is minuscule.' (Holm, Molutsi and Somolekae, 1996: 49).

In addition, they observed that the groups were non-partisan and hardly engaged the state (Holm, Molutsi and Somolekae, 1996). That is, they did not align with any political party and distanced themselves from party politics. These were findings based on the 1991 survey.

In contrast, the 'Civil Society and Democracy in Botswana' conference of 1995 sought: (a) to examine the relationship between the state and civil society; (b) to explain why civil society remained weak in many post-colonial African societies; (c) to establish whether the solution to the weakness of civil society lay in external intervention or in internal organisation; and (d) to establish the extent to which different interest groups worked together to influence government policy (Somolekae, 1996). The conference was based on a survey conducted in 1994. Patrick Molutsi's presentation at that conference focused onto the structure of the civil society in Botswana. He began by discussing the origins of the concept of civil society, linking it with George Hegel's dichotomisation of society into the political and the non-political, and finally arriving at civil society. Molutsi's essay also explored the origin of the concept in Africa linking it with the 'Civil Society Project in Africa', that was initiated by donor agencies through the conference on 'Civil Society, Democracy and Development' that was held in Washington D.C in 1994. His argument was that civil society was imported by donor agencies into Africa in response to the crisis of the African state. This fair observation links African NGOs to their western counterparts who are sometimes also the sponsors.

Patrick Molutsi also studied the structure of civil society in Botswana, observing that 'more striking about the structure of Botswana's civil society is that some 78 per cent of the organisations fall under what can be called "apolitical welfarist organisations". While it is controversial to classify organisations in terms of political and apolitical and while the reality is more fluid, past experience supports the general conclusion that most of the organisations in the three categories of burial, sporting and religious have on the whole been more inward looking and less engaging when it comes to policy issues' (Molutsi, 1996: 61). Patrick Molutsi's finding on the non-partisan character of Botswana's NGOs was confirmed in a workshop organised by Botswana Council of Non-Governmental organisations in 2002, where leaders of civic organisations were conspicuously non-partisan in their outlook. But does it really mean that non-partisan civic organisations have an insignificant role in the democratisation process, as Patrick Molutsi suggests? For instance, has the role of the non-partisan DRP and other non-partisan civic organisations, been insignificant in the democratisation process in Botswana? This issue occupies the central focus of this chapter.

Mpho Molomo's presentation at the 'Civil Society and Democracy' conference also discussed the origins of the civil society concept, tying it to the liberal philosophical traditions of Thomas Hobbes and John Locke on the one hand, and to the communitarian ideas of George Hegel, Karl Marx and Antonio Gramsci, on the other. He further discussed state-civil society interaction in Africa and observed that 'because of the wanting political and economic situation, it would appear organs of civil society are always on a war path with the state. Another factor that appears to be a thorn in the flesh of most governments in Africa is the sympathy that the organs of civil society enjoy from donor agencies and international organisations' (Molomo, 1996: 46). According to Molomo, the worsening political and economic situation in Africa has combined with the fact that donors favour civil society, to generate confrontational politics between civil society and the African states. This may be the case in other African settings, but Molomo did not discuss the supposed confrontation, or lack of it, between civil society and the Botswana state. This leaves a gap that should be filled.

Yet some authors in other settings, such as Sierra Leone, observed 'exit', where families and businesses disengaged from the economically failing and oppressive state, and engaged in the politics of avoidance, such as through informal businesses, tax evasion, voter apathy etc. This chapter will test whether 'exit' was a viable option in Botswana's democratic politics.

More important is the fact that the surveys that provided the material for both the joint article by Holm, Molutsi and Somolekae, by Molutsi and by Molomo were conducted at the beginning of the democratisation movement that was sweeping the whole world some twenty years ago. Other material from these authors was based on findings from surveys in 1991 and 1994. There is no doubt, therefore, that the material needs updating. Democratisation has been ongoing since the late 1980s. Thus, there is no doubt that Botswana's socio-economic and political settings have changed over the years, and that civil society has changed its orientation. In the next section, the role of civic organisations in the democratisation process is discussed.

CIVIC ORGANISATIONS IN THE DEMOCRATISATION PROCESS

This section considers the democratising activities of the Democracy Research project (DRP), Emang Basadi, Ditshwanelo, Botswana National Youth Council, trade unions and the Botswana Council of Non-Governmental Organisations. It shows that these have shed their image of weakness and that they have played an important role in the process of democratising the various sectors that constitute the Botswana society.

DRP and the democracy process

In 1987, John Holm of Cleveland State University of the USA cooperated with nine University of Botswana academics in a year-long study that culminated in a national symposium. From this was established the Democracy Project, now known as the Democracy Research Project (DRP). This group of academics has literally led the democratisation process in Botswana. The non-partisan, multi-disciplinary DRP research group derived its membership from the faculties of social sciences and humanities and has carried out nationwide surveys on indicators of democracy in Botswana.

The DRP conducted a national symposium in 1988, bringing together academics from the region, civil servants, politicians and journalists to discuss, 'Botswana's experience with democracy since independence' (Molutsi and Holm, 1989: 2). The DRP's non-partisan orientation was primarily responsible for bringing together different stakeholders who would otherwise never meet. In fact, the organisers expected that, 'the debate at the symposium would set in motion discussion about ways in which Botswana's democracy might be improved' (Molutsi and Holm, 1989: 3). Thus, the non-partisan organisers sought to, and did, spark a democratisation debate nationally.

Three things stand out from the initial symposium: (i) non-partisan academics, organised on an 'adhocracy' basis, had conducted a survey whose findings served as the backbone for the historic symposium on the state of democracy in Botswana. That is, an ad hoc and non-partisan academic research group set the agenda for the whole democratisation process; (ii) for the first time in the democratic history of Botswana, politicians, academics, civil servants, journalists and traditional chiefs, were brought together in a forum in which government politicians and officials did not exercise control over its proceedings. Academics, rather than state officials, exercised leadership over this historic symposium that enabled the stakeholders to interact and publicly deliberate on the state of democracy in Botswana; and (iii) academics from the African continent and those from the most mature working democracy in Africa, Botswana, were brought together. This unique experience compelled the former to re-think the application of democracy in Africa. Thus, the DRP, a civic academic group acted as a democratising force for the whole African continent.

The DRP was later consolidated into a formal group of indigenous academics whose activities were sponsored neither by the government nor by the university. It continued to rely on donor funding. Moreover, the DRP's membership remained full-time employees of the university. Thus, the DRP did not enjoy the 'organisational development' that John Holm, Patrick Molutsi and Gloria Somolekae assumed was crucial for impacting on state policy. However, it must be acknowledged that the DRP's 'adhocracy' status hindered it from growing into a formal 'democracy research institute' such as the electoral institute of southern Africa. It has therefore not become a formal autonomous institution, with a full-time director and permanent staff who could have taken it to greater heights, fully commercialised and with a self-supporting budget based on the services it offered.

However, the 'adhocracy' structure and donor-based sponsorship of the DRP did not deter it from influencing the democratisation process. It continued to conduct surveys, organise conferences and workshops on various aspects of democratisation and it continued to actively encourage debates among councillors and parliamentarians on ways of improving democracy in Botswana. The DRP organised separate workshops for councillors and parliamentarians on 'mass mobilisation and campaign strategies' in 1989. Such separate workshops were significant in another sense as not only did the workshop for the councillors provide the ingredients for autonomous development, it also provided the ingredients for checks and balances between councillors and parliamentarians. Indeed, the councillors called for the right to be heard over the state-run Radio Botswana which has previously been dominated by parliamentarians. Councillors insisted that 'Radio Botswana should develop a programme for the councillors, a facility which is presently a monopoly of parliamentarians' (Molomo and Mokopakgosi, 1990: 20). In other words, the DRP was giving councillors a forum to debate national and theoretical issues and to voice their grievances. Such a democratising process was significant for Botswana where democracy is highly centralised.

The DRP also introduced debates on the electoral system, particularly on proportional representation and on gender. In the latter case, the DRP was well positioned because two of its leading members – Dr Ataliah Molokomme and Dr Gloria Somolekae are renowned gender activists who had also formed the *Emang Basadi* women's association in 1986. The DRP introduced gender concepts to Botswana politics and provided the empirical data that enriched the democratisation debates. Furthermore, the DRP observed primary elections and general elections at a time when the international community gave little attention to the Botswana political system. These were important political areas that were at the heart of the democratisation process. In 1990, The DRP also released its 'Report on the primaries held in 1989 in Botswana'. This report that was authored by Mogopodi Lekorwe and Patrick Mgadla, made important observations that helped in further democratising the primaries in subsequent years.

The DRP organised a conference on 'civil society and democracy in Botswana at the end of 1995 where detailed discussions were conducted on the theory and structure of civil society organisations in Botswana. DRP academics presented papers and different NGO leaders made comments. By organising such a conference, the DRP helped to establish what constituted civil society, and brought different civic organisations together for the first time. The indirect result of this was the formation of the Botswana Council of Non-Governmental Organisations (BOCONGO) that has become a significant player in the policy process. Lastly, the DRP has now authored a book, the impact of which will be felt over many years.

Ditshwanelo

(Much of what follows is based on an interview between the author and the Director of Ditshwanelo on 17 April 2003)

Ditshwanelo is a non-partisan and non-membership NGO that focuses on the protection of human rights. It does not rely on a large base of human rights activists in the manner that trade unions do with employees and has no membership to fund its activities. It is a small service NGO that seeks to protect the marginalised and the poor. It distances itself from political parties and does not take any government funding even if it could be offered. It is a small and seriously under-resourced NGO that finds it extremely difficult to raise funds locally, as the local business community always wants to know the position of government on a particular issue before donating funds. But Ditshwanelo has played a central role in the democratisation process in Botswana.

One of Ditshwanelo's biggest constituencies, and a central focus of the organisation, has been the marginalised community of the Basarwa, or San, who faced eviction and forced removals from the Central Kalahari Game Reserve (CKGR), their ancestral lands. Ditshwanelo was also concerned about the human rights violations of the Basarwa in other areas. The Department of Wildlife officers suspected the Basarwa of poaching, but Ditshwanelo accused the Department of Wildlife of heavy-handedness in its dealings with the Basarwa.

Ditshwanelo also targeted its campaigns on the death penalty. Following the execution of a human rights activist in Nigeria in 1994, Ditshwanelo has placed the death penalty on the Botswana national agenda. At the time of the execution, Ditshwanelo issued a press statement condemning the death sentence and organised panel discussions on the death penalty. The execution by the Botswana government of Marietta Borsch, a white South African woman accused of murdering her friend, provided Ditshwanelo and other sectors of the international community with powerful material to emphasise the worst side of the death penalty. The hanging was carried out in secret, disregarding her relatives' appeals for mercy to the president. It was also done hastily at a sensitive time when President Festus Mogae was promoting 'diamonds for development' in Europe. The news of the execution, which took place over the weekend was only released on the following Monday, coinciding with the time when President Mogae would have boarded his flight back to Botswana, thus avoiding European journalists. However, this did not prevent a domestic and international uproar against Botswana's death penalty. Ditshwanelo and the print media seized on the opportunity presented by irregularities in the execution to keep the issue of the death penalty on the national agenda for some time. It is however interesting to note that a law reform commission convened after the execution of Borsch found that the majority of Batswana still favoured the death penalty.

Ditshwanelo has also focussed on protecting people living with HIV/AIDS and this has presented an additional constituency for it to work for and protect. Ditshwanelo issued press statements on the human rights of people living with HIV/AIDS and lobbied against mandatory testing, and the discrimination of HIV/AIDS patients by health staff and in the work place. It stressed that health staff should treat patients equally and without favour and also emphasised the importance of confidentiality by health staff who were treating HIV/AIDS patients. Ditshwanelo made the point that testing was a personal decision which only the individual had the right to make, and that the revelation of one's HIV/AIDS status was an individual choice and human right.

However, Ditshwanelo has concerns that the Botswana government is still not committed to the protection of human rights. 'Ditshwanelo has not succeeded in bringing a different orientation in the thinking of government on issues of human rights. It is very difficult to find a meeting point when discussing human rights with government officials'. If Botswana cannot change its orientation and adopt a positive attitude towards human rights, globalisation will bring in international organisations such as Survival International. These organisations engage in tough tactics which could include staging vigils at Botswana's embassies abroad and at international forums where members of the Botswana government are in attendance.

The Botswana National Youth Council

The Botswana National Youth Council (BNYC) can be described as a quasi-NGO. It was set up through a Presidential Directive in 1974. However, its policy making structure, the Annual General Assembly, is elected from leaders of affiliate youth organisations and of District Youth Councils. The Botswana government largely funds the BNYC, but does not fund its political empowerment programme. Thus donors, particularly the Friedrich Ebert Foundation, wholly funded the BNYC's 2003 political empowerment programme which involved holding workshops for youth intending to contest the primary elections and the 2004 general election. Around a hundred youthful politicians from different political parties attended the BNYC empowerment workshops held in Gaborone, Palapye, Jwaneng and Maun between April and May 2003. These workshops had a revolutionary effect in that the youth came out to demonstrate their intention to be leaders of today not of tomorrow – as is made clear in the BNYC mission statement.

When the BNYC held its fourth political youth empowerment workshop in Maun on the 20-21 May 2003, the main political parties were already reacting negatively, which indicated that the workshops were having an impact. For instance, the ruling BDP reacted by establishing nomination fees for candidates wishing to contest in the party primary elections. The fee was a non-refundable P500.00 for primary election candidates whose success would enable them to stand for council wards in the 2004 general election (*Mmegi Monitor*, 21st May 2003). The other fee was fixed at a high figure of P1 000.00 for candidates wishing to stand for primary elections that would allow them to contest for parliamentary seats in the 2004 general election. By fixing the nomination fees so high, the BDP was trying to control the 'influx' of young people who would have been encouraged by the BNYC political empowerment workshops.

In the case of the BNF some party leaders such as the late Information Secretary, Mareledi Giddie, accused the BNYC of inciting young people for purposes of destabilising opposition parties. These influential BNF leaders were of the view that the veteran BNF politicians should be given priority in order to enter parliament and represent the party mission properly.

The BNYC has also played a crucial role in democratising the Botswana public health system to help make it youth-friendly. 'Our health system was hostile and not youth-friendly. Health staff would ask embarrassing questions to the youth, such as, how could you have contacted venereal diseases when you were so young'. The BNYC intervened to influence the public health system to make it user friendly to the youth. Such intervention is already bearing fruits. For instance, recently, the government asked the Botswana Family Welfare Association to set up youth health clinics. One has been set up at the Botswana Youth Centre in Gaborone. The BNYC has convinced the Family Health Division of the Ministry of Health, to re-train nurses to ensure they have a positive approach towards the youth. They are re-training them and this is a major success' (The Director of BNYC, personal interview with the author, 17 April, 2003).

The other area where the BNYC has proved itself concerned the government proposals to reform the Land Board Act, intending to increase the age entry point for those who could be elected. The BNYC opposed the age entry point of 30 years that was proposed by the government and instead proposed 18 years as the age entry point. The BNYC issued a press release on the issue, and mobilised a group of young people to visit the Minister of Lands, Margaret Nasha. It also mobilised young people to attend kgotla (traditional village assembly) meetings and to oppose the government proposals. The BNYC addressed district council meetings in a number of places, urging councillors to oppose government proposals that were youth-unfriendly. The end result was a compromise decision, fixing the age entry point at 26 years.

Trade Unions

Trade unions are internationally recognised as an important element of organised civil society. They are 'membership' organisations that partly depend on membership dues to finance their activities. The most significant unionised sector has proved to be the teaching profession. The teachers unions, the Botswana Teachers Union (BTU) with 11 000 members, the Botswana Federation of Secondary Teachers (BOFESETE with 3 000 members and the Botswana Primary Teachers association (BOPRITA) have flourished. While BOFESETE and BOPRITA represent the interests of secondary and primary teachers, respectively, BTU represents those of primary, secondary and tertiary teachers. The teaching establishment stands at 22 000. This is a large constituency deserving two or three unions.

Yet the Botswana educational system was such that teachers neither participated in the policy-making organs nor in designing the syllabuses that they taught (The vice president of BOFESETE, personal interview with the author, 15 April, 2003). In the early period of Botswana's independence each administrative district council hired and fired its own teaching staff and hence, the conditions of service varied. Even the transfer of teachers was localised to each administrative district council. Even after 35 years of independence, teachers in the Gantsi District Council were denied the right to be transferred to other districts.

Recently in the Okavango and Nhabe areas, teachers were denied the same rights of transferring outside the district. They were being circulated in the same district. The BTU wants the district-based transfer system to be democratised such that a teacher could be transferred to any part of the country. It met the ministry of education officials and suggested that teachers should stay in one school for three years and school heads should stay for five years after which they should be transferable anywhere in the country (the administrative secretary of BTU, personal interview with the author, 14 April, 2003). In contrast, BOFESETE was of the view that transfers were used for punitive purposes to punish some teachers who lost favour with the transferring officers (the vice president of BOFESETE, personal interview with author, 15 April, 2003). The above noted that transfer problems happened despite the fact that the Teaching Service Management was the central employer for all teachers. It had replaced the Unified Teaching Service, the successor to the district-based employment system.

The teaching management that encompasses school heads was also active in the BTU as it faced transfer problems emanating from the principle of the 'level of operation'. According to this principle, schools are classified according to the number of students and fall in three categories. Those with student numbers above a certain level are classified as 'Group One' schools. Others are 'Group Two' and 'Group Three' schools, proportionately to their student population. The result of the classification is that head teachers are not transferable between different categories of schools (the administrative secretary, BTU, personal interview with the author, 14 April, 2003). The different categories of schools even determined the pay rates for the head teachers. The BTU was opposed to a categorisation system that brought divisions into the teaching fraternity. These were some of the central democratisation issues that the teaching unions were sponsoring. But it should be emphasised that all the teaching unions were able to maintain their non-partisan approach, although they also failed to form an umbrella body. The need for an umbrella body is evidenced by BOFESETE which has now joined BOCONGO.

Botswana Council of Non-Governmental Organisations

In 1995, Botswana's NGOs met and decided to form an umbrella body where they could share experiences and chart a common destiny. The mother body came to be known as the Botswana Council of Non-Governmental Organisations (BOCONGO). It is a non-partisan council, consisting of over 70 NGOs from various fields, such as youth, human rights, health, trade, environment, publishing and so on. BOCONGO's goals are to assist member NGOs through capacity building, networking and information dissemination, and policy advocacy. However, BOCONGO has no political empowerment programmes and does not mobilise resources for purposes of influencing voting in the general elections. This may be explained by the fact that the Botswana government funds half the salaries of BOCONGO's secretariat and donors such as the African Development Foundation, fund specific projects (Networking and Information Dissemination Officer of BOCONGO, personal interview with the author, 26 May 2003).

This does not mean that BOCONGO has no role in the democratisation process. It sits in the 2016 Vision Council. This is the organ that is tasked with monitoring the implementation of Botswana's long-term vision that defines what the country would want to look like in 2016. Thus, through BOCONGO, the NGO sector has a permanent representation in the 2016 Vision Council and its views form part of the vision. BOCONGO also participated in the electoral reform workshop organised by the Independent Electoral Commission in February 2002 and observed the 1999 general elections. It also participated in the Emang Basadi political empowerment workshops that the Electoral Institute of Southern Africa facilitated in May 2003.

BOCONGO organised a breakfast show in which it invited political researchers

(Doctors Ian Taylor and Zibani Maundeni) from the University of Botswana to address NGO leaders on the Iraq war. Two important things took place at the breakfast show: The first was that after the researchers had given their presentation, NGO leaders released a press statement on the war. The second thing was that BOCONGO alerted the NGO leaders of, and urged them to attend, the 'war prayers' organised by the main churches in front of the parliament building. These activities demonstrated the NGOs' opposition to the war.

In November 2002, BOCONGO also organised an NGO week in Maun village, some 900 kms away from Gaborone. Maun was chosen because BOCONGO had planned to take the NGOs to the people. The NGO week was meant to sensitise ordinary people to the activities of NGOs and how they could benefit them and to the New Partnership for Africa's Development (NEPAD). By taking NGOs and NEPAD to the rural areas, BOCONGO was providing a forum through which rural people could learn more about them and about what Africa was doing to uplift itself from poverty.

Above all, BOCONGO has assisted member NGOs to improve their administrative capacity and their networking with other agencies involved in the development of the country. For instance, 'since the beginning of 2002, BOCONGO has completed training courses in the following areas: financial management, organisational development, marketing skills, public policy analysis, facilitation techniques (training of trainers), networking and secretariat coordination, advocacy and lobbying, NGO management and governance, project design and proposal writing, fundraising and participatory development methodologies' (BOCONGO, 2002: 10). BOCONGO has also provided computer courses, such as utilising the internet and e-mail facilities, to its member NGOs. It has access to websites of international NGOs where it taps information for use by its member NGOs. These benefits that NGO members enjoy from the parent body help to improve their capacity and help them to participate actively in the national policy process and the development of the country.

CONCLUSION

This chapter has analysed the involvement of organised civil society in the democratisation process in Botswana. One crucial point emerging is that 'exit', or disengaging from the formal sector, has not been an option for the non-partisan organised civic organisations which have been surveyed in Botswana. Engaging the state in a non-partisan manner has been a characteristic of all these organisations. All of them have actively promoted the interests of their constituencies and have engaged the state in order to achieve their goals.

The second point is that Botswana's civic organisations have been less confrontational with one another and with the state and have been more integrated in working together and with the government. They formed BOCONGO bringing more than 70 civic organisations together and they have participated in shared forums with government officials. Thus, the 'war' that Mpho Molomo observed in other parts of Africa was absent in the context of Botswana where there was less aggression from either the government or the NGO sector.

The third point is that the Botswana Government partly funded some NGOs and international donors have wholly funded others. In contrast, membership-based civic organisations such as trade unions remained free of both government and international donors. However, non-membership-based organisations which turned down government funding remain ill-resourced. It is not clear whether the source of funding had an effect or not on the character of the civic organisations concerned. The fact is that Botswana civic organisations engage in mass action only as a last resort, regardless of the source of funding. The other fact is that since the withdrawal of most donors from the Botswana economy, funding has become an extremely scarce resource and the government is increasingly becoming the main sponsor of NGO non-political activities.

REFERENCES

BOCONGO, (2002) Annual Report, Gaborone: BOCONGO

Administrative Secretary, BTU, personal interview with the author, 14 April 2003.

Networking and Information Dissemination Officer, BOCONGO, personal interview with the author, 26 May, 2003.

Holm, J. (1989) 'How Effective Are Interest Groups' in J. Holm and P. Molutsi (eds) *Democracy In Botswana*, Gaborone: Macmillan Botswana: 142-155.

Holm, J. and P. Molutsi (1992) 'State-Society Relations In Botswana: Beginning Of Liberalisation'; in G. Hyden and M. Bratton (eds) *Governance In Africa*, Boulder and London: Lynne Rienner: 75-95.

Holm, J., P. Molutsi and G. Somolekae (1996) 'The Development of Civil Society in a Democratic State: the Botswana Model', *African Studies Review*, 39,2: 43 – 69.

Mokopakgosi, B.T and Molomo, M.G. (Ed) (1991) *Multi-Party Democracy in Botswana*, Harare: Sapes Books

Molomo, M. (1996) 'Theoretical and Conceptual Issues about Civil Society', in G. Somolekae (Ed) *Civil Society and Democracy in Botswana: Proceedings of a conference held from 25 – 27 October 1995*, Oasis Motel: 35 – 51.

Molutsi, P. (1996) 'The Civil Society and Democracy in Botswana' in G. Somolekae (Ed) *Civil Society and Democracy in Botswana: Proceedings of a conference held from 25 – 27 October 1995*, Oasis Motel: 52 – 66.

Molutsi, P. and J. Holm (1989) 'Introduction' in J. Holm and P. Molutsi (eds) *Democracy In Botswana*, Gaborone: Macmillan Botswana: 1-7.

The Director of BNYC, personal interview with the author, 17 April 2003.

The Director of Ditshwanelo, personal interview, 17 April 2003.

Vice President of BOFESETE, personal interview with the author, 15 April, 2003.

CHAPTER 11

WOMEN'S REPRESENTATION IN PARLIAMENT AND COUNCIL: A COMPARATIVE ANALYSIS

Dolly Ntseane and Joel Sentsho

INTRODUCTION

The starting point for this chaptrer is that the under-representation of women in politics and in decision-making is not unique to Botswana. Few women throughout the world occupy positions of power, despite the fact that by 1987 most women were granted the right to vote and to be elected into office by their respective countries (UN, 1988; 1992; 1994; 1995(b); Government of Botswana, 1995; Inter-Parliamentary Union, 1995). In Botswana the recognition of the rights for women to vote and to be elected coincided with independence in 1965. Since then, women have been making strides to gain recognition as equals in decision-making structures. This chapter provides a comprehensive review of the achievements made so far. The analysis begins with a brief discussion on the rationale for equal representation. The international and regional norms that legitimise political participation and representation are then reviewed. Despite numerous political ratifications both at the international and national levels, women are still significantly under-represented in politics, not only in Botswana but also worldwide. A comparative analysis of the participation of women around the world helps us to appreciate the situation of women in the political arena and to learn lessons on how to expand women's representation in Botswana. We conclude by examining barriers and obstacles that contribute to under-representation and suggest ways in which women's participation can be enhanced.

WHY EQUAL REPRESENTATION?

A number of arguments have been advanced as to why women should have equal representation in the political decision machineries. The first commonly cited reason is that women constitute more than half of the voting population in Botswana. As a result, it is in the interest of democratic and egalitarian principles that they should be represented in proportion to their numbers (Republic of Botswana, 2003). President F.G Mogae rightly articulated the point that, 'equality of access to positions of power and decision-making is a matter of fundamental human rights and pre-requisite to democracy' (SADC, 1999:19).

The second argument in favour of equal access to positions of leadership is that women play an active role not only in mobilising support for their political parties but they also vote in large numbers compared to their male counterparts. Data is used from a recently published study on voter apathy which shows that more women were involved in the 1999 voter registration than their male counterparts. Altogether, there were 266 449 registered women voters compared to 214 522 registered male voters (IEC, 2002:51). A closer look at the above figures shows interesting comparisons across districts. For example, the North West district had 24 549 women to 19 941 men who had registered. Kgatleng had 12 808 women and 9 609 men who registered and Central had 80 269 women to 54 286 men. In contrast, more men than women registered to vote in urban centres such as Francistown (11 685 men to 11 017 women), Gaborone (21 643 men to 16 917 women), Lobatse (5 006 men to 4 864 women) and Gantsi (5 252 men to 5 224 women). The figures show that although there is high voter apathy country wide, more women exercised their right to vote in 1999 than men (IEC, 2002). It therefore follows that they are psychologically ready to make a meaningful contribution in parliament and council.

The third argument is that women in Botswana have made significant contributions in the socio-economic, political and cultural development of the nation despite their multiple roles, heavy workloads and work/family strains. Women constitute an important pool of talent and ability as well as a rich reservoir of experience and wisdom. They are the backbone of the nation - 'thari ya setšhaba'. Hence their integration into the political process recognises their value as partners in the developmental process. To deny them the power to hold legislative positions robs the nation of an important human resource. It also leads to the adoption and implementation of policies and programmes which are inappropriate and costly since women do not have a voice in the identification of needs and in the design of national programmes (WNGOC, 2002; Makanya, 1995:53; Government of Botswana, 1995).

191

The final argument is that Botswana government has made a commitment that the realisation of equal rights for men and women at all levels of the socio-economic and political spectrum will contribute to the achievement of a just and caring nation as well as the attainment of social justice in line with Vision 2016. Further, the government has ratified a number of international and regional treaties that legitimise women's participation in decision-making structures namely: the Convention on the Elimination of All Forms of Discrimination against Women, the Nairobi Forward Looking Strategy, the Beijing Platform for Action and the SADC Declaration on Gender Development. These conventions place heavy responsibility and commitments on government to play an active role in enhancing women's empowerment and to facilitate their equal representation in decision-making. These conventions and treaties are discussed and their significance in advancing the participation of women in parliament and council structures is outlined below.

INTERNATIONAL AND REGIONAL TREATIES

The Convention on the Elimination of All Forms of Discrimination against women was adopted by the United Nations General Assembly, Resolution 34/180 of 18 December 1979. Botswana government ratified this convention on the 13 August 1996 respectively (UN, 2001). Within the context of this convention, discrimination against women is defined as:

> 'Exclusion or restriction made on the basis of sex which has the effect or purpose of impairing or nullifying the recognition, enjoyment or exercise by women, irrespective of their natural status, on a basis of equality of men and women, of human rights and fundamental freedoms in the political, economic, social, cultural, civil or any other field' (United Nations, 1979).

With respect to the participation of women in political and public life of the country, Article 7 of the Convention commits state parties to ensure that women have the right: to vote in all elections and public referenda and to be eligible for election to all publicly elected bodies; to participate in the formulation of government policy and the implementation thereof and to hold public office and perform all public functions at all levels of government; to participate in non-governmental organisations and associations concerned with public and political life of the country (United Nations, 1979)

In contrast, the Nairobi Forward Looking Strategy for the Advancement of Women was adopted at the 3rd World Conference on Women held in Nairobi in July 1985. The conference was convened to review and appraise achievements of the UN Decade for Women. The Forward Looking Strategy was adopted to reaffirm the International concern regarding the status of women and to provide a framework for renewed commitment to the advancement of women and to the elimination of all forms of gender based discrimination (UN, 1985). In addition, the strategy emphasised the need for the promotion of equality of participation by women in all national and legislative bodies. It also stressed the achievement of equity in the appointment, election and promotion of women to high-level posts in the executive, legislative and judicial branches (UN, 1995:206).

Following the Nairobi conference, the 4th World Conference on women was convened by the United Nations in September 1995 at the Beijing International Conference Centre, Peoples Republic of China. The conference focused on the crosscutting issues of equality, development and peace and analysed them from a gender perspective (UN, 1985). Participants adopted the Beijing Platform for Action aimed at accelerating the implementation of the Nairobi Forward Looking Strategy and removing obstacles to women's active participation and equal share in economic, social, cultural and political decision-making (United Nations, 1995(a): 17). With respect to women in power and decision-making, the Platform of Action committed governments to take the following actions: ensure women's equal access to, and full participation in, power structures and decision-making; increase women's capacity to participate in decision-making and leadership; create or strengthen national machineries for women and other government bodies; integrate gender perspectives in legislation, public policies, programmes and projects; generate and disseminate gender-disaggregated data and information planning and evaluation.

Building upon the commitments made in Beijing, SADC Heads of State adopted and signed the SADC Declaration on Gender Development in Malawi in 1997. By doing so, Heads of State reaffirmed their commitment to the Nairobi Forward Looking Strategy and the Beijing Declaration. Specifically SADC Heads committed themselves to: promoting the equal representation of women and men in the decision-making of member states and SADC structures at all levels, and the achievement of the target of at least 30 per cent of women in political and decision-making structures by the year 2005 (SADC, 1999:21). As a follow-up to this declaration, the SADC Council of Ministers approved the strategic plan for the promotion of equality between women and men in decision-making. Of critical importance, is that the plan commits the SADC Secretariat to conduct periodic monitoring and evaluation of the implementation strategy (SADC, 1999:5).

These international and regional treaties have played a key role in creating an enabling environment for the promotion of gender equality in power sharing and political representation. Advocacy and lobby groups such as Emang Basadi, Botswana Women's NGO Coalition, Women and Law in Southern Africa, Ditshwanelo and other civil society organisations have used these instruments to lobby effectively for the enhancement of the status of women. As a result of pressure from these groups, government has adopted a series of measures to address some of the critical concerns. These include: the adoption of the National Policy on Women and Development, the launching of the National Gender Programme and the amendment of national laws which affect the rights of women. These measures are briefly discussed in the next section.

NATIONAL STRATEGIES FOR PROMOTING GENDER EQUALITY

The government of Botswana instituted a National Policy on Women and Development (1996) to facilitate the promotion of gender equality aimed at empowering women in all spheres of social, economic and political life of the country. The adoption of this policy marked a major milestone in recognising the important role of men and women in decision-making (Republic of Botswana, 2003). Further, the National Gender Programme (1998) launched by His Excellency President Festus Mogae has also prioritised power sharing between women and men as one of the six critical areas of concern for Botswana. In addition, Vision 2016 commits government and other stakeholders to ensure that positive measures including affirmative action in favour of women are taken to enable them to participate fully in positions of power, leadership and decision-making at all levels of the society (Presidential Task Force, 1997:53). Finally, Botswana has amended some national laws which affect the rights of women and act as a barrier for their active participation in politics namely; the Public Service (Amendment) Act 2000, Affiliation Proceedings (Amendment) Act 1999, Deeds Registry (Amendment) Act 1996, Employment (Amendment) Act 1996 and Citizenship (Amendment) Act 1995.

The critical question is, given the commitment made by government to address fundamental obstacles that hinder women, are we there yet? The next section evaluates the progress made to translate these policy commitments into action. This analysis begins by taking stock of progress made regarding participation at parliament level.

As noted earlier in the chapter, despite the numerous political ratifications at both the international and regional levels, women are still significantly under-represented in the Botswana parliament and councils. In order to assess the progress made by Botswana, this section will make a comparative analysis of the participation of women in parliament globally and regionally and show Botswana's achievement in relation to the emerging global trends. It will further assess the requirement to increase women's representation in Botswana's parliament in order to achieve the SADC minimum 30 per cent quota.

Figure 11.1 below depicts women's representation in parliament globally. It can be seen that women's representation in parliament is still very small in both developing and developed countries. Except for the Nordic countries where women's representation in parliament comes to about 40 per cent, on average, women's representation in parliament is less than 20 per cent across all the seven regions in the chart. Interestingly, for Europe, even when the Nordic countries are included, the average comes to about 17 per cent.

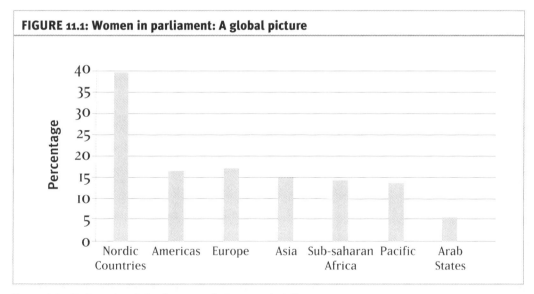

FIGURE 11.1: Women in parliament: A global picture

Source: Inter-Parliamentary Union (1995, 2003) plus own calculations.

Apart from the Nordic countries, women's representation in parliament is higher at about 18 per cent in the Americas and lowest at about 6 per cent in the Arab countries. Sub-saharan Africa, where Botswana belongs, ranks as number five out of the seven regions. Therefore, overall, women's representation in parliament is quite small.

However, since aggregation tends to hide individual country differences, Botswana is now compared with other countries in the SADC region in **Table 11.1** below. The Table shows each country's number of seats in parliament, the number of men and women in parliament, the proportion of women in parliament relative to the 30 per cent target and, most important, the absolute numbers and percentages required for each country to achieve the minimum 30 per cent women representation quota by 2005. The table reveals that two countries, Mozambique and South Africa, have already achieved the minimum requirement of 30 per cent women representation in parliament. We further show that the countries with the least representation in parliament are Swaziland and Mauritius at 3 per cent and 6 per cent respectively.

SADC Country	Number of seats in parliament	Men	Women	Percentage of women in parliament	Required incr. to reach 30 per cent quota Number	Percentage
Mozambique	250	175	75	30	0	0
South Africa	399	280	119	30	0	0
Namibia	72	53	19	26	3	4
Tanzania	274	213	61	22	22	8
Botswana	44	36	8	18	5	12
Angola	220	186	34	16	31	14
Zambia	158	139	19	12	28	18
Lesotho	120	106	14	12	22	18
Zimbabwe	150	135	15	10	30	20
Malawi	193	175	18	9	41	21
DRC	129	118	11	9	27	21
Mauritius	70	66	4	6	17	24
Swaziland	65	63	2	3	18	27

Table 11.1 Women's participation in parliament in SADC countries (1999-2002)

Source: Inter-Parliamentary (1995, 2003) Union plus own calculations.

When the countries are ranked in terms of the largest percentage of women in parliament, Botswana comes out as number five, after Mozambique, South Africa, Namibia and the United Republic of Tanzania. Under the current parliamentary structure[41], we note that Botswana would have needed to increase the 1999 women representation in parliament by 12 per cent to achieve the SADC 30 per cent quota by 2005. This means that Botswana women Members of Parliament would have to increase to 13 during 2004 general elections. However, Botswana dismally failed to live up to the challenge in the 2004 election.

41 This analysis does not use the number of parliamentary seats defined under the Delimitation Commission recommendations since these have not yet been implemented. Under the Delimitation Commission, Botswana will have 57 elected MPs and 4 specially elected MPs. Therefore, the above figures are likely to change after the 2004 elections

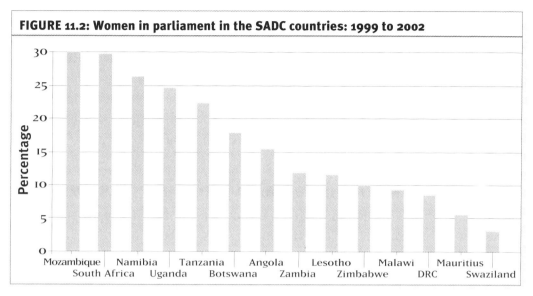

FIGURE 11.2: Women in parliament in the SADC countries: 1999 to 2002

Source: Inter-Parliamentary Union (1995, 2003) plus own calculations.

Figure 11.2 makes a graphic illustration of each SADC country's women representation in parliament relative to the 30 per cent quota. Half of the SADC countries have not yet achieved even half of the required minimum of the quota.

WOMEN REPRESENTATION IN LOCAL GOVERNMENT: SADC

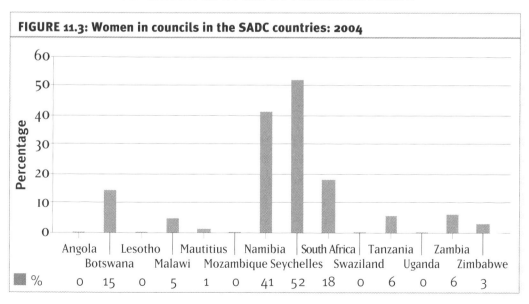

FIGURE 11.3: Women in councils in the SADC countries: 2004

Note: Zero denotes countries where data was not available. Source: Morna, C. L, 2004. Women's Political Participation in SADC, Institute for Democracy and Electoral Assistance (IDEA).

It has been found that the representation of women in local government (councils) is no different from that of parliament. Where data is available (see **Figure 11.3**)[42], the data from the Institute for Democracy and Electoral Assistance (IDEA), 2004 shows that women representation in local government in SADC ranges from as low as 1 per cent in Mauritius to as high as 52 per cent in Seychelles. Botswana remains an average performer at 18 per cent representation. Overall women representation in SADC local government is just as small as that in parliament.

WOMEN REPRESENTATION IN BOTSWANA PARLIAMENT OVER TIME

The objective in this section is briefly to sketch the trend in the representation of women in the Botswana Parliament. Women MPs in both the ruling Botswana Democratic Party (BDP) and the most popular opposition parties in Botswana are compared, with the analysis based on **Table 11.2** below:

Table 11.2: Representation in Parliament by Gender and Party Affiliation since Independence

	1965		1969		1974		1979		1984		1989		1994		1999	
	M	F	M	F	M	F	M	F	M	F	M	F	M	F	M	F
BDP	31	0	30	0	26	1	28	2	28	2	29	2	27	4	29	8
BPP	3	0	3	0	2	0	1	0	1	0	1	0	0	0	0	0
BIP	0	0	1	0	1	0	0	0	0	0	0	0	0	0	0	0
BNF	N/A	N/A	0	0	0	0	2	0	5	0	5	0	13	0	6	0
BCP	N/A	N/A	N/A	N/A	N/A	N/A	N/A	N/A	N/A	N/A	N/A	N/A	N/A	N/A	1	0
BAM	N/A	N/A	N/A	N/A	N/A	N/A	N/A	N/A	N/A	N/A	N/A	N/A	N/A	N/A	N/A	N/A

Source: Emang Basadi (2002) The Position of Men and Women in decision-Making in SADC: Botswana

The table above shows that the first ten years of Botswana's post-independence era were characterised by few women MPs in the ruling BDP and no women MPs in the opposition parties. Within the BDP, the next twenty years were characterised by either one or two women MPs. These increased to four and eight during the 1994 and 1999 elections respectively. This means that, for these two periods Botswana increased women MPs by 100 per cent in each case. Since the required increase to reach the minimum SADC requirement of 30 per cent women representation in parliament is

---

42 There is no data on women representation in Local Government in Angola, Lesotho, Mozambique, Swaziland and Uganda

significantly less than this, Botswana should have comfortably achieved this target during the 2004 general elections.

For the opposition parties, both male and female representation in parliament has generally been small over the years. The BPP started with three MPs in 1965 and achieved a maximum of six in 1974 before declining to one and finally zero in subsequent general elections. In all these cases, it was never represented by a woman. On the other hand, the BIP never had more than one MP over the years and none was a woman. The BNF, which for some years was a big challenge to the BDP, rose from two MPs in 1979 to a maximum of thirteen in 1994, before declining to six in 1999. Interestingly, over the last 37 years of the BNF's existence, none of its MPs was a woman. This is a major concern, given that the evidence suggests that women's participation rate is higher than that of men in both voting during elections and mobilisation of support for respective parties (Voter Apathy Study, 2002).

It has been made evident in this analysis that even though Botswana compares fairly well with global trends, its record when compared to other SADC countries is not particularly good. The country ranks behind countries such as Mozambique, Namibia, South Africa and Uganda, all of which have just emerged from many years of protracted civil war or liberation struggle. Botswana has been ahead of all these countries in terms of economic achievement and political stability and should be able to empower women fairly easily. But the fact is that the growth of women MPs over the years has not been impressive in Botswana. Disappointingly, the BDP has achieved only eighteen per cent women representation in nearly four decades, while the opposition parties achieved zero in the same period. It is therefore important that both the ruling BDP and opposition parties target the SADC 30 per cent quota of MPs for the 2004 general elections.

WOMEN'S REPRESENTATION IN TOWN/CITY/DISTRICT COUNCIL

Local government is made up of district and urban councils. In the previous section we concentrated on the participation of women in leadership positions at national government level, in this section the focus will be on women's participation at the local government level. Just like Members of Parliament, councillors are elected every five years and in addition, the Minister of Local Government is empowered to nominate additional councillors into respective councils across the country.

Figure 11.4 below shows the number of both elected and nominated councillors for the years 1997 and 2002.

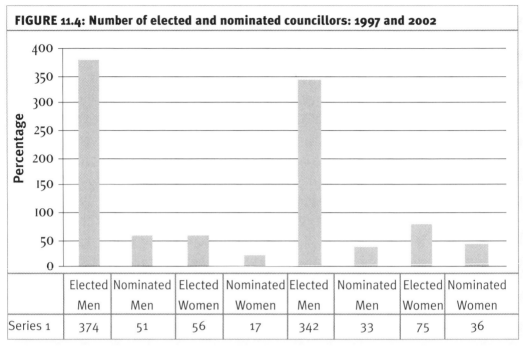

FIGURE 11.4: Number of elected and nominated councillors: 1997 and 2002

	Elected Men	Nominated Men	Elected Women	Nominated Women	Elected Men	Nominated Men	Elected Women	Nominated Women
Series 1	374	51	56	17	342	33	75	36

Source: Government of Botswana, 2002. Botswana National Report on Women in Politics and Decision-Making. Women's Affairs Department, Ministry of Labour and Home Affairs.

It also shows that both the number of elected and nominated male councillors declined after the 1999 elections. For instance the number of elected male councillors declined by 9 per cent whereas the number of nominated male councillors declined by 35 per cent. On the other hand, the number of elected women councillors increased by 34 per cent while that of nominated women councillors increased by 112 per cent. It is acknowledged that women councillors have held important positions of power at several points in Botswana's post-independence era. For instance, Gaborone City Council had a woman Mayor at one point, while Kgatleng and Central Districts had a woman Council Chairperson and woman Deputy Council Chairperson, respectively. As the Women's Affairs Department in the Ministry of Labour and Home Affairs has observed (Ministry of Labour and Home Affairs, 2002), this positive change towards the empowerment of women in local government decision-making reflects the political will and lobbying of women for positions of leadership and political power. However, lobbying should be strengthened so that this change would also occur at higher levels of political power, namely at the parliamentary levels and ultimately, cabinet.

OBSTACLES TO WOMEN'S POWER SHARING AND DECISION-MAKING

The foregoing discussion has provided concrete evidence that women throughout the world are under-represented in parliament and councils. The available data has shown that in general women who want to enter politics find that the political, public and social environments are often unfriendly or even hostile to them (Ashworth, 1996; Shevdova, 1998; Lovenduski & Karam, 1998; Regional Bureau for Africa, 1999; Tamale, 2000). Below, we briefly discuss the obstacles or hindrances faced by Batswana women which prevent them from entering councils and parliament. We focus specifically on: social-economic constraints, lack of appreciation regarding the capabilities of women, lack of capacity to train aspiring politicians and lack of vision and party commitment.

Our observation is that the road to council and parliament is determined largely by availability of adequate personal income (President Mogae, 1999; Makanya, 2000; SADC, 2001; India West, 2004). Available data indicates that despite an impressive developmental record there is persistent income inequality and poverty among women (Republic of Botswana, 1995). Data obtained from the 1991 census suggest that women household heads in a rural setting are more likely to have no cash-earning member in the family as compared to their male counterparts (Republic of Botswana, 2003). This means that women are seriously disadvantaged when it comes to commanding economic power and are limited in their opportunities to participate in politics as a result of the lack of necessary resources. It is important to acknowledge that the Plan of Action for the National Gender Programme aims to reduce women poverty by 20 per cent and to increase access to top management positions in economic decision-making by 35 per cent (WAD, 2003). The achievement of this goal will require considerable efforts on the part of government.

Despite efforts made by Emang Basadi and Botswana Caucus for Women in Politics to educate the general public about the role of women in politics, there is still a general lack of appreciation of the capabilities that woman have to run for political office[43]. At the local levels, where initial nominations and selections occur, women are often overlooked largely because of traditional cultural values which perceive men as the sole legitimate heirs to positions of leadership (Republic of Botswana, 2003). As a result of these obstacles, women are not voted for in large numbers even though they constitute the majority of voters (DRP, 1999).

As indicated in Chapter 13 in this book, since 1994, Emang Basadi has mounted a political education programme aimed at equipping women politicians with skills to

---

43 See Chapter 13 for more information on Emang Basadi's Political Education Project as well as the activities of the Botswana Caucus for Women in Politics

venture into the male-dominated arena of political decision-making (Machangana 1999). Women have been trained in the areas of campaign management, lobbying and advocacy, leadership and fundraising (Ibid: 88). The role played by the Botswana Caucus for Women in Politics has reinforced these efforts specifically to prepare women for the 2004 general elections. Despite these commendable efforts, more training is needed to reach the majority of the women residing in rural and remote areas. Training is particularly crucial in the areas such as leadership skills, campaign strategies, public speaking, advocacy, lobbying and fund-raising.

To a large extent the leadership of political parties seems to be supportive of the women's movement. This is evidenced by the fact that party manifestos are increasingly becoming gender sensitive.[44] However, this has not yet translated into concrete actions. For example, the achievement of a 30 per cent quota is still regarded by some male politicians as a women's ideal that cannot be achieved overnight. Women feel that there is need for an enabling political environment and change of attitude from party leadership that will allow them to succeed in their quest to enter parliament and council.

The struggle to advance the woman's cause, has gained some momentum in Botswana despite the prevailing obstacles and challenges. As a way forward, it is suggested that some practical measures be put in place in order to ensure the full representation of women in parliament and council. The following are some practical strategies that need to be adopted and /or strengthened to help realise this process:

It is recommended that there should be on-going training on women's political empowerment with greater emphasis on the following skills: leadership, communication, assertiveness, public speaking and fund-raising and effective campaign strategies. Female youth aspiring to political decision-making positions should be identified and targeted for such training. Further, some women councillors who are doing their best to participate are often unable to make meaningful contributions to the debates due to low literacy skills. These women should be given special assistance through the provision of adult education courses and seminars.

It is also suggested that women politicians need to build on a record of successful political leadership at the neighbourhood, ward, village and district levels. They should inspire people and build a record of high achievement and show compassion for, and interest in, the issues that women care about. The presence of women parliamentarians and councillors should be felt at local levels as motivators

44 See BDP 1994 and BNF 1994 Election Manifestos

and role models. In addition, mature, experienced women, particularly those in parliament and other decision-making bodies, should provide guidance and mentoring to inexperienced, aspiring politicians to induct them into the culture of politics.

We recommend that affirmative action should be put in place to remove direct and indirect discrimination practices and procedures that hinder the advancement of women in the political system. Born of the civil rights movement in the US three decades ago, affirmative action programmes call for special consideration to be given to women and minorities in employment, education and other decision-making structures (Skrentny, 2001; Fobanjon, 2001). Affirmative action has shown success in Namibia where the number of women parliamentarians increased from seven to fourteen in 1997. Similarly, the ruling ANC reserved 30 per cent of parliamentary seats and 50 per cent of local government for women (SADC, 2001). Other countries, for example, Sweden, India, Uganda, Nepal and Bangladesh have introduced quotas for women candidates and this has accelerated women representation in parliament and councils (Dahlerup, 1998; Tamale, 2000). Over the years, Emang Basadi has been lobbying for affirmative action policies and programmes that include national quotas (Emang Basadi, 1996; 2002). Political parties should consider adopting this strategy to correct current imbalances in parliament and council.

It is clear that the caucus needs more resources to implement its activities and to promote the collective rights and interests of women[45]. Full time personnel across party lines should be recruited to run the office. In addition there is need to strengthen database and research capabilities of the caucus and increase financial sustainability and credibility. The caucus should also establish linkages with women's organisations locally and in the region to exchange information and identify best practices. Research experts in local academic and research institutions should be utilised to build the knowledge base and to act as a 'think tank' for the caucus. Finally, it is suggested that the caucus should work closely with men to gain credibility, support, solidarity and respect.

It is recommended that seats should be reserved for women. It has been discovered that the majority of women politicians in Botswana prefer a mixed electoral system of constitutional quota, proportional representation and constituency based (Emang Basadi, 2002:27). They rightly feel that this strategy will provide an enabling environment for women to enter parliament. Indeed, Molomo's chapter on electoral systems has shown that the list proportional representation system helps to promote

---

45 See the next chapter for more details on the role of the Botswana Caucus for Women in Politics

women representation. But Maundeni's concluding chapter has also shown that India has successfully reserved seats for minorities under the FPTP system. So whatever system is adopted, the recommendation is that seats should be reserved for women politicians. The lesson learnt from the region, as shown by Molutsi, is that women representation can be improved.

CONCLUSION

This chapter has provided an overview of women representation in parliament and council. Central to the discussion is that women constitute more than half the voting population and therefore equal representation is imperative. The other argument is that Botswana has ratified international and regional treaties that bind the country to fulfil these commitments. These include the Convention on the Elimination of All Forms of Discrimination against Women, the Nairobi Forward Looking Plan, the Beijing Declaration, the Platform for Action and the SADC Declaration on Gender and Development. Global and regional trends in women's participation in parliament and local government have been analysed. Overall, the analysis revealed that not much has been achieved to integrate women into politics despite signing international declarations mentioned earlier. Amongst developed countries, Nordic countries are in the lead with 40 per cent women representation in parliament. At the regional level, Mozambique and South Africa have achieved the 30 per cent quota recommended by SADC Heads of States. But Botswana ranked number six with only 18 per cent women representation in parliament after the 1999 election and this has since declined further after the 2004 election. The analysis of women representation in local government both regionally and in Botswana shows that there is not much difference in women under-representation even at that level.

REFERENCES

Ashworth, G (1996) 'Gendered Governance: *An Agenda for Change' Gender in Development Monograph Series # 3*

Antrobus, P (2000) 'Transformational Leadership: Advancing the Agenda for Gender Justice' *Gender and Development 8 (3)*

Dahlerup, D (1998) 'Using Quotas to Increase Women Political Representation' in Karam (ed.) *Women in Parliament Beyond Numbers* Stockholm: International IDEA

DRP (1999) 'Results of Opinion Polls' DRP, University of Botswana Gaborone

Emang Basadi (2002) 'National Conference on Women Political Empowerment: Setting an Agenda for 30 per cent minimum of female representation in parliament and council by 2004' Gaborone 19th – 21st June

Emang Basadi (1998) *Political Education Project: A Strategy that Works*, Lentswe La Lesedi, Gaborone.

Emang Basadi (1996) *Strategic Planning Document* (1996-2000), Gaborone

Fobanjong, J (2001) *Understanding the Backlash Against Affirmative Action Science* Huntington: Nova Publishers

Government of Botswana (2002) *Report on the Delimitation Commission*, Gaborone: Government Printer

Government of Botswana (2002) *Botswana National report on Women in Politics and Decision-Making. Women's' Affairs Department, Ministry of Labour and Home Affairs*, Gaborone.

Government of Botswana (1995) *Policy on Women in Development* Gaborone

Government of Botswana (1998) *The National Gender Program* Gaborone

IEC (2002) Voter Apathy Report Gaborone: Government Printer

Inter-Parliamentary Union (2003) Women in Parliament 1945-2003: A World Statistical survey. Geneva: IPU. Found in http://www.ipu.org/wmn-e/classif.htm

Inter-Parliamentary Union (1995) Women in Parliament 1945-1995: A World Statistical survey. Geneva: IPU

Lovenduski, J & Karam, A (1998) 'Women in Parliament: Making a Difference' in Karam (ed.) *Women in Parliament Beyond Numbers* Stockholm: International IDEA

Makanya, S (1995) 'Situation analysis of women in politics in selected SADC countries' in SADC *Women in Politics and Decision-making in SADC: Beyond 30 per cent in 2005* Gaborone: Printing and Publishing Co

Morna, C. L, 2004. *Women's Political Participation in SADC*, Institute for Democracy and Electoral Assistance (IDEA).

Presidential Task Force (1997) *Long Term Vision for Botswana: Towards Prosperity for All* Gaborone

Republic of Botswana (2003), International Conference on Population and Development, Country Report, Botswana.

Regional Bureau for Africa (1999) 'Women in Africa: Profiles of Leadership' *United Nations Development Program* New York

SADC (1999) *Women in Politics and Decision-making in SADC: Beyond 30 per cent in 2005 Report of the proceedings of a conference held in Gaborone 28 March – 1st April* Gaborone: Printing and Publishing

SADC (2001) 'SADC Gender Monitor: Monitoring Implementation of the Beijing Commitments by SADC Member States' Issue # 2 SADC Gaborone

Shevdova, N (1998) 'Obstacles to Women's Participation in Parliament' in Karam, (ed.) *Women in Parliament Beyond Numbers* Stockholm: International IDEA

Skrentny, J.D (2001) *Color Lines: Affirmative Action, Immigration, and Civil Rights Options for America* Chicago: University of Chicago Press

Tamale, S (2000) 'Point of Order, Mr Speaker: African Women Claiming their Space in Parliament' *Gender and Development* 8 (3)

United Nations (2001) 'Status of the Convention on the Elimination of all forms of Discrimination against Women' *United Nations* New York A/56/328

United Nations (1995:a) *Beijing Declaration and Platform for Action* United Nations New York

United Nations (1995:b) *From Nairobi to Beijing: Second Review and Appraisal of the Nairobi Forward Looking Strategy for the Advancement of Women* New York: United Nations

United Nations (1994) *Fifth African Regional Conference on Women: Summaries of National Report* 16th – 23rd Nov. Senegal

United Nations (1994) *Fifth African Regional Conference on Women: Summaries of National Report*' 16th – 23rd Nov. Senegal

United Nations (1992) *Women in Politics and decision-making in the late Twentieth Century: A United Nations Study* Boston: Martinus Nijhoff Publishers

United Nations (1988) *Changing Socio-Economic Conditions of Women in Africa in the Context of the Nairobi Forward Looking Strategy for the Advancement of Women* New York

United Nations (1985) *Report of the World Conference to Review and Appraise the Achievement of the United Nations Decade for Women: Equality, Development and Peace* United Nations, New York

United Nations (1979) 'The Convention on the Elimination of all forms of Discrimination against Women' *United Nations* New York

WAD & WNGCO (2003) 'Botswana Country Report' *Women's Affairs Department* Gaborone

WNGCO (2002) 'Botswana Women's NGO Coalition Strategic Plan 2002-2006' Gaborone.

CHAPTER 12

YOUTH AND ELECTORAL PARTICIPATION IN BOTSWANA

Tidimane Ntsabane

INTRODUCTION

This chapter examines trends in electoral participation of the youth. However, as pointed out elsewhere (Ntsabane and Ntau, 2000), this is a narrow view of political participation as the youth have other modes of participation in the political process. It is however, noted that there is growing concern over the quality and long term sustainability of electoral democracy especially in the light of the low voter participation rates of recent years (see **Table 12.1**). Voter apathy is worrying as it limits the extent to which the voting population is able to influence who is elected and with what policies and programmes. Also of concern is that if a significant part of the population lose confidence in the elections then the rulers and the electoral system lose their legitimacy and democracy becomes unsustainable (Mackenzie,1967).

Young people in Africa have historically played important roles in the political process. For instance, young people such as Tshekedi, Kgari and Tawana were crowned chiefs in colonial and post-colonial Botswana and have gone on to exert enormous influence. Young people elsewhere also played crucial roles in the various struggles by African nationalist movements for political independence from the 1950's to 1990's, for example in the Soweto uprisings of 1976, and they have also played leading roles in the struggle for democracy. They have been elected to parliament and local authorities, become involved in house-to-house campaigns on behalf of individual candidates and political parties, organised fund raising events and rallies and constituted the youth wings of political parties. The ultimate, however, is the extent to which they are able to influence who is elected as elections provide an important opportunity for the electorate to express their preferences on the policies and programmes of both the government of the day and those of the other contenders for political office (Mackenzie, 1967). A growing concern, however, is that young people have withdrawn from public activities, including national elections.

The youth currently represent a significant part of the population in Africa. Demographic trends in the continent show that about 50 per cent of Africa's population is below the age of eighteen years and an extraordinarily high percentage is between the ages of 15 to 25. Botswana is no exception to these trends. According to the 1991 census, the youth represent 36 per cent of Botswana's population and represent a significant part of the voting population. What norms, values and beliefs or political culture they hold are very important, as they serve as a guide to behaviour in general and electoral behaviour in particular (Prewitt,1971).

CONCEPT OF YOUTH

The concept of youth has varied in meaning across societies and cultures over time. Chronological age is the most common and primary criteria. Botswana's National Youth Policy for instance defines youth as those aged 12 to 29. The Botswana Democratic Party (BDP) defines its youth as the 16 to 35 year cohort while the Botswana National Front (BNF) and the Botswana Congress Party (BCP) define it in terms of the 16 to 39 year cohort. This indeed is a useful though broad indication of the beginning and the end of youthfulness or adolescence but age alone cannot provide a precise definition as no one can precisely say when adolescence starts and ends. This is especially so in today's complex and multicultural world that places increasing challenges in education, training and social skills on the adolescent road to successful adulthood.

Rogers (1985) notes other common markers of youth across cultures. Some cultures identify it as a period of physical development and thus a biological phenomenon. It indeed is a period of rapid biological transition associated with puberty, changes in body shape, hormones and sexuality. But it is also a socio-cultural phenomenon marked by the acquisition of the attitudes, values and other skills that will carry young people into good adulthood whilst avoiding those negatives which will limit their future potential (Ntsabane and Sechele, 2003).

In traditional Tswana society, however, youth was marked by an elaborate series of rites known as Bogwera (for men) and Bojale (for women). Schapera (1970;105) notes that '...a man who had not passed through them was always regarded as a boy or girl, no matter how old he might actually be; he was not allowed to marry or take part in tribal discussions, and was regarded with contempt by the women'.

All cultures and societies have universally recognised a period between childhood and adulthood, often referred to as youth or adolescence. The word adolescence comes from Latin and means 'to grow into maturity'. It is a stage of growth that has brought contrasting images across time and cultures. As early as the 5th century BC, Socrates stated: 'Our youth now love luxury. They have bad manners, contempt for authority; they show disrespect for their elders and love chatter in place of exercise. They contradict their parents, chatter before company, gobble up their food and tyrannise their teachers.'(Osei-Hwedie, et. al 1989:88). Other images are those of the youth as movers, adventurers, conquerers and martyrs: from David's sling that killed Goliath right up to the 1976 Soweto uprisings.

SIGNIFICANCE OF THE YOUTH IN BOTSWANA

Botswana is a country with one of the fastest growing populations in the world. Population statistics from the three post-independence censuses show that the de facto population in 1971 was 596 944 growing to 941 027 in 1981, 1 326 796 in 1991 and 1 678 891 in 2001. These figures imply growth rates of 4.7 per cent between 1971 and 1981 and 3.5 per cent between 1981 and 1991. The growth rates are not only high but also indicate a high growth potential. The proportion of the population aged from under fifteen years has consistently remained high, 44 per cent in 1971, 48.8 per cent in 1981 and 42 per cent in 1991. The 1991 census further shows that 60 per cent of the population is aged less than 30 years of age. The 10 to 29 year age cohort in 2001 comprised 43.6 per cent of the nation's population. Botswana's population, as indeed is true of Africa as a continent, is thus a youthful one with implications for the demands on education, training, health, housing and jobs. Despite these demographic statistics, the young still remain either marginal or excluded from mainstream political, social and economic processes of society. They are often viewed as belonging to 'the future' or, at worst, belonging to a period of sexual, emotional and social disorientation needing parental, school and state guidance and control (Harvey, 1993).

SITUATION OF THE YOUTH IN BOTSWANA

Botswana's population characteristics show a young and highly dependent population, with serious implications for the provision of social services such as education, health and employment. The youth's situation in contemporary Botswana is a picture of good and bad news. The positive side is that Botswana has done exceptionally well in the past two decades to provide services in the form of schools and health facilities. At present at least 80 per cent of the primary school age population is at school and more than 80 per cent of those who finish seven years of primary education are able to proceed to junior secondary schooling. In the health sector impressive progress has been made. Some 85 per cent of the population is within fifteen kilometres of the nearest health facility. Life expectancy at birth has risen to 67 years, making it among the highest in the region (CSO, 2001). The Infant Mortality Rate (IMR) has declined over the years from a high of 100 per 1 000 live births in 1971, to 71 per 1 000 live births in 1981, to a low of 46 per 1 000 live births in 1991 (CSO, 1971, 1981 and 1991).

These impressive gains in health are a result of increased national investment in better nutrition, health and income generating programmes established to counter the effects of drought in Botswana between 1982-1988 (CSO, 1989:71). There was also wider use of immunisation reaching 80 per cent of children injected with all vaccines. There are however limitations to these gains. Principal among these is the impact that the growing HIV infection rate has on the access to care and its quality due to the growing numbers of patients. Contrary to previous projections, the HIV prevalence rates continue to worsen (GOB, 2003). For 2002 it was estimated that approximately 35.4 per cent of the general population were infected with HIV and that in the 15 to 49 years age group almost 300 000 people were infected (GOB, 2003).

YOUNG PEOPLE AND HIV/AIDS

Botswana's HIV/AIDS prevalence rate statistics at 35.4 per cent show that the country is the worst affected in the world. When disaggregated by age, the youth are the hardest hit (GOB, 2003). In 2002 the overall prevalence rate was 35.4 per cent, with 21 per cent in the 15 to 19 years age group and 37.4 per cent in the 20 to 24 age group (GOB2003). The future is not promising either. Young people have been associated with the most risky sexual behaviours and habits and the most negative attitude towards HIV/AIDS (Government of Botswana, 2003). While knowledgeable on HIV/AIDS they have not translated this into corresponding behavioural change. This is a worrying situation as the youth are not only the present but also the future productive members of society.

YOUTH AND UNEMPLOYMENT

Unemployment has been identified as another of the greatest problems facing the youth. Labour statistics show that unemployment among young people is very high and that young women are far more disadvantaged in this regard than are young men (Abasi et al, 2005). In 1994 statistics showed that the unemployment rate among young people aged 15 to 19 and 20 to 24 was 49 per cent and 27 per cent respectively. The 1998 statistics showed that the situation was not improving as 35.4 per cent and 38.9 per cent of those aged 15 to 19 and 20 to 24 were unemployed respectively (Abasi et al, 2005 :11). These are all outcomes of the demographic and economic changes of the past three decades that not only increased in the number of young people in the population but also brought new challenges with the changes in the labour market.

EDUCATION AND TRAINING

There is a growing number of young people who are not participating in any form of education and training. The 1991 Census indicated that 17 per cent of young people aged between seven and thirteen were not enrolled in school. There is also a growing number of youths who have dropped out of the school system, either out of poor performance or lack of places to continue to the next level of the education system. They are all of school age and in the most impressionable period of their lives but they are spending this time out of school. This has obvious implications for their chances in the job market now and in the future.

Young people also feature very prominently in crime statistics. Juvenile crimes are on the increase. They commit offences such as traffic violations, malicious injury to property, common theft, house breaking, common assault, armed robbery, rape, murder and use and traffic in habit-forming drugs. Young men tend to be the main offenders and in addition, young people are also known to be leading alcohol and substance abusers (Molamu and Manyeneng, 1988). These drinking and smoking patterns have obvious implications on their health and well being.

Young people are also victims of abuse by older members of society as they have a lower social status than their older compatriots. They are subject to many kinds of abuse and discrimination, which include child labour, physical and sexual abuse and exclusion from decision-making on issues that concern them. Age, gender and their own social skills and knowledge of the law however influence the extent of abuse and discrimination. Many of these social and economic problems have combined to affect the youth as individuals and as a group.

The last three decades have witnessed phenomenal social, economic and political changes globally. Consequently the world has become increasingly more complex and more multicultural, placing more challenges on the youth in terms of education, training and better skills to cope (Ntsabane and Sechele, 2003). In Botswana these have combined to affect the youth in ways that are unprecedented in the country's recent past and have affected their personal circumstances and social environment. Some have resorted to negative coping strategies like alcohol and substance abuse and other social ills and even suicide. The route to adulthood is no longer a simple one of transition through Bogwera and Bojale. It has increasingly become less clear, more complex and longer. There is however a consensus that the current and future well-being of any society is dependent on the raising of a generation of skilled, competent and responsible adults.

YOUTH AND ELECTIONS IN BOTSWANA

Elections, narrowly conceived as a process of choosing between individuals to fill an office, have not long been a feature of many African political systems. Much of pre-colonial Africa, Botswana being no exception, was characterised by the predominance of chiefdom politics where the most significant political office was that of chief. Chiefdoms had elaborate traditional procedures for filling this office (Ngongco,1989). This system may not have been fully transparent, as the final decision was often taken by a small council of elders, but it did allow for a lively interest and strong opinions. Political institutions allowed very limited access to traditionally excluded groups such as women, minorities and children. These were marginalised as only the elders, males and dominant tribal groups held sway.

The advent of colonialism in Africa brought with it a new system of rule. In some parts of the continent, however, it left chiefly rule ('indirect rule') largely untouched for as long as it was applied to the African population and not the Europeans. Botswana was in this category of countries. Legislatively there was the European Advisory Council and the Native Advisory Council, both of which were advisory bodies to the Colonial Administration. The Native Advisory Council was made up of chiefs and 'councillors' appointed in Kgotla. As Mgadla and Campbell (1989) note, there was in practice no effective participation as chiefs nominated these councillors without adequate popular participation at the Kgotla. The council reflected some element of continuity with the pre-colonial order in two ways. First, it was done through nomination and not election and secondly, it continued the exclusion and political marginalisation of youth, women and tribal minorities.

Independence was marked by the advent of a new constitution which ushered in a competitive, multi-party electoral system guaranteeing open, free and fair elections every five years for citizens meeting the minimum voting age. There have been such elections in 1969, 1974, 1979, 1984, 1989, 1994, 1999 and more recently 2004.

Elections, as institutionalised procedures for the choosing of officeholders, have historically carried different meanings to both the rulers and the ruled. To the rulers they are a key instrument of legitimacy and consent. To the ruled the question of what motivates them to participate is answered according to their understanding of the meaning of elections. Their answer may be different from the reason why the rulers may want them to participate. Under the liberal democratic dispensation in the West, voters vote out of the need to express a preference for alternative leadership and programmes. What then is the extent of youth electoral participation in Botswana and what is the meaning of this participation or the lack of it?

ELECTORAL PARTICIPATION IN THE LAST THREE DECADES

It is acknowledged that generally, Botswana recorded fairly high levels of electoral participation though the 1974 and 1969 elections saw the lowest and second lowest voter turnouts of 31.2 per cent and 54.9 per cent respectively. Turnout for the other years as shown in **Table 12.1**, has been over 65 per cent. Turnout here is defined by the number of those registered to vote versus those who actually voted. When the number of eligible voters is used as the common denominator then the voter turnout percentage drops significantly.

Table 12.1: Electoral Statistics, 1965 – 1994

	1	2	3	4	5	6
Year	Potential No. of voters	No. of electorate registered	Percentage of electorate registered	No. of electorate who voted	Percentage of 4/1	Percentage poll=4/2
1965	243 365	188 950	78,0	140 789	58,0	74,0
1969	267 647	156 428	58,5	92 965*	34,7	54,9
1974	309 810	236 848	76,4	95 809*	30.9	31.2
1979	362 515	343 483	67,3	147 658	40,7	60,6
1984	416 996	293 571	70,4	227 756	54,6	77,6
1989	507 569	367 069	72,3	250 487	49,4	68,2
1994	609 000	370 356	60,8	281 931	46,3	76,1
1999	800 000	460 500	57.6	336 982	42.1	77.6

Source: IEC Election Reports *These figures include the registered voters from uncontested constituencies. We have treated the latter as if they all voted, which has inflated the poll percentage for 1969, 1974 and 1979. The actual poll percentages for these elections were 54.9; 31.2 and 58.4 respectively.

The data shows that Botswana does not fare very well when compared to other democracies with competitive elections. A recent electoral participation survey of 177 countries across the world by the Institute on Democracy and Electoral Assistance (IDEA 1998) shows an increasing trend in overall participation in competitive elections across the globe between 1945 and 1990. Some 140 countries out of 189 have multi-party elections and 2/3 of the world's population lives in countries which have multi-party elections. In comparison to other African countries in the IDEA survey, which have held two or more elections between 1945 and 1997, Botswana's turnout was below 14 of them. These countries were Mauritius' six elections with 82.5 per cent, Namibia (2) with 80.4 per cent, Comoros (2) with 75.7 per cent, Cape Verde (2) with 75.6 per cent, Madagascar (4) with 72.5 per cent, Togo (4) with 69.3 per cent, Lesotho (3) with 65.2 per cent, Benin (2) with 60.1 per cent, Zimbabwe (5) with 58.8 per cent, Cameroon (3) 56.3 per cent, Gambia (6) with 55.6 per cent, Uganda (3) with 50.6 per cent, Nigeria (3) with 47.6 per cent and Sierra Leone (3) with 46.8 per cent. Clearly Botswana might be said to suffer from more entries than all these countries. Taking the latest elections conducted after 1990, however, the 44.5 per cent voter turnout still falls below that of fifteen African countries.

YOUTH ELECTORAL PARTICIPATION

There has been interest in the subject of youth participation in politics in general, and in elections in particular, for some time. Voter apathy among the young deserves thorough investigation. The concern about the youth's low electoral participation is recognised as a problem area for the country's political system. These include the Independent Electoral Commission, political parties and the Botswana Youth Council; newspaper editorials and political commentators have also expressed concern. It is not unique to Botswana: South Africa, Japan, the United States of America and other mature democracies are faced with this problem. A recent survey in the United States of America called 'America Unplugged' reports that 69 per cent of young Americans see government as irrelevant to their lives yet those aged 65 and older seem to feel politically disenchanted (Ntsabane & Ntau, 2000). Massey (1967) also raises the same problems about Japanese youth. These trends are not surprising as whatever the minimum legal age for office-holding, government is always in the hands of middle-aged and older people. The youth are a category not normally associated with political decision-making, because most cultures view youth as belonging to 'the future'. The assumption is that as today's rulers retire, young politicians become rising stars and spokespersons for a new generation. There is some consensus that youth and politics do not mix but there are, however, contrasting and often conflicting theories as to why that is so. One common school of thought is that youth have a low interest in politics and therefore their level of participation measured through voter turnout statistics and through membership of political parties is low. It is argued that this is because politics does not appeal to them as politicians and political institutions are not 'youth-friendly'. This suggests a need for the creation of a youth-centric or youth-oriented political culture. Another school of thought argues that young people throughout history have been politically involved in the various struggles for liberation democracy and elections.

It has been noted that while the overall voter turnout in most of Botswana's recent elections shows participation rates upwards of 65 per cent, recent Democracy Research Project surveys do show lower levels of participation among the youth (see **Tables 12.5** and **12.6**). This lower trend is more present among men compared to women. This is especially surprising as the youth are a relatively better educated generation of voters, have lived all their lives under the present multi-party system and are thus free from the excesses of the past and seem to prefer the current election system over chieftaincy (see **Table 12.3**). Many adult voters are said to be reluctant to vote at every election because, in their opinion, they determined who should lead them at the very first election in 1965. In their view the tradition is that once a chief has been confirmed, he occupies office until he dies. This tradition of hereditary leadership, which is discussed extensively by Maundeni in another chapter, is an important factor limiting political participation in Botswana (BDP 1974). As **Table 12.3** illustrates, this explanation cannot hold true for the youth as they have an overwhelming preference for the current electoral system over chieftaincy and most of them were born under the current electoral system.

Table 12.2: Age Distribution of the Sample Population

Constituency	YEARS				
	21–30	31–40	41-50	51- 60	61–70
Nkange	52 (22.2)	64 (27.4)	51 (21.8)	28 (12.0)	19 (8.1)
North East	38 (16.2)	58 (24.8)	70 (29.9)	29 (12.4)	20 (8.5)
Francistown	56 (26.0)	64 (29.8)	40 (18.6)	27 (12.6)	18 (8.4)
S/Phikwe	58 (29.4)	62 (31.5)	54 (27.40	13 (6.6)	3 (1.5)
Mochudi	60 (28.0)	39 (18.2)	37 (17.3)	19 (8.9)	20 (9.3)
Lob/Barolong	68 (33.0)	59 (28.6)	43 (20.9)	21 (10.2)	7 (3.4)
Ngwaketse South	50 (21.3)	65 (27.7)	55 (23.4)	24 (10.2)	20 (8.5)
Kanye	52 (21.8)	69 (29.0)	41 (17.2)	29 (12.2)	29 (12.2)
Molepolole	55 (22.0)	80 (32.0)	55 (22.0)	31 (12.4)	15 (6.0)

Table 12.2: Age Distribution of the Sample Population

Constituency	YEARS				
	21 –30	31 –40	41-50	51- 60	61 –70
Maun/Chobe	39 (30.0)	36 (27.9)	31 (24.0)	11 (8.5)	5 (3.9)
Kweneng West	51 (20.6)	71 (28.6)	61 (24.6)	20 (8.1)	16 (6.5)
Gaborone South	105 (45.9)	62 (27.1)	34 (14.8)	17 (7.4)	5 (2.2)
Gaborone North	111 946.3)	56 (23.3)	40 (16.7)	15 (6.3)	7 (2.9)
Total	797 (27.8)	785 (27.3)	612 (21.3)	284 (9.9)	184 (6.4)

Source : DRP Opinion Poll Study 1999.

Table 12.3: Age and Preferred Form of Government

AGE	Democratic election system	Chieftainship
21-29	83,2	16,9
30-39	74	26
40-52	70,1	29
53-64	60,9	39,1
65+	46,4	53,6

Source : DRP Opinion Poll Study 1999.

During the March 1999 Opinion Poll, respondents were asked whether they had registered to vote in the October 1999 election. A significant majority (74.1 per cent) of those aged 18 to 20 years indicated that they had not registered. Only 46.7 per cent of those aged between 21 and 30 years, indicated that they had registered. From the poll results a substantial number of the youth (18 to 30 years) said that they had not registered compared to the elderly population which recorded 70.6 per cent.

Table 12.4: Registered to vote in Elections by Age Groups 1999 Poll

Age	Registered to Vote		
	Yes - n (per cent)	No - n (per cent)	Total
18-20	146 (25.9)	417 (74.1)	563
21-30	685 (46.7)	783 (53.3)	1468
31-99	1614 (70.6)	671 (29.4)	2285
Total	2445 (56.6)	1871 (43.4)	4316

Respondents who participated in the March 1999 Opinion poll were further asked whether they would vote in the 2004 elections. It seems the recently enfranchised eighteen to twenty age category is yet to take advantage of the 1998 electoral reforms. Young people aged between eighteen and twenty years fared badly as compared to other age categories recording only 42 per cent compared to 80 per cent among respondents aged thirty-one years and above (see **Table 13.5**). Generally the youth were not enthusiastic about casting their vote in the polls in October 1999.

Table 12.5: Intention to Vote by Age Groups 1989 Poll			
Age	Intending to vote		
	Yes - n (per cent)	No - n (per cent)	Total
18-20	239 (42.4)	252 (44.7)	564
21-30	913 (62.1)	402 (27.3)	1 470
31-99	1 836 (80.4)	274 (12.0)	2 284
Total	**2 988 (69.2)**	**928 (21.5)**	**4 318**

PARTY SUPPORT AMONG YOUTH

The 1989 DRP opinion survey showed the BNF supported by some 36 per cent of the people aged 21 to 30 years compared to the BDP's 22.9 per cent. The BPP rallied behind with 19 per cent.

Table 12.6: Party Support by Age 1989				
Age	None – n (per cent)	BDP – n (per cent)	BNF – n (per cent)	BPP – n (per cent)
21 – 30	51 (37.2)	334 (22.9)	270 (36.8)	39 (19.0)
31 – 40	36 (26.3)	399 (27.4)	214 (29.2)	47 (22.9)
41 – 50	23 (16.8)	354 (24.3)	127 (17.3)	51 (24.9)
51 – 60	11 (8.0)	160 (11.0)	54 (7.4)	32 (15.6)
61 – 70	5 (3.6)	109 (7.5)	32 (4.4)	21 (10.2)
71+	4 (2.9)	65 (4.5)	20 (2.7)	10 (4.9)
Total	**137 (100)**	**1457 (100)**	**733 (100)**	**205 (100)**

Table 12.7 below shows party support based on the 1999 DRP opinion results. BNF popularity seems to have diminished. From the poll results, young people aged 21 to 30 showed their preference for the BDP over the BNF. The BDP led other parties by

40.4 per cent support. The BNF, which fared better in the 1989 polls among the youth, came behind the BDP with 21.5 per cent in the 1999 poll. The Botswana Congress Party (BCP) and Botswana People's Party obtained 7.2 per cent and 1.2 per cent respectively. A similar pattern is repeated for the 18 to 20 year olds. The lowering of the voting age from 21 to 18 would not it seems benefit the BNF, which over the years has been attracting young people to its rallies. The BNF strongly advocated for electoral reforms, which included the lowering of the voting age.

Despite these shifts in party support among young people, most political parties have ignored the youth and youth issues in their manifestos (Raditlhokwa, 1999). The BDP and the BNF for instance did mention the plight of women, children and other vulnerable groups but made no direct reference to the youth. The BNF went further and pledged to reserve 30 per cent of all eligible positions for women but said nothing about the youth. In 1999 however, the BDP did attempt to appeal to the youth vote through some innovative youth targeted advertising

Table 12.7: Party Support by Age 1999

Age	BCP	BDP	BLP	BNF	BPP	BPU	BWF	IFP	MELS	UAP	UDF	PUSO	No Answer
18-20	43 (7.7)	252 (44.9)		98 (17.5)	14 (2.5)			4 (.7)					150 (26.7)
21-30	106 (7.2)	592 (40.4)	3 (.2)	315 (21.5)	17 (1.2)	1 (.1)	1 (.1)	6 (.4)	2 (.1)	2 (.1)	1 (.1)	1 (.1)	418 (28.5)
31-99	120 (5.3)	1152 (50.7)		451 (19.8)	51 (2.2)	5 (.2)		7 (.3)	1 (.0)			1 (.0)	486 (21.4)
Total	269 (6.3)	1996 (46.4)	3 (.1)	864 (20.1)	82 (1.9)	6 (.1)	1 (.0)	17 (.4)	3 (.1)	2 (.0)	1 (.0)	2 (.0)	1054 (24.5)

The explanation for youth voter apathy may be found in African societies' traditional political culture that does not, as Ngcongco (1989) notes, consider public affairs a domain for women and youth. Traditionally, political power is based on age and was centred on a person's social standing. The young, as Somolekae (1989) notes, are traditionally believed to be insufficiently mature and so they were, and are still, excluded from the political process. This culture remains strong and influences who is elected into political and civic office. This lack of a democratic ethic tends to permeate all major social institutions of society and is a survivor from pre-colonial times through the colonial period and into post-colonial society. Youth, are considered as minors whether in the family, polity, economy, religion or education. Whenever the youth attempt to have an impact on policy-making there is often mistrust due primarily to differences in political values and behaviour. Elderly males often made key decisions on their behalf. The pre-independence and post-independence periods of transition did not provide sufficient socialisation to break this lack of a democratic ethic amongst these marginalised groups in society.

The point is that a political culture in general, and a democratic culture in particular - as is true of all norms, values, beliefs and attitudes held by a society - are a product of a complex process of socialisation. The human infant is born a political *tabula rasa* and acquires the necessary political values, beliefs and attitudes through political socialisation. Somewhere between the years of early childhood and late adolescence the youth are expected to learn the skills and values which prepare them for adulthood. Key to this process, are social institutions such as the family, the schooling system, media and political parties.

The family is the most fundamental of all the agencies of socialisation and is often referred to as the 'nursery of our humanness'. If we owe so much of our humanness to the family surely it must play an important role in the process of political socialisation. The question is whether the family in Botswana preaches and practices democracy and electoral politics that might be broadly referred to as a democratic ethic. That is, does the Botswana family provide opportunities for learning and living values and attitudes that are democratic? The data indicates that the family in the traditional Tswana society was not one of the most democratic institutions. Youth and women, as is true in other institutions in society, were regarded as being incapable of making major decisions. They could thus never learn and live democratically nor could they develop the right sets of values and attitudes that can be referred to as a democratic ethic. The Tswana family values and practices seem to have been carried on into the new post-independence political culture. The modern Tswana family is also hampered in two other ways in breaking with this past. First, it competes with other agencies of socialisation such as the school which, as Priwitt (1971:14) notes 'monopolises the time and instruction of youth during the impressionable years of late childhood and early adolescence. The youth tend to spend most of their early years in formal institutions such as schools and have increasingly become products of these agencies rather than of the family. Secondly, parents, as key agents of socialisation in the family, are also new to the post-colonial political culture. They have been educated in the past but have to teach the youth in the present.

It is clear that the education system is also an important agency of political socialisation. This is more so in contemporary society as it is widely accessible and where the young spend their most impressionable years and where they can learn and live democratically. In practice, however, students are commonly regarded as young and immature and therefore incapable of exercising their discretion properly. They are supposed to learn about democratic institutions and how they work and also gain a knowledge and understanding of Setswana culture and traditions. These may contradict one another. The predominant view is one that seems to be in line with Tswana culture and tradition and summed up by Ramatsui when he says: 'Pupils because of their relative immaturity, can be given only a limited voice in any important decisions affecting the school community' (Ramatsui, 1989:pp.90).

I share the same view as Phorano (1989), who, amongst others, decries the present education system in Botswana, seeing it as authoritarian and lacking in the development of a democratic culture. This authoritarianism is enforced through a hierarchical system that expects the head teacher and teachers to instil and enforce discipline and places the student on the passive, receiving end of the system. The classroom culture is also one of teacher dominance and he/she is seen as a custodian of the truth and the fountain of unquestionable knowledge. Critical thinking and questioning by the students is discouraged and seen as disrespectful. It is an attitude that pervades all levels of the educational system. It is only at the level of tertiary education that there is an element of representative governance in student affairs, though even here the head of the institution still reigns supreme on all matters pertaining to the school. Students in these tertiary institutions are still viewed by authorities with suspicion and mistrust when they challenge decisions. In my view, this limits the development of democratic practice and governance.

Political parties are also important in the socialisation process. They are central institutions of electoral politics and are expected to organise the voters into registered party members and encourage them to participate in political events including elections. However, the evidence gathered from DRP opinion polls is that political parties tend to attract very few registered members especially from among the youth. Their main strategies of attracting supporters, including the 'freedom square', study groups, leaflets and house to house campaigns, have failed to reach the youth. For instance, freedom squares have proved to be of limited appeal to the youth. Their timing and use of improper language may be the big turn off to the young voter and may appeal more to those already affiliated. Study groups as a mobilisation strategy is of very limited appeal as it is sparingly used and is often targeted at party membership.

House to house campaigns are a recent phenomenon to most parties and their use has been limited to periods immediately before the general elections. While it may be too early to judge their utility, it is evident that it is not the most appealing to the young voter as authority patterns in the home centres around the parents or the oldest person at home.

The media is yet another institution of importance in political socialisation, with the potential to be very influential in spreading values and beliefs. The youth are relatively more educated than their parents' generation and better placed, materially, to access newspapers, radio, television and magazines. The critical question is, how much political content should the media present and with what audience in mind?.

CONCLUSION

Although the youth are relatively better educated than the older generation, they are still lacking in democratic culture. This is a very worrying trend especially in a society where some 60 per cent of the population is under the age of 30 and are not only the voters of the present but also of the future. One of the important ways of ensuring the survival of any electoral system is not only in applying the law to the letter but also in enlisting the development of a democratic culture. What the average citizen and the youth in particular think about elections and the electoral system is of importance in how citizens view their leaders and what may motivate them to go to the polls when so required. Should a significant part of the population lose confidence in the electoral system, as the youth are in Botswana, then the future of democracy becomes uncertain. I suggest that the family, school system, media and political parties should play a bigger role in promoting a democratic culture. Voter education, especially one that targets the youth, should take these factors into account.

REFERENCES

Abasi et al (2005) 'The state, globalisation and the survival of the urban informal sector in Botswana.' Paper presented at the 5th Biennial Congree of the African Association of Political Science (AAPS) held in Cairo, 27 – 29 June 2005

Botswana Democratic Party (1994) Election Manifesto. Printing and Publishing Company, Gaborone.

Botswana National Front (1994) Manifesto for General Elections.

CSO (1989) *Selected Economic and Social Indicators: 20th Anniversary Issue*, Gaborone: Government Printer

Democracy Research Project, Opinion Poll Reports.

Government of Botswana (2003) *Botswana HIV Sero-Prevalence Sentinel Survey Results*, Gaborone: Government Printer

Harvey, E. (1993), *Youth and the welfare state in Weimar Germany*. Oxford : Clarendon Press.

Hayward, F. (1987) *Elections in Independent Africa*, Westernview Press.

Holm, J. (1987) 'Elections in Botswana: Institution Alienation of a New System of Legitimacy, in Hayward, F. *Elections in Independent Africa*, pp. 122-147.

Holm and Molutsi (ed.) (1989) *Democracy in Botswana*, Gaborone: Macmillan Botswana.

Mackenzie and Robinson (1960) *Five Elections in Africa*, Oxford: Oxford University Press.

Mackenzie, W.J.M. (1967) *Free Elections*, George Allen and Unwin Ltd.

Massey (1967) *Youth and politics* Lexington: D. C. Heath and Co.

Mgadla and Campbell (1989) 'Dikgotla, Dikgosi and the Protectorate Administration', in Holm and Molutsi (ed.) *Democracy in Botswana*, pp. 48-56.

Molama and Manyeneng (1998) *Alcohol use and abuse in Botswana* Gaborone: Government Printer.

National Research Council & Institute of Medicine (2002) *Community Programmes to Promote Youth Development.* Washington D.C. National Academy Press

Ngcongco, L.D. (1989) 'Tswana political tradition: how democratic?' in Holm and Molutsi (ed.), *Democracy in Botswana.*

Ntsabane, T. & C.Ntau (2000) 'Youth and Electoral Participation in Botswana' in *PULA; Botswana Journal of African Studies* Vol. 14 No.1 2000. pp. 85-94.

Ntsabane, T. (1993) 'Issues and Debates in Botswana's Electoral System in Molutsi and Otlhogile (ed.), *Consolidating Democracy: The Electoral Process under Scrutiny*. Democracy Research Project Report.

Ntsabane, T. (1985) *The Botswana Economy, Society and Polity in the Post-colonial Period*, University of Botswana Election Study Project Research Report.

Ntsabane, T. and Selhele (2003) *Youth and elections in southern Africa: some lessons from Botswana* (unpublished)

Parson, J. (1984) *Botswana: Liberal Democracy and the Labor Reserve*, Tata McGraw-Hill.

Parson, Cliffe (et al) (1984) *The 1984 Botswana General Elections: Class Politics and Competitive Elections*, University of Botswana Election Study Project Research Report.

Picard, Louis (1987) *The Politics of Development in Botswana: A Model for Success?* Boulder: Lynne Rienner Pubications.

Phorano, G. (1989) 'The School System: Should it be Teaching Democracy?', in Holm and Molutsi (ed.), *Democracy in Botswana*, pp.93-98.

Prewitt, K. (1971) *Education and Political Values*, Nairobi: East Africa Publishing House.

Raditlhokwa, L. (1999) 'Reasons for Low Participation In Botswana's Politics' *The Youth Enquirer* Vol.1 Issue no.2.

Ramatsui, P.T. (1989), "The School System: Is It Teaching Democracy? In Holm and Molutsi (ed), *Democracy in Botswana*, pp. 89-94.

Rogers (1085) *Adolescents and Youth* Englewood Cliffs: Prentice Hall.

Schapera, I. (1947) *Migrant, Labour and Tribal Life: A Study of conditions in the Bechuanaland Protectorate*, London: Oxford University Press.

Schapera, I. (1970) *A Handbook of Tswana Law and Custom* London: Frank Cass and Company Ltd.

Somolekae, G. (1989) "Citizen Participation in Democratic Politics", in Holm and Molutsi (ed.), *Democracy in Botswana*, pp. 89-92.

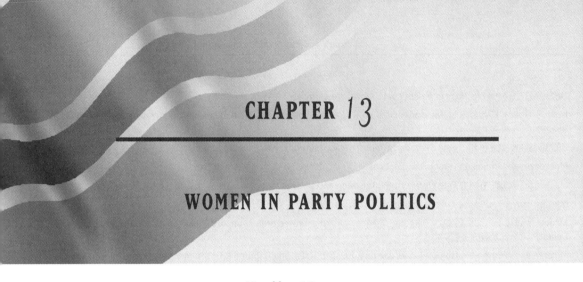

CHAPTER 13

WOMEN IN PARTY POLITICS

Dolly Ntseane

INTRODUCTION

This chapter examines women's representation in different sectors of political parties. Data for this analysis is based on a case study of three political parties namely, the Botswana Congress Party (BCP), the Botswana Democratic Party (BDP) and the Botswana National Front (BNF). The rationale for selecting these three parties was based on the premise that they currently have representation in the National Assembly. They were compared with other political parties and they all command a large following in their women's wings countrywide. Information for this chapter was collected through in-depth interviews with women in leadership positions in these parties as well as key stakeholders. In addition, relevant literature and party documents were consulted to supplement the above material.

The chapter provides a brief analysis of the situation of women in Botswana and gives the context and background for understanding the complexities and challenges that surround the participation of women in politics. It then outlines a historical review of the women's movement in Botswana. It is argued that the active participation of women in politics was to a large extent linked to the successful challenge of the Citizenship Law of 1982-84. There is an in-depth analysis of the achievements made by women politicians following the 1994 and 1999 general elections. Specific attention is paid to the functions and activities of women's wings, the involvement of women in the Central Committee as well as the role played by the Botswana Caucus for Women in Politics (BCWP). The chapter concludes by examining challenges and obstacles facing women in realising their political goals with recommendations for a positive way forward.

BRIEF SITUATION ANALYSIS OF WOMEN

Demographic indicators show that, out of a population of about 1.7 million, women in Botswana comprise 52 per cent of the population (CSO, 2001). Life expectancy for females has dropped from 67 per cent in 1991 to 57 per cent in 2001. This is largely due to the high prevalence of HIV infections and other chronic illnesses. Indicators also show that despite impressive progress in the health sector, maternal mortality is unacceptably high. Secondly, teenage pregnancy continues to be a major source of concern. According to the 2001 census, out of a population of 621 961 children aged 5 to 19, about 41 308 (6.8 per cent) dropped out of school before completing Junior Certificate or Cambridge Certificate. Pregnancy accounted for 38 per cent of all the secondary school dropouts (CSO, 2001). In essence, teenage pregnancy acts as a barrier to the educational and career advancement of the girl child and for her future participation in power and decision-making.

The data on marriage and family relationships shows an overall decline in marriage. For example, the proportion of married females declined by 14.3 per cent from 1981 - 1991 and by 9.3 per cent from 1991 - 2001. The overall decline in the proportion of married females between 1981 and 2001 is 23 per cent (Mookodi, 2003). As a result of the decline in marriage, the data show that 46 per cent of household heads are females. Overall, female-headed households tend to be poorer than their male counterparts due to lack of resources, access to capital and land (BIPDA, 1997).

In terms of economic activity and employment situation men constitute 60 per cent of those in paid employment, while women account for 40 per cent (CSO, 2001). Overall, women tend to be crowded in the jobs labelled as 'women's jobs'. For example, women still dominate in the category of clerks (67 per cent), technicians and associate professionals (64 per cent) and service and sales (52 per cent) (Siphambe, 2003). Although female enrolment has increased in secondary and tertiary institutions, female students prefer arts and social sciences as areas of concentration as opposed to science and technology (Republic of Botswana, 1995; 2003). Efforts are currently being made to eliminate gender discrimination in the education system by promoting access to vocational and technology areas, making curricula and teaching materials gender sensitive, encouraging female students to take science subjects and strengthening career guidance and counselling in schools (Republic of Botswana, 1995; 2003).

Finally, in spite of regional and international treaties that have been ratified by Botswana government, women are still accorded subordinate status when it comes to certain rights and freedoms. The low social status of women stems predominantly from traditional and cultural practices that perceive a woman as a minor and a homemaker. Consequently, women often shy away from participating actively in politics due to fear that this role clashes with these traditional expectations. It is, however, significant to note that progress has been made over the last few years to change the negative socio-cultural practices that militate against women's full participation in politics. For example, a number of national laws which affect the rights of women have been amended namely; the Public Service Amendment Act, (2000), Affiliation Proceedings Amendment Act, 1999, Penal Code Amendment Act, 1998, Criminal Procedure and Evidence Amendment Act, 1997, Deeds Registry Amendment Act, 1996, Employment Amendment Act, 1996, and the Citizenship Amendment Act, 1995 (Republic of Botswana, 2003).

It is clear that remarkable progress has been achieved in the improvement of the status of women. However, much still has to be done in the areas of economic empowerment, education and skill training, health and reproductive issues, power sharing and decision-making and the promotion of gender awareness in development planning. These areas are the essential ingredients for the full participation of women in politics. The next section reviews briefly the historical developments and milestones of the women's political movement in Botswana.

A BRIEF HISTORY OF THE WOMEN'S MOVEMENT

Information about the history of the women's political movement is very scanty and fragmented as issues on gender and politics have not been given much attention by scholars and researchers. Also the quality of the existing data is not sufficiently disaggregated to allow proper analysis along gender dimensions (Madisa, 1990; Kamau, 1999). However, despite these limitations, the available literature has been used and supplemented with interviews in an effort to unravel the unique role of women in politics since independence in 1966.

From Independence (1966) to 1986

Batswana women have had the right to vote since independence. However, this right was not coupled with political education and economic empowerment (Madisa, 1990). Consequently, from the early sixties to the late 1980s, women's participation in politics can be classified as predominantly passive or dormant as far as political activism is concerned. For example, although three major parties were formed in the early sixties namely, the Botswana People's Party (BPP), Botswana Democratic Party (BDP), and the Botswana Independence Party (BIP), it was not until 1977 that a women's wing was launched by the Botswana National Front. The BDP followed ten years later in 1987 and the BCP women's league came into existence in 1998 when the party was formed.

The analysis of the election manifestos of BDP and BNF reflects that it was only during the preparation of the 1994 general elections that these parties articulated their commitment towards women's political empowerment. Prior to this, women were not accorded any meaningful attention although they played a critical role in mobilising party support by organising at grass-root level and raising funds for the parties. Traditionally women did not take part in the political affairs of the tribe prior to independence and political offices were kept exclusively in the hands of the men. Overall, women were regarded as socially inferior to men and were treated as minors (Schapera, 1984). With the advent of modern education, women have become more aware of their rights and obligations as partners in national development and a few women have played a pivotal role in decision-making structures, for example: Dr G. Chiepe, the former Minister of Education and Mrs Mannathoko, the former Mayor of Gaborone. Furthermore, women's organisations such as the Botswana Council of Women and the Young Women's Christian Association were instrumental in the early sixties in addressing issues facing women and children and lobbying and advocating for women's issues in general.

Mobilising Women for Political Rights: 1986 to 2003

Here it is noted that the mobilisation for women's political discourse was spearheaded by the successful challenge of the Citizenship Law of 1982-1984 by Unity Dow in 1995 (Molokomme, 1991;Selolwane, 1998; Van Allen, 2001). Dow argued that Sections 4 and 5 of the Citizenship Act discriminated against women contrary to the provisions of Section 3 of the Botswana Constitution (Dow, 1995). According to Sections 4 and 5 of the Act, 'a person born in Botswana shall be a citizen of Botswana by birth and descent if at the time of birth; a) his father was a citizen of Botswana; b) his mother was a citizen of Botswana'. Further, that 'a person born outside Botswana shall be a citizen of Botswana by descent if at the time of birth; a) his father was a citizen of Botswana or b) in the case of a person born out of wedlock, his mother was a citizen of Botswana (Republic of Botswana, 1984).

There is a view that the existence of this discriminative law brought together women activists to adopt a common strategy to challenge the state on what was considered a fundamental human right issue (Molokomme, 1998; Van Allen, 2001). Various women's rights activists grouped together to form Emang Basadi (stand up women) to lobby for political reforms and respect for human rights. Invariably, the Citizenship Act became the primary campaign issue. In 1995, the Citizenship Act was successfully challenged and was found to be in violation of the Constitution by both the High Court and the Court of Appeal (Dow, 1995).

Emang Basadi was not started as a political movement although it paved the way for political reforms. Launched in 1986, a women's research group met informally to share ideas about fundamental issues affecting women nationally and internationally. Members of this group observed that government departments discussed women's issues in an uncritical manner usually perceiving them in terms of welfare rather than politics (Molokomme, 1991:848). They also realised that the 'insistence by women organisations that the activities of women are non-political resulted in the further de-politicisation of women' (Ibid: 848). Determined to make a meaningful difference, the group decided to form a new organisation that would provide a platform for serious advocacy for women's human and political rights. One of the key objectives of the association was to influence the state policy to remove discriminatory provisions in the law. Realising that there was lack of positive response from government, the association changed its strategy to focus on political empowerment of women (Emang Basadi, 1994).

Following these historic events, Emang Basadi started a lobbying and advocacy campaign to challenge politicians to introduce political reforms. A major achievement was the launching of the Political Education Project (PEP) in November 1993 with the aim of ensuring greater participation of women in the political process. Another specific challenge was to lobby for at least 30 per cent female representation in both parliament and local government (Emang Basadi, 1998). Three major accomplishments of the PEP included the production of the 1994 Women's Manifesto, the running of constituency workshops and, finally, the training of prospective women candidates (Ibid: 4).

The 1994 Women's Manifesto drawn by various women's organisations articulated succinctly, critical issues facing women. With regard to participation of women in politics, the Manifesto called upon political parties to adopt the following strategies:

- change the existing structures in order to give women a chance to participate at all levels
- establish a quota system to ensure that equity is maintained between male and female candidates
- build awareness of women's political rights
- support competent women candidates
- His Excellency the President to nominate competent female MPs who are sensitive to women issues as specially elected members of parliament.

Most importantly, the drafting of the Women's Manifesto was instrumental in ensuring that women's issues were taken on board during the 1994 general elections (Selolwane, 1998; Emang Basadi, 1998). For example, for the first time in their history, the BDP and BNF 1994 Election Manifestos had a specific section on women and politics. These parties made a commitment to address sex discrimination and inequality and to work towards repealing all laws that discriminate against women. Parties also committed themselves to encourage and support women in all spheres particularly the political arena and other policy-making bodies. Interestingly, the BNF pledged to reserve 30 per cent of the eligible positions to women and to leave 70 per cent to be contested by women and men (BNF, 1994:10). It is noted with disappointment that this pledge has not been honoured. In the same vein, following the 1994 general elections, President Masire nominated two women to parliament bringing the female representation from a maximum of five per cent to 9.1 per cent.

Another historical benchmark arising from the Women's Manifesto of 1994 was the implementation of the decision of the Court of Appeal in the case of Attorney General vs. Unity Dow through the enactment of the Citizenship Amendment Act of 1995. Further, in 1996, Parliament adopted the National Policy on Women and Development. During the same year, government ratified the Convention on the Elimination of All Forms of Discrimination Against Women, which had been passed by the UN General Assembly as early as 1979 (United Nations, 1979). The ratification of this convention played a pivotal role in enhancing the empowerment of women and ensuring that they are recognised as active and equal participants in nation building.

In order to prepare women for the 1999 general elections, Emang Basadi implemented the second phase of the PEP project. A strategic plan was drawn targeting four components namely: training and empowering prospective women candidates, mobilising and training women's wings of political parties, forming a women's Inter-Party Caucus and developing a research and data base on women in decision-making (Emang Basadi, 1998:10). Also, the second edition of the Women's Manifesto was developed preparing women for the 1999 general elections. A specific addition to the 1994 manifesto was the chapter on economic empowerment and violence against women and an expanded chapter on women and family. It is clear that one cannot talk about political emancipation of women without making reference to these issues and concerns (Madisa, 1990; Byanyima, 1996 Nzomo, 1993; Selolwane, 1998; Emang Basadi, 1998; Hassim, 2000).

In concluding the analysis of the history of the women's movement, it is evident that Emang Basadi played a pivotal role in igniting women's political consciousness. Women activists and politicians embraced this development and joined hands with Emang Basadi in the formulation of the Women's Manifesto which had a strategic influence on party manifestos. Acknowledging the role of Emang Basadi in this regard Hon Phumaphi, in a speech delivered at the National Conference for Women and Politics, reiterated that it was through the guidance of the association that women managed to develop determination and self confidence as well as lobbying skills and campaign strategies to counteract threats by men and to generate and win the support of the general public (Phumaphi, 1997).

The SADC Gender Unit should be commended for the advocacy role it has played in bringing the issues of women's empowerment to the forefront. Through the efforts of this unit, member countries have been challenged to make radical constitutional reforms to bring more women into positions of power and decision-making and improve the conditions that hinder the development of women (SADC, 2001). In 1999, the Unit organised a historic regional conference that drew the attention of key politicians in the region to the need to work towards increasing participation of women in politics. The conference adopted a Regional Programme of Action for Women in Politics and Decision-making. Amongst other things, this programme identifies actions and strategies that must be adopted at the national and regional level if the 30 per cent target is to be achieved (Ibid; 15). Women from different political parties have used the recommendations of this conference as a platform to lobby for change in their respective constituencies.

Against the backdrop of these events, the extent to which women have succeeded in pursuing their dreams is examined, first by taking stock of the role played by women in women-wings of political parties, then evaluating their role in central committees and key leadership positions. In addition, the chapter briefly discusses the participation of women in key decision-making positions, concluding by highlighting the role of the Botswana Caucus for Women in Politics and how it positioned women politicians for the 2004 general elections and beyond.

Women Wings of Political Parties

As noted earlier, the BNF established a women's wing of the party in 1977 – the first political party to do so. The BDP women's wing was formed in 1987 whilst the BCP women's wing came with the formation of the party in 1998. Although these parties differ in philosophies and ideologies, the women's wings share a common vision that women's democratic rights should be protected and promoted and that political parties should democratise their structures to ensure that both men and women are adequately represented.

After the 1995 evaluation of the political education programme, Emang Basadi decided to target women wings of political parties as a strategy to enhance the leadership capacity of women. The association realised that women's wings were better placed to influence the agendas of political parties since they operate from within. Seemingly, they were viewed as a unique avenue to enable women to infiltrate decision-making structures such as council and parliament (Emang Basadi 1998:18). As a result, phase II of the political education project began with a needs assessment to identify how women's wings or leagues could be strengthened. The result of this assessment revealed that women wings required training on gender issues and on lobbying and advocacy skills. Other critical areas requiring attention included: training workshops on campaign management, fundraising, assertiveness and confidence building skills (Ibid: 19). As a follow-up to this, Emang Basadi organised a workshop on 'effective use of women's wings'. Being the first workshop of its kind, it gave women politicians guidance on how to address women's issues within political parties. Women were also guided on how to ensure that their members were focused on enhancing the political status of women (Ibid: 19).

Through the assistance of Emang Basadi and other international organisations, notably the Forum for Women in Democracy (FOWODE) of Uganda and the Friedrich Ebert Stiftung, women's wings/leagues have developed a clear focus and direction. Despite inevitable obstacles, women wings/leagues in BCP, BDP and BNF have grown in strength to move away from providing welfare functions to perform the following activities: sensitising women on political issues by giving lectures and through workshops, conferences and seminars; mobilising women and motivating them to participate actively in party and national politics; promoting and protecting women's rights; inculcating among women the spirit of self- confidence and self reliance by encouraging them to address political rallies and community initiatives; encouraging women to articulate and defend their rights through their involvement in village activities and non-governmental organisations; ensuring that women's interests are considered in every major decision of all party structures in the interest of gender equality through advocacy and active lobbying; mobilising party support through door to door campaigns, choirs and other strategies; participating in fund-raising activities and community projects that promote the party image; sensitising their female colleagues about the benefits of becoming involved in party politics; lobby and advocate for the inclusion of 30 per cent quota in the party and national constitution.

To a large extent, the participation of women in the political women's wings has also enhanced women's confidence level and willingness to run for political office. **Table 13.1** below, shows the number of women in positions of responsibility following the 1999 general elections.

Table 13.1: Women in Positions of Responsibility since 1999

	Central Committees		Councillors		Members of Parliament		Ministers/ Assist Ministers	
	Men	Women	Men	Women	Men	Women	Men	Women
BCP	19	5	16	11	1	0	0	0
BDP	12	6	389	97	32	8	11	5
BNF	18	8	82	11	6	0	0	0

It is evident from this table that although disparities still exist, women now constitute at least one third of the central committee membership across political parties. This trend is very significant given the fact that these figures were considerably lower after the 1994 general elections. The figures for council and parliament are comparatively very low. Nevertheless, a momentum for political reform has been generated. Party leaders are becoming increasingly gender sensitive. Seemingly, there is now a realisation that women have the necessary talents, skills and potential to make a meaningful difference in the political discourse. For example, the BCP elected a woman to assume the position of Regional Chairperson for the first time in 2002. Another woman was elected as Regional Deputy Chairperson. In addition, a member of the BNF women's league became the first woman chairperson. Currently, a woman is holding an executive position as the BNF party Deputy Secretary General. Yet another BNF woman was holding the position of Deputy Mayor of Gaborone. Finally, within the ruling BDP, there were eight women parliamentarians out of 32 (25 per cent) of whom five (15 per cent) were cabinet ministers.

I conducted interviews on whether a woman vice president or presidential candidate would be acceptable among female politicians. Responding to this question, women in leadership positions in all three parties (BDP, BNF and BCP) agreed that women have clearly proved their potential at council, parliamentary and ministerial levels and hence have the capability to take up these positions. In the same vein, the results of the 1999 opinion poll conducted by the Democracy Research Project showed that 64 per cent of the respondents in a sample of 3 365 selected nationwide indicated their positive support for a woman vice president or president. A third of the respondents (36 per cent) reported that women are not yet ready. Overall, 71 per cent of the respondents reported that women are as capable as men to hold these positions. (DRP,1999). My interpretation of the results of the opinion poll is that gender stereotypes are gradually being replaced by a more inclusive approach which is advocating for equal representation between men and women in positions of leadership.

Finally, in the areas of decision-making and management, my research shows that women are making steady progress in moving into professional and high visibility jobs. Women for example currently constitute 27 per cent of the positions in the super-scale hierarchy (D1 and above) (Republic of Botswana, 2003). Out of these, women make up 30 per cent of the deputy permanent secretaries, 50 per cent of the directors and 35 per cent of the deputy directors. Women ambassadors or high commissioners are 5 out of a total of 33. The number of women judges has increased to three and the number of magistrates has also increased to sixteen (Republic of Botswana, 2003).

Overall, at the levels of decision-making and management, women have exceeded the 30 per cent mark recommended by the Beijing Platform of Action (UNDP, 2003; WAD & Botswana Women's NGO's Coalition, 2003). The involvement of women in decision-making is critical because this is where they gain skills that are essential in the political arena such as leadership and management skills, policy development skills and analytical skills.

The Botswana Caucus for women in Politics

The Botswana Caucus for Women in Politics (BCWP) is the brainchild of Emang Basadi and it was officially launched in April 1997. Women councillors and parliamentarians from different political parties saw the need to form a unified force despite their opposing philosophies and ideologies. They also recognised the reality that party structures did not provide opportunities for women to get the necessary training on political leadership and empowerment. Invariably, from its inception, the mission of the caucus was to see to it that women, across party lines, were given strategic skills to empower them to lobby and advocate for power sharing between men and women. Another major vision of the Caucus was to strive to increase political awareness of women so that by the year 2004, women would have reached the minimum 30 per cent level of representation in council, parliament and party structures (BCWP, 2002). It should be understood that the whole purpose of this initiative was to enable individual Caucus members to become skillful in the political field rather than becoming representatives of their parties.

In order to translate these broad goals into activities, the Caucus has embarked on a project called 'Positioning Women Politicians for 2004 and Beyond. The main thrust of this project was to prepare women to stand for the 2004 elections in larger numbers. With this aim, the Caucus has conducted regional seminars and workshops covering topics such as the right to share power with men, changing voting trends, interpersonal skills, campaign logistics, public speaking, presentation skills as well as managing critics. The Caucus also conducted research into difficulties facing women in standing for political office. It now intends to become active in lobbying parliament to amend the national constitution to facilitate reservation of special seats for women, youth and other special groups; to lobby the media to be gender responsive in their reporting; to empower women politicians through training on standing for positions of power; to train women to vote for other women; to empower youth through training and to encourage them to stand for leadership positions (Emang Basadi, 2002).

Challenges and Obstacles

While efforts made by BCWP are commendable as an inter-party structure, women political leaders as well as key stakeholders acknowledge that it faces enormous challenges. First, there has been reluctance, mainly from the leadership of the opposition parties, to allow their party members to join the Caucus because they see it being dominated by women from the BDP who want women from opposition parties to vote for them. Secondly, some people argue that influential MPs within the Caucus are also likely to exert unfair influence and pressure over women from the opposition. Others have expressed the view that even the content of the materials used to train women is driven by the dominant forces within the Caucus who happen to be BDP members. Thirdly, some women within the Caucus feel that there is a lack of democratic governance and transparency within the Caucus. For example, they feel that power sharing and decision-making rests with a few individuals. This apparent lack of ownership by some Caucus members is likely to undermine its capacity to develop into a powerful force which can advance women's issues across party lines.

Fourthly, it has been found that some male politicians are generally suspicious and therefore not fully supportive of the Caucus developing into a strong women's movement. Some feel threatened that women want to start their own political party while others have gone to the extent of demanding regular feedback on the issues discussed during Caucus meetings. This lack of trust and suspicion is likely to act as an enormous obstacle for women as they aspire to mature in political leadership. As articulated by Shvedova in her study of obstacles to women's participation, 'men dominate the political arena; men formulate rules of the political game; and men define the standards for evaluation. The existence of this male dominated model results in either women rejecting politics altogether or rejecting male-style politics' (Shvedova, 1998:20).

Fifthly, it is apparent that the Caucus has very limited capacity to empower women politically. Currently for example, the Caucus does not have any full-time staff to run its activities. Women politicians who are already in the forefront have enormous responsibilities as full-time councillors, MPs and business persons. In addition, due to the restructuring of the roles and responsibilities, Emang Basadi does not seem to be playing an active role in advancing the activities of the Caucus. Lack of capacity may significantly hinder the Caucus to carry out its lobbying and advocacy functions effectively.

Finally, what is also a serious stumbling block is that the majority of women, particularly those residing in the rural areas, are poor. Because of their low economic status, many women are likely to work against the mission of the Caucus due to the fact that they get rewarded when they support men. Some women have argued that men generally assist them materially whereas women work for the advancement of their families (*'mosadi ene o berekela lwapa lwa gagwe'*). Another threat is that because of cultural orientations and gender stereotypes, some women do not believe that women can hold political office; as a result, they prefer to vote for male candidates even when they are ignorant of their political backgrounds and capabilities. Hence, women find themselves trapped by cultural stereotypes that 'men are leaders and women are followers'. Invariably, besides awareness building and education, the Caucus needs to focus on activities that address poverty alleviation and gender mainstreaming and empowerment.

I have highlighted the major obstacles and challenges specifically facing the Women's Caucus and this section concludes by discussing other challenges facing women politicians in general. Among those that feature prominently are: socio-cultural stereotypes, ideological and psychological setbacks, lack of party support and finally, lack of education and access to information.

SOCIO-CULTURAL STEREOTYPES

Research shows that women do not dominate leadership of political parties because of conservative traditions and cultural stereotypes. Despite social change, traditional attitudes still prevail which relegate women to subordinate roles. Some women feel too uncomfortable to pursue political careers because they tend to perceive politics as a domain reserved for men. Women are also kept away from participating effectively in politics due to the fact that they have multiple responsibilities as wives and mothers and are also involved in subsistence production. The advent of the HIV and AIDS pandemic has made the situation worse as the burden of care rests solely on women. Coupled with these multiple roles, there is resistance from men in supporting women who want to advance in political leadership. When women are given positions of power and responsibility, this is usually in the traditional female fields such as health, education, welfare, tourism, social security, culture and home affairs. The general perception is that women would feel more comfortable and confident in these areas.

My interviews have established that often women internalise the socio-cultural expectations and stereotypes and then lose confidence and a sense of competence. Some women even begin to perceive politics as a 'dirty game' that is played by women who are bold and tough (*'basadi ba ba diganka'*). As a result of ideological and psychological orientations, women become fearful of the unknown and feel easily intimidated from standing for elections. They begin to fight amongst themselves and undermine the capabilities of others. Commenting on this aspect, Nasha (1999:18) contends that the most 'vicious de-campaigners of other women are women themselves'. In addition, the negative manner in which the media portrays women often reinforces feelings of insecurity and lack of confidence. The 'pull her down' syndrome that was discussed earlier emanates from these underlying contradictions.

It must be emphasised that running for political office requires party support and commitment from the leadership. This could be in the form of financial support, transport to organise political rallies in the constituency, training opportunities, gender sensitivity and an enabling environment where women feel secure to develop without experiencing any form of intimidation and harassment. It has been demonstrated that party support is critical to the survival of the Women's Caucus and other party structures. Interviews with women politicians have also revealed that lack of party support is a major setback in the advancement of their full participation in party politics.

LACK OF EDUCATION AND ACCESS TO INFORMATION

Access to education and information is a critical component in advancing participation of women in party politics. As articulated by Shawa, a woman Member of Parliament in Pakistan, 'education is the most important channel for encouraging women to speak up' (Shawa, 1998:27). I share the view that women need to have a certain level of education to articulate issues, to read and understand policy papers and to have a certain level of appreciation of political issues around the world. I consider lack of education and access to information to be serious challenges for women in Botswana particularly those who reside in rural and remote areas of the country. Most government policy documents, legislative instruments, reports and other public papers are written in English and this makes it very difficult for a less well-educated woman to understand or even to offer meaningful comments during political debates. It is also clear that women and young girls lack political education and awareness. Although Emang Basadi has done a tremendous job in this area, most women are still ignorant about their political rights and their role in politics. Consequently, when women talk about political participation this is often in terms of participation in choirs and fund-raising activities. Only a few educated women address political rallies.

THE WAY FORWARD

As a way forward, there are a number of measures that can be adopted to address these challenges namely, review of institutional arrangements, education and awareness building, lobbying and advocacy, economic empowerment, resource mobilisation, networking, coalition building and finally the positive involvement of the media. These measures are discussed below.

Concrete strategies need to be put in place to remove all those cultural stereotypes, beliefs and attitudes that relegate women to subordinate positions. This can be done by repealing all laws and policies that discriminate against women, by promoting educational campaigns that portray positive achievements made by women, mainstreaming gender in all sectors including educational institutions and by empowering women through resource allocation to organisations that are devoted to training and economic development.

Women need political education in areas such as, the role of women in politics, the role of women as voters, the role of women in drafting party manifestos and policies, political development, socio-economic issues affecting the society and other areas of national interest. In addition, women need to be made aware of the concrete roles they can play in the political discourse that goes beyond participating in choirs, cooking and party fund-raising activities. I suggest that political education projects initiated by Emang Basadi should be intensified to reach more women. As much as possible, young women and rural women should be strategically targeted. Education and awareness building should have a gendered approach and therefore should also aim at targeting men.

Women's wings should intensify their lobbying and advocacy campaigns at party level for the inclusion of the 30 per cent quota in the national constitution. They should also continue to lobby both the President and other key stakeholders to nominate more women in council and parliament.

ECONOMIC EMPOWERMENT

Solid strategies should be adopted to create employment opportunities for women through income generating projects, development of agriculture, tourism, irrigation schemes and provision of financial resources and expertise to facilitate economic development. Women's wings should go beyond party structures in mobilising resources for political advancement of women. They should strengthen existing relationships with Friedrich Ebert Stiftung and approach other sponsors and donors both within SADC and abroad. In addition, women's wings should strengthen linkages with political movements in the region and beyond. This will enable them to share areas of common concerns and lessons learned. The role and function of the Women's Caucus needs to be clarified in order to give it credibility and sustainability as it has great potential to mobilise politicians and other women in civil society to address critical issues affecting women as well as ensuring that the Beijing Platform of Action is fully implemented. Efforts should continue to be made to sensitise the media about women's issues and, where feasible, a network should be formalised between the media and women politicians to ensure that women's issues are promoted and portrayed positively. The media should also play an active role in sensitising the nation about the need for gender equality.

CONCLUSION

In this chapter I have given an overview of the role of women in party politics beginning with a discussion of the historical development of the women's movement in Botswana. The activities of Emang Basadi have been highlighted and the drafting of the Women's Manifesto which played such a critical role in transforming party manifestos to address issues of gender inequality in the party structures. Attention was then given to the functions of women's wings and the Women's Caucus and I have highlighted the role played by these structures in building leadership capacity. It is clear that, despite achievements being made on the road to equality, women are still facing major constraints that prevent them from participating fully in decision-making. With that in mind, the chapter ends by examining possible intervention strategies which could be implemented to overcome these challenges.

REFERENCES

Alexander, E (2002) 'The Case of Women in Politics in Botswana' in S. Kaye, L. Machacha and T. Maundeni (eds) *Gender: Opportunities and Challenges. 1st Conference of the Gender and Policy Program Committee* October 2001 Associated Printers.

Byanyima, W.K (1996) Speech delivered by Honorable Byanyima MP Uganda at Emang Basadi 10th Anniversary Celebrations Fund Raising Dinner. Boipuso Hall, Gaborone.

BCWP (2002) 'Positioning Women Politicians for 2004 and beyond' BCWP, Gaborone.

BCWP (2003) 'Regional Workshops Materials' BCWP, Gaborone.

Botswana Congress Party (1994) *Election Manifesto*, Gaborone.

Botswana Democratic Party (1969) *Election Manifesto* 1969, Gaborone.

Botswana Democratic Party (1974) *Election Manifesto* 1974, Gaborone.

Botswana Democratic Party (1989) *Election Manifesto* 1989, Gaborone.

Botswana Democratic Party (1994) *Election Manifesto*, Gaborone.

BIDPA (1997) 'Study on Poverty and Poverty Alleviation in Botswana', BIDPA, Gaborone.

Botswana National Front (1994) *Manifesto for the General Elections*, Gaborone.

Botswana National Front (Pamphlet # 1).

CSO (2001) 2001 *Population and Housing Censu*s Government Printer.

Dow, U (1995) *The Citizenship Case: The Attorney General of the Republic of Botswana vs. Unity Dow, Court Documents, Judgement, Cases and Materials* Gaborone: Lentswe la Lesedi.

DRP (1999) *Results of Opinion Polls*, DRP, University of Botswana Gaborone.

Emang Basadi (1994) *The Women Manifesto: A Summary of Botswana Women's Issues and Demands* Gaborone: Lentswe la Lesedi.

Emang Basadi (1998) *Political Education Project: A Strategy that Works* Gaborone: Lentswe la Lesedi.

Emang Basadi (2002) 'Setting an Agenda for 30per cent Minimum Female Representation in Parliament and Council by 2004' *Report of the National Conference on Women and Political Empowerment* June 2002 Gaborone.

Hassim, S (2000) 'South Africa: A Strategic Ascent' *UNESCO Courier*, 53 (6) 20-22.

Kamau, M (1999) Speech delivered at the Conference on Women in Politics and Decision-making in SADC: Beyond 30per cent in 2005 28th March – 1st April 1999 SADC Gender Unit, Gaborone.

Madisa, M (1990) 'Few Women participate in the political process' *Southern Africa 3* (7).

Molokomme, A (1991) 'Emang Basadi' Signs: *Journal of Women in Culture and Society* 16 (4) 846.

Mookodi, G (2003) 'Marriage and Nuptiality' in *CSO 2001 Population and Housing Census Dissemination Seminar* September 2003 Government Printer.

Nasha, M (1999) Speech delivered at a Conference on Women in Politics and Decision-making in SADC: *Beyond 30 per cent in 2005 SADC*, Gender Unit, Gaborone.

Nzomo, M (1993) *Strategies for empowering Kenyan women in the post 1992, multi-party era*. Institute of Diplomacy and International Studies. University of Nairobi, Kenya.

Phumaphi, J (1997) Speech delivered at the official opening of the National Conference on Women in Politics. 'Women preparing to run for political office' Boipuso Hall, Gaborone.

Republic of Botswana (1984) Citizenship Act of 1984 Cap 01 01.

Republic of Botswana (1995) Policy on Women and Development, Women's Affairs Department, Gaborone.

Republic of Botswana (2003) International Conference on Population and Development: Country Report, Gaborone.

SADC (2001) 'Monitoring Implementation of the Beijing Commitments by SADC Member States' *SADC Gender Monitor*, Issue 2 March 2001.

Schapera, I (1984) *A Handbook of Tswana Law and Custom* Great Britain: Frank Cass and Company LTD.

Shawa, R (1998) in Karam (ed.) *Women in Parliament Beyond Numbers* Stockholm: International IDEA.

Selolwane, O (1998) 'Equality of citizenship and gendering of democracy in Botswana' in W. Edge & M. Lekorwe (eds) *Botswana Politics and Society* Pretoria Schaik Publishers.

Siphambe, H (2003) 'Economic Activity by Labor Force' in *CSO 2001 Population and Housing Census Dissemination Seminar* September 2003 Government Printer.

Shvedova, N (1998) 'Obstacles to Women's Participation in Parliament' in Karam (ed.) *Women in Parliament Beyond Numbers* Stockholm: International IDEA.

United Nations (1979) 'The Convention on the Elimination of all Forms of Discrimination against Women' United Nations New York.

UNDP (2003) *Human Development Report: Millennium Development Goals- A compact Among Nations to end Poverty* New York: Oxford University Press.

Van Allen (2001) 'Women Rights Movement as a Measure of African Democracy' *Journal of Asian and African Studies* 36 (1) 39-64.

WAD & BNCO (2003) 'Botswana Country Report' Women's Affairs Department, Gaborone

CHAPTER 14

CONCLUSION:
RE-CONSIDERING DEMOCRACY
IN THE SOUTHERN AFRICAN REGION

Zibani Maundeni

The chapters of this book have analysed numerous issues, ranging from democratic leadership in the region, electoral systems, transparency in the administration of elections, electoral reforms, internal organisation of political parties, succession rules, electoral performance of political parties, the role of civil society in the democratisation process and in voter education and the roles of women and youth in politics. This concluding chapter reviews the material in the book and provides new arguments for the purpose of establishing whether Botswana is still the leading democratic nation in the continent. It will also isolate a few central issues from the different chapters and either emphasise what the different authors noted or broaden the debate to give a balanced view of different situations.

The question that has arisen since the advent of new democracies in southern Africa and in the world is whether Botswana is still the leading democratic nation or whether it has been overtaken by others? Many of the contributors to this book acknowledge that Botswana has pursued democratic politics throughout its post-colonial period, avoiding the monarchical/military/one-party dictatorships that have characterised the African continent and the third world for three decades. But some authors hold the view that Botswana's democratic history has not been used positively or proactively to influence democratic change in the region. What is most discomforting to them is the observation that Botswana still suffers from the same problems that are facing new democracies.

However, it has been observed that Botswana has regressed in terms of succession laws. Its presidential succession laws, which allow automatic succession by the vice president in the case of a vacancy before the expiry of the term of office of the incumbent president, were a step backward in the democratisation process. But equally, it can be argued that other countries have not done much better in this regard. They have not successfully democratised the presidential succession process and it is here that democratisation faces a possible reversal. The question of succession split the BNF and led to the emergence of the New Democratic Front. The observation is that many more political parties, including ruling ones, may suffer the same fate over the question of succession. However, I am inclined to believe that the intense debates around succession rules that are raging in Botswana (other countries in the region are not discussing it with the same intensity) have the capacity to propel Botswana to be the leading democratic nation in terms of reforming its succession rules.

Some authors in the book have noted positive changes in the administration of elections but they also noted some serious challenges emerging from Botswana's electoral system. I would add that, on a general level, any electoral system translates the votes cast in a general election into seats won by parties and candidates, determines who is elected and which party gains power, shapes the type of party system in the country (either encouraging factionalism or coherence), influences the way parties conduct their campaigns and encourages the losers either to work within or outside the system (Reynolds and Reilly, 2002).

It has also been shown here that the type of electoral system that a country operates crucially determines the methodology for converting the popular vote into elected seats. The authors made a systematic comparison between the FPTP system and PR, and the evidence showed that while the former produced stable governments (though not in India anymore, I would argue), it was less equitable in the distribution of elected seats (including giving a seat bonus to the ruling party), promoted one-party predominance, marginalised the small parties and was wasteful in terms of popular votes. The authors of this book have also exposed the danger posed by the FPTP system in Botswana, noting the possibility that the ruling party could lose the popular vote and yet still win the majority of the elected seats, leading to a serious questioning of the fairness of the system and, possibly, a constitutional crisis. In addition to their observations, I would add that such questioning of the fairness of the elections plunged Mongolia in 1992, and Lesotho in 1998, into a constitutional crisis, leading to sharp electoral reforms.

But the main point is that both Mongolia and Lesotho had no real history of democratic politics and toleration and are therefore different from Botswana which does have an entrenched democratic culture. I think Britain offers the correct example for Botswana. 'Twice in Britain (in 1951 and 1974) the party winning the most votes in the country as a whole won fewer seats than their opponents, but this was considered more a quirk of a basically sound system than an outright unfairness which should be reversed' (Reynolds and Reilly, 2002: 11). So, while other authors see the dangers posed by the electoral outcome of the 2009 election, in the event the ruling party wins the most seats but loses the popular vote, I foresee the likelihood of the nation accepting the results and considering the outcome as a quirk and the electoral system as sound. My impression is that Botswana's democratic culture is now more entrenched and resistant to the kind of constitutional crisis that visited Mongolia and Lesotho. If my interpretation of Botswana's democratic culture is correct, its implication is that the predicted constitutional crisis may never happen.

I would also point out that South Africa, which practises a List Membership Proportional system, has not avoided the predominance of the African National Congress (ANC) and neither has the Mixed Member Proportional system (MMP) solved Lesotho's one party predominance. In the 2002 election, the ruling Lesotho Congress for Democracy (LCD) won 79/80 FPTP seats with 54.8 per cent popular vote and was excluded from the 40 MMP seats. The largest opposition, Basotho National Party [BNP] won 1/80 FPTP seats with 22.4 per cent of the popular vote and was awarded 21/40 MMP seats. The rest of the 19 MMP seats were distributed between the smaller opposition parties with the party with 6.9 per cent of the popular vote getting five seats, another with 5.5 per cent popular vote getting five seats, another with 2.9 per cent popular vote getting three seats and so on (Kabemba et al, 2005: 21). Overall, the ruling LCD controls 79/120 parliamentary seats and the combined opposition controls the other 41/120 seats. This is a significant improvement for Lesotho, but its unstable politics are also directly linked to disloyal security forces and an adversarial and violent political culture that cannot be addressed through electoral reforms.

> 'Changes to the electoral system from the FPTP to MMP and restructuring of the armed forces have substantially reduced the risks of the rejection of election results and political violence in Lesotho. However, there is a need for continued vigilance. Lesotho's political culture remains adversarial and the problems of political violence and poor accountability should not be regarded as solved' (Kabemba et al, 2005: 53).

The point is that despite reforming its electoral system, the future of democracy in Lesotho is still uncertain. The implication for Botswana is that electoral reforms would help the small parties to enter parliament, but would not help the opposition to win state power unless they solve other issues such as opposition unity and good internal party governance which have been discussed extensively in this book.

The other central point is that South Africa started well with the proportional system: proportionality was followed to the letter.

> 'South Africa used a classically proportional electoral system for its first democratic elections of 1994 and with 62.65 per cent of the popular vote the

ANC won 63 per cent of the national seats. The electoral system was highly proportional and the number of wasted votes (i.e. those which were cast for parties who did not win seats in the Assembly) was only 0.8 per cent of the total' (Reynolds and Reilly, 2002: 17).

But South Africa too has degenerated into the predominant party system despite its continued use of the list PR.

'On 14 April 2004 post-apartheid South Africa conducted its third set of national and provincial elections. First, although there was a marked increase in the number of political parties contesting the elections the ANC increased its support and concomitant legislature majority. Second, the NNP virtually collapsed, the IFP was defeated in KwaZulu Natal, the DA increased its support and a new party, the Independent Democrats (ID), made its appearance count. Third, there was a marked convergence of the campaign issues highlighted by the political parties. And fourth, the percentage of women in parliament increased reaching the 30 per cent quota target' (Hendricks, 2005: 66).

Thus, the same list PR system has produced dramatically opposed results in South Africa, at different times. So, despite the fact that Botswana practices one electoral system, Lesotho another and South Africa yet another, the predominance of one party and the un-viability of the opposition is present in all of them. The mushrooming of political parties is common in all these countries, including South Africa where 19 parties contested the 1994 election, 16 contested the 1999 election and 21 contested the 2004 election.

However, this book has demonstrated that the FPTP electoral system is no longer adequate to address the electoral needs of Botswana as it works against minority parties and women and gives 'seat bonuses' to the ruling party. But it should be noted that the FPTP system has been positively modified in India where 'the constitution reserves 22 per cent of the 400 seats for historically disadvantaged groups known as the "Scheduled Castes" (79 reserved seats) and "Scheduled Tribes" (41 reserved seats). In these constituencies, only a member of the Scheduled Castes or Tribes may contest the polls, although the electors have voting rights. This has ensured that their parliamentary representation is in line with their proportion of the population' (Reynolds and Reilly, 2002: 35). Thus, although South Africa and India practised completely different electoral systems, they were both able to reserve seats for historically disadvantaged groups. Thus, Botswana has the choice of retaining the FPTP system but reserving seats for historically disadvantaged groups such as women and youth as happens in India, or of introducing PR in some form and insisting on a quota system for the historically disadvantaged groups. Reforming the electoral system in either direction would address some of the current weaknesses and assure Botswana's leadership in the league of democratic nations in the region and in the world.

However, I would argue that while reforming the electoral system is a partial answer to one-party predominance, building the opposition into a formidable force is the most important task. In Botswana, South Africa, Zambia and Tanzania it is becoming increasingly clear that rebuilding the opposition (in whatever form, including the Indian and Kenyan way) rather than reforming the electoral system, seems to be the better option. Fortunately, Botswana is most likely to regain its leadership in democratic politics in the southern Africa region with opposition unity on the cards for the 2009 election. Unity talks had become the buzz word in opposition politics by the time this book was finalised. But it should also be remembered that individual opposition parties, which had formed broad alliances of interests, won state power in Zambia and Malawi and a coalition of opposition parties won state power in Kenya. In all these cases, no significant improvement occurred from the manner in which the countries were run by previous regimes. The only change in Zambia was the prevention of former president Kenneth Kaunda from standing for the presidency in 1996 and this was democratically insignificant. The implication of all these examples is that Botswana should not be too optimistic about the changes that an opposition takeover could bring.

The management of elections in Botswana has undergone tremendous positive shifts over the years: from permanent secretary to the president; to the supervisor of elections and to the IEC. In terms of election management, Botswana and South Africa are very much in the forefront of democratisation. With Namibia having experienced a national recount of ballots in 2005 amid allegations of serious irregularities and Lesotho still struggling to institute transparent and fair elections, Botswana and South Africa are way ahead in modernising their election administration. But in terms of peace and tranquillity during elections, Botswana is definitely leading South Africa where research shows that violence there can be reduced but not eliminated altogether. Thus, even the reduction in the level of violence in Namibia, KwaZulu-Natal in South Africa, in Lesotho and in Zimbabwe during elections, cannot compare with the peaceful elections in Botswana.

The point here is that there are still bottlenecks in the management of elections in Botswana, particularly in regard to setting the election date. Uncertainty over election dates in Botswana has a history of causing confusion. An election audit report noted that such a confusing situation over the date of the elections did not promote transparency and good electoral governance (Dundas, Maundeni and Balule, 2004). It has been made clear that it was the uncertainty over the election date in the 1999 election, that caused around 67 000 voters who had registered through the supplementary registration process nearly to be disenfranchised. This compelled the president to declare a 'state of emergency' in order to recall Parliament to legislate to prevent the likely disenfranchisement of these voters. The audit report further stated that the legal implications of such a situation were huge, compelling the president to institute a commission of inquiry to investigate the root cause of the confusion, leading to a near court case between the President and the Attorney General (Dundas, Maundeni and Balule, 2004). While there were no serious legal implications during the 2004 election, the possibility of their occurrence remains. Thus, there is need for Botswana and the region to reconsider the issue of fixing the election date in the constitution to remove uncertainty.

State funding of political parties, non-transparent campaign contributions and the use of public resources by ruling parties are emerging as important issues for southern Africa. In the first instance, the weakness of the opposition parties partly derives from poor finances and there is a strong perception (among researchers, opposition parties and civil society) that state funding could reverse it. But it has been convincingly demonstrated that state funding has a tendency to entrench the dominance of ruling parties.

In the second instance, my observation is that non-transparent campaign contributions are becoming controversial in both Botswana and South Africa. For example, 'Since the ANC was voted into power, rumours have continuously surfaced regarding campaign contributions made to the party on condition that certain actions be undertaken (or not undertaken as the case may be). The clearest single example of this form of "back-room politics" came in 2002 when Taiwan's last officially recognised ambassador to South Africa, Eugene Loh I-cheng, confirmed that the Taiwanese government had made substantial financial contributions to repay debts incurred in the ANC's 1994 election campaign with the attached condition that the ANC continue to recognise Taiwan's diplomatic status in favour of mainland China for at least two years' (Masterson and Letsholo, 2005: 96). It should be acknowledged that little state funding (20 per cent of the IEC budget goes to political parties) has not positively improved the status of the opposition parties in South Africa. In addition, substantial state funding of opposition parties supplemented non-transparent campaign contributions to significantly improve the status of the ruling party in Zimbabwe. State funding of political parties largely benefit the ruling parties in Namibia, South Africa and Zimbabwe. In contrast, there is no state funding of political parties in Botswana and Zambia and its role is not easily discernable although it is preferred. The major issue then is not so much state funding of political parties - which benefits ruling parties more than the opposition

- but transparency in election contributions. Un-declared election contributions are a threat to clean government and tend to promote corruption. Therefore, it is important to make it a requirement that significant private-election contributions and expenditure are registered and that such records should be accessible for public inspection.

REFERENCES

Dundas, C.W., Z. Maundeni and T. Balule (2004) Audit of the Independent Electoral Commission's (IEC) Preparedness to Conduct Legitimate and Credible Elections in October 2004, International IDEA, Sweden.

Hendricks, C (2005) 'Party Strategy Not Popular Prejudice: Electoral Politics in South Africa' In L. Piper (ed) *South Africa's 2004 Election: The Quest for Democratic Consolidation*, EISA Research paper No 12, EISA.

Kabemba, C., et al (2005) *From Military Rule to Multi-party Democracy: Political Reforms and Challenges in Lesotho*, EISA Report No 2, EISA.

Masterson, G and S. Letsholo (2005) 'The New Challenges of Democracy Assistance in South Africa', in L. Piper (ed) *South Africa's 2004 Election: The Quest for Democratic consolidation*, EISA Research Paper No 12. EISA.

Reynolds, A and B. Reilly. 2002. *The International IDEA Handbook of Electoral System Design*, Stockholm: International IDEA.